AFRICAN NOVELS
AND THE QUESTION
OF ORALITY

AFRICAN NOVELS AND THE QUESTION OF ORALITY

Eileen Julien

Indiana University Press

BLOOMINGTON AND INDIANAPOLIS

"Prayer to the Masks" and "Night in the Sine," from *The Complete Poetry of Léopold Sédar Senghor*, trans. Melvin Dixon, University Press of Virginia, 1991. Reprinted by permission.

The paper used in this publication meets the minimum requirements of American National Standard for Information Sciences—Permanence of Paper for Printed Library Materials, ANSI Z39.48-1984.
⊗™

Manufactured in the United States of America

Library of Congress Cataloging-in-Publication Data

Julien, Eileen, date.
    African novels and the question of orality / Eileen Julien.
      p.   cm.
    Includes bibliographical references (p.   ) and index.
    ISBN 0-253-33101-3 (cloth : alk. paper). — ISBN 0-253-20702-9 (paper : alk. paper)
    1. African fiction (French)—History and criticism. 2. African fiction (English)—History and criticism. 3. African fiction—20th century—History and criticism. 4. Oral tradition in literature. 5. Oral tradition—Africa. I. Title.
PQ3984.J85   1992
809.3—dc20   91-24020
1 2 3 4 5   96 95 94 93 92

*For Birago Diop and Edris Makward,
and for Edward and Mae*

CONTENTS

Preface

Research often has as its object the revelation of unknown facts—the data and documents that we have unearthed, the history that we have pieced together. At other times, we do research in an effort to reconsider facts already at our disposal, to shift the way the elements of a theory or system are perceived. This book is of the latter sort. I bring no bypassed novels or details about orality to the attention of readers but propose instead a different view of those novels and facts already at our disposal, for the issue of orality and the African novel is not a relationship left out of critical studies, but one I believe to be misapprehended.

The novel is a genre "in the making," Mikhail Bakhtin tells us, and it is this aspect of African novels which I should like to explore and to stress: their dynamism, creativity, process. As is frequently the case with research projects, the direction and issue with which I began have led me to a consideration of yet other issues that culminates in these analyses. My original topic was one familiar to researchers and readers of African literatures, the links between the oral traditions of Africa and the novel, the heritage (as it is often described) owed by the novel to the tale or epic. It began as a search for the aesthetic origins of the African novel but has shifted from what now seems to me a deterministic, evolutionary approach to a more open-ended examination of how aesthetic, cultural, and social needs are met by reference to and imitation or parodying of the structures of oral genres. Thus, as Part I demonstrates, my question is no longer the extent to which the African novel is derivative of oral traditions, but rather the extent to which such references hold the means of imaginative solutions to problems of aesthetic and ideological dimensions (Part II). Because this approach accords writers more liberty and assumes they are thinking architects rather than prisoners of a cultural heritage, it allows for richer, more complex interpretations.

ACKNOWLEDGMENTS

This book is the culmination of a project begun in 1985–86, when I was a Carnegie Fellow at the Bunting Institute of Radcliffe College. The Institute provided not only a room of my own but an extraordinary atmosphere of congeniality and collaboration. The Boston University Humanities Foundation also funded my research in fall 1986. I am grateful to Jacqueline Boltz for technical support and to Tammy Iralu for her invaluable assistance in preparing translations of the French texts. For advice and support at various stages of the writing, I am deeply indebted to Karin Barber, Ava Baron, Richard Bjornson, Melvin Dixon, Jane Guyer, Lemuel Johnson, Janis Mayes, Kitzie McKinney, Kipre Nea, Micheline Rice-Maximin, Peter Schofer, Eunice Smith, Pam Solo, and Sandra Zagarell.

PART I

Of Origins and Orality

1

The Search for Continuity and Authenticity

As our awareness of African oral art has grown in recent years, many scholars of written literary texts have begun to consider the possible links of these texts with African oral traditions. At their best, such studies may mean the exploration of the interplay or evolution of aesthetic forms in varying social contexts, but studies of written and oral African texts are frequently sidetracked by another more compelling objective. It is surely a *quest for continuity* in African verbal arts which has brought researchers to comparative studies of this type: we have been working to challenge and dispel the widespread perception that written African literature is discontinuous with the oral. Thus Harold Scheub begins and concludes his "Review of African Oral Traditions and Literature," commissioned by the African Studies Association for presentation at the 1984 annual meeting, with an emphatic statement of the unity of those arts: "There is an unbroken continuity in African verbal art forms, from interacting oral genres to such literary productions as the novel and poetry. . . . [T]he early literary traditions were beneficiaries of the oral genres, and there is no doubt that the epic and its hero are the predecessors of the African novel and its central characters" (1). Scheub's view of the unity of African verbal arts is one that makes good sense, for African verbal arts, like Asian or European verbal arts, are unquestionably related and continuous. The truth of this assertion, put so plainly, seems obvious and tautological to us, needing no evidence or argument. Yet, in the history of African literary criticism, this simple fact has often been obscured by prevailing wisdom—from whence the insatiable need to assert and defend it.

As is well known, older African texts, written in French and English, were usually and are still sometimes viewed as satellite literatures of the literatures to the north. Camara Laye was, above all, the heir of Kafka, Achebe of Conrad, Sembène of Zola, Senghor of Claudel and Saint John Perse, and so on. It was not, of course, by chance that the texts of these and other writers were seen as belonging to the cultural spheres of England

and France, since the texts were written in European languages and intended, in their protests of colonial ideology and policy, for European as well as African readers. There could be no doubt of the intertextuality and affinity of African texts with European texts, but, as we know, Eurocentric views of African literature did not stop at intertextuality and affinity; they appropriated African literature and "colonized" it completely.

The reading public has grown more conscious of the biases in such criticism, but these biases have not lost their centrality in the discourse on African and diaspora texts and art, although they are perhaps less blatant and sometimes lurk in other forms. Two examples make the point. In 1984 at the Venice Film Festival, for example, Euzhan Palcy's film *La Rue Cases-Nègres* was described by journalists as representing alternately "un nouveau courant . . . au sein de la production *française*" and "un nouveau territoire d'origine" (Ménil 97, emphasis added) ["a new trend within French production" and "a new country of origin"].[1] Under which rubric did it, in fact, belong: Martinique or France?

Similarly, the multiple designations for African literatures, including terms such as *francophone* and *of French expression*, have ideological significance, as Guy Ossito Midiohouan demonstrates in *L'Idéologie dans la littérature négro-africaine d'expression française* (14–22). His careful discussion reveals the acuity of this issue, which is bound to be with us as long as African writers write in European languages and the geopolitical order remains what it is. The problem is, of course, extremely complex because, apart from the issue of one's place of birth and the language in which one writes, artists frequently have had a great many experiences outside the culture of their birth. Thus the urge to demonstrate the continuity of African verbal arts has had great urgency for readers and scholars. While there can no longer be any doubt about the continuity in African verbal arts, we nonetheless have not been content to assert that continuity exists: we seem compelled to search for and prove it. Given that objective, an important question becomes, Where do we situate the beginnings of continuity? Where does it originate?

For many practitioners of African literature and criticism, continuity has meant most often a search for a heritage from oral traditions to the new literatures written in European and African languages, the "passage from orality to writing." Orality is a complex concept to which we shall give considerable attention, but here let us note simply that scholars of written African literature generally have looked for the origins of continuity in those genres which existed centuries before the colonial period and the writing of novels: poetry, proverbs, riddles, narratives, epics articulated and performed orally—the so-called indigenous and authentic genres.

Among the first to signal the continuity of African verbal arts was Léopold Senghor. In *Ethiopiques*, published in 1956, Senghor includes among his poems the essay "Comme les lamantins vont boire à la source." He states with regard to French influences in his poetry and that of other poets included in his *Anthologie de la nouvelle poésie nègre et malgache* (1948): "Si l'on veut nous trouver des maîtres, il serait plus sage de les chercher du côté de l'Afrique" (156) ["For those wanting to discover our mentors, they would do best to look toward Africa"]. As is well known, throughout his poetry, beginning with *Chants d'ombre* in 1945, Senghor frequently alludes to the oral tradition in the titles of poems ("Que m'accompagnent koras et balafongs" ["For koras and balafongs"], "Prière aux masques" ["Prayer to Masks"]) and in parenthetical, italicized scripts that are the equivalent of musical directions:

Prière des tirailleurs sénégalais
(woï pour deux koras)

[Prayer for the Tirailleurs of Sénégal
(lament for two koras)]

Readers familiar with African oral traditions and with Senghor's comments tend to view the breath and rhythm of Senghor's verses and their "traditional"—that is to say, culturally specific and nature-based—imagery also as derived from oral poetry. Senghor thus aims—with what might be called "une volonté de transparence" ["willed transparence"]—to situate his poetic practice vis-à-vis oral traditions and to guide the reception of his poems.

Mohamadou Kane responds nearly twenty-five years later to the same issue with regard to African novels. In "Sur les formes traditionnelles du roman africain," Kane states that "l'originalité du roman africain doit être cherchée plus particulièrement dans ses rapports avec les formes de la littérature orale. . . . [U]ne plus grande attention aux rapports, aux liens de continuité des littératures orales et écrites permet de mieux comprendre les problèmes du roman africain" (537) ["the originality of the African novel must be found more specifically in its relationship to forms of oral literature. . . . Greater attention to the relationships, to the links of continuity between oral and written literatures would allow one to better understand the problems of the African novel"]. Kane's objective is to explain why the form of African novels is different from (and sometimes regarded as inferior to) that of their European counterparts and to elaborate the underlying unity of the African novel.

Mbwil a Mpang Ngal takes this issue still further. In *Giambatista Viko ou le viol du discours africain* (1984), the African intellectual Giambatista is haunted by the dream of amalgamating the oral tale and the written novel:

Apprivoiser le discours occidental paralysé, refoulé, me paraît vraiment génial!
. . . Accoucher d'un roman! C'est en effet tenir un discours occidental. C'est évoluer dans l'espace visuel. Faire évoluer un récit dans la dimension spatio-temporelle. Carcan qui limite étrangement la liberté

de l'écrivain; les possibilités du discours. Le pouvoir du mot très amoindri perd de cette efficacité que lui connaît l'univers magique de l'oralité.

. . . Aucune rigidité pareille à celle du roman! Véritable cercle infernal, l'espace romanesque! Je rêve d'un roman sur le modèle du conte. D'un roman où coexistent des éléments d'âges différents. (12–13)

[Taming the crippled and inhibited discourse of the West seems to me really ingenious!

. . . Giving birth to a novel! That is, in fact, to hold a Western discourse. To evolve in visual space. To make a story evolve in a spatial-temporal dimension. Shackles that strangely limit the liberty of the writer, the possibilities of discourse. The power of the word so diminished loses the efficacy that it holds in the magical universe of orality.

. . . No rigidity like that of the novel! A truly vicious circle, the novel's space! I dream of a novel on the order of the tale. A novel where elements of different ages coexist.]

The texts of both Kane and Ngal are alike in their premise of two juxtaposed "worlds." Giambatista's obsession to unite tale and novel is, however, different from Senghor's and Kane's assertions of continuity, which are meant to rectify what they see as a misperception on the part of literary critics. Giambatista's desire is, in fact, an explicit acknowledgment of discontinuity and implies, at odds with Kane's assertion, that there is no automatic heritage from tale to novel: what has been written heretofore by African writers has not been determined by their past.

We infer that for Giambatista "novel" and "tale," "orality" and "writing" are both causes and consequences of differing social universes. The question of the interaction of literary forms poses a greater question of sensibility and values. Does reconciliation between forms suggest, metonymically, a possible reconciliation between world views? Giambatista comes close to pinpointing what is for me the fundamental issue in debates on narrative form: the causes and effects of the different forms of narrative. For Giambatista, the novel is Western; by implication then, "Africanness" is located in the oral universe of the tale. The novel will have been "tamed" or domesticated when it will have been touched and modified by orality.

We will refer again to the issues raised by Senghor, Kane and Ngal. I have cited these writers here to convey, first of all, the widespread interest in the issue of continuity in African verbal arts, oral and written. I have cited them also to show their emphasis on *orality* as the source from which continuity between oral and written arts must flow. As Alioune Tine states in his article "Pour une théorie de la littérature africaine écrite," "la littérature africaine se définit comme une littérature située entre l'oralité et l'écriture. Cette idée a permis la réalisation d'un vaste consensus qui va des critiques africanistes aux écrivains" (99) ["African literature can be defined as a literature situated between orality and writing. This idea has given rise to a vast consensus that includes both Africanist critics and authors"]. Since we situate the tale's particularity in its orality and the novel's particularity in its writing and subsequent printing, it follows that if there is continuity between the two, the novel must contain or reveal orality. It is this assumption, orality as origin and authenticity, which must be examined.

An Accidental Fact and an Essentialist Myth

It is important, for the purposes of this analysis, to distinguish between the concrete conditions in which African verbal arts are produced and the way in which those conditions are represented in critical discourse. The primarily oral character of traditional African verbal art is of the first order. It is a fact, but it is a fact whose significance and implications are, I believe, often misrepresented. This study treats the issue of how that fact has been discussed and written about, how that treatment affects the way we think, how it enables us to see certain things, to see only certain things. The issue at hand, then, is not the orality of Africa but rather the intellectual categories of orality and writing that we construct and use. The discourse on orality has been articulated both by the West and by Africans. We must consider how the category of "African orality" permeates literary criticism, how it is subject to ideological pressures, and how it has come to define and confine the scope of our interest in and perception of African writing.

As late as 1960, the activity of writing in Africa—and especially serious, sustained writing—was generally assumed in the popular Western view and even by Africanists to have begun with the arrival of Europeans on the continent. Janheinz Jahn, a pioneer of African studies, who problematized terms such as *African literature* and *black literature*, could declare nonetheless with regard to orality and writing that

> une littérature qui ne témoigne d'aucune influence européenne et qui donc n'est pas écrite n'appartient pas à la littérature néo-africaine mais à la littérature africaine traditionelle. La frontière entre les deux est facile à tracer: c'est la frontière entre littérature orale et littérature écrite. (*Manuel* 16)

> [a literature that does not bear witness to any European influence and that therefore is not written does not belong to neo-African literature but to traditional African literature. The dividing line between the two is easy to trace: it is the line dividing oral literature from written literature.]

The fact that writing did exist in Africa before the arrival of the first Europeans and had no connection with the Roman alphabet is a matter of record with which most of us are now familiar, thanks to the efforts of a number of scholars.[2] My point, however, is neither that oral language and art were not dominant in Africa nor that modes of language do not affect social and cultural mores. What is striking above all is that Jahn, like many others, equates an accidental phenomenon (mode of language) with essence: writing is European, orality is African.

The dominance of oral language in Africa is obviously a matter of material conditions and not of an "African nature," but more than a few literary critics take this accidental fact for an essential one and assume almost invariably that there is something ontologically oral about Africa and that the act of writing is therefore disjunctive and alien for Africans.

When we consider the critical reception of African poetry and narrative, the contours of this assumption begin to reveal themselves. In modern Western thought from Romanticism through Surrealism, poetry is the trace of a state of trance. The poet is moved to create by "inspiration," intuition, or the power of the unconscious. Written poetry by Africans, then—even, it might be argued, that of the modernist Soyinka and Okigbo—does little to challenge the discourse in which Africa is assumed to be ontologically oral. This is because poetry is perceived as perfectly compatible with the category of "oral," which connotes spontaneity, rapture, intimacy with *being* and the spiritual, as in this comment by Senghor: "Le Nègre singulièrement . . . est d'un monde où la parole se fait spontanément rythme dès que l'homme est ému, rendu à lui-même, à son authenticité. Oui la parole se fait poème" ("Comme les lamantins" 154) ["The Negro singularly . . . is in a world where the word spontaneously becomes rhythm as soon as a man is moved, returned to himself, to his authenticity. Yes, the word becomes a poem"]. Such allusions to the "instinctive poetry of the native African" are commonplace.

What seems to be overlooked in such assessments of African music and poetry, however, is consideration of their context and material conditions and reference to *traditions* of poetic practice. Presented abstractly, with no reference to their context, "accidental" attributes take on the force of essentialist, ontological truths. Just as it has seemed not only plausible but altogether *natural* that African-Americans should express themselves in music—spirituals, blues and jazz—it has seemed inevitable (and, perhaps, even reassuring) that Africans and their descendants should express themselves in poetry. Apart from questions of "God-given talent," African-American musical expressions may seem singularly prominent because of the lesser participation of black Americans in other *less accessible* realms—political, scientific, or otherwise.

Although attitudes on the part of Europeans toward the musical and poetic talents of Africans have ranged, of course, from Gobineau's condescension, "parmi tous les arts que la créature mélanienne préfère, la musique tient la première place, en tant qu'elle caresse son oreille par une succession de sons, et qu'elle ne demande rien à la partie pensante de son cerveau. Le nègre l'aime beaucoup, il en jouit avec excès" (474) ["among all the arts that the melanistic creature prefers, music holds first place, inasmuch as it caresses his ear by a succession of tones and requires nothing of the thinking part of his brain. The Negro loves it very much and indulges in it to excess"] to Cendrars's admiration, "L'esprit souffle où il veut et n'est-ce pas le théoricien et le fondateur du racisme aryen, le comte de Gobineau, ce contempteur des races de couleur, qui, sur la tête maudite du Nègre pose la couronne de la poésie" (100) ["The spirit blows where it will, and was it not the theorist and founder of Aryan racism, the count of Gobineau, this hater of races of color, who, on the wretched head of the Negro, places the crown of poetry"], the flattering view that Africans are born to poetry tends to go unnoticed and unexamined. There are surely several reasons. It is perhaps a view espoused by all, and, above all, there may be tacit consensus about the usefulness of "oral" rhythms, metaphor and personification in the creation of poetry. Thus, in discussions of written African poetry, the assumption of an underlying orality is so commonplace as to go inarticulate. And when it is articulated, it is greeted enthusiastically because of the consensus that holds it to be useful to poetic practice.

On the other hand, in debates on the novel—the only genre, according to Bakhtin, to come into existence since writing and the book—the assumption of African orality can be readily perceived. It is surely one of the reasons for the many perennial controversies surrounding the African novel: there has been an unspoken belief that novels were not for Africans (because oral forms were) and that African writers needed guidance in perfecting this craft, or, alternatively, that truly African novels are and in fact need to be "oral" in some fashion. (We will examine the latter criterion with greater scrutiny in the following chapter.) An example of the first tendency is Adrian Roscoe's statement in *Mother Is Gold*:

> The novel . . . has no history in Africa . . . is not a fact of the African past. . . . The African child . . . is faced in school with a *written* literary form imposed on him. . . . He may acquire a taste for the novel; but his life, his society's history—in a word, his culture—pre-dispose him *naturally* to the story. (75–76, emphasis added)

Since the discourse on orality and writing has a life of its own, apart from the evidence, the argument set forth by Roscoe cannot be dismissed simply by pointing out that there are innumerable African novels. Indeed the thrust of Roscoe's comment lies elsewhere. The fact that Africans can and do write and read novels does not challenge his assumption that novels are inappropriate for them because writing is imposed and because the novel is not natural in Africa.[3] He argues that regardless of what they actually do write, writers should be writing short stories. The biases in Roscoe's argument become apparent, then, when one asks rhetorically, Does the absence or presence of a literary form in one's past determine the extent to which it might exist in one's future? Do we wish that Virgil had not written because his inspiration and his models were Greek? Was the sonnet forbidden to Ronsard because Villon had not used it? Should Cervantes not have written *Don Quixote* because the Spanish past did not predispose him to it *naturally*? Roscoe has an essentialist view both of the concept "African" and of the concept "novel" (as well as of their supposed opposites).

Paradoxically, the assumption of the profoundly oral nature of African life and art is expressed more subtly in the expectation or requirement that novels be leavened with the appropriate African yeast of orality. Alioune Tine writes that "ce qui constitue le trait spécifique de la littérature africaine est . . . la notion d'oralité feinte" (102) ["what constitutes the singular characteristic of African literature is . . . the idea of feigned orality"]. Mohamadou Kane states similarly, as we have seen, "Il est donc opportun de montrer que l'originalité du roman africain doit être cherchée plus particulièrement dans ses rapports avec les formes de la littérature orale de l'Afrique Noire" ("Sur les formes" 537) ["It is therefore opportune to show that the originality of the African novel must be found more particularly in its relationship to forms of oral literature from Black Africa"]. Indeed, African novels could be studied profitably in their relationship to all other African verbal, plastic and performance arts. Scheub's discussion of oral and written literature, to which I referred earlier, is just such an effort. But to say this is not to say that the originality of African novels is determined by the extent to which they echo oral traditions. The implication is that the novel is European until it inscribes orality and thereby becomes African.

It is this bias, it seems to me, which reveals our thinking that an African essence can be found in, and indeed is bound to, orality. In fact, it is often not a hidden assumption at all and is stated forthright as in Honorat Aguessy's important essay "Visions et perceptions traditionnelles," where he notes that "l'une des caractéristiques des cultures africaines traditionnelles, leur caractéristique essentielle, même à certains égards, c'est l'oralité" (162) ["one of the characteristics of traditional African cultures, even in some respects their essential characteristic, is orality"]. The question here, as in many instances, is how to signal particularity without losing sight of common ground and how to describe the "accidental" without its becoming "essential." In Aguessy's case, he tempers his statement by adding that orality in African cultures is "a dominant characteristic" and not "an exclusive one," but in general such nuances are lost. "Orality" has become a metonymy for "African."

A Polyvalent Symbol: Beauty and the Beast

If essentialist views of "African" and "the novel" complicate the task of comparative studies of oral and written forms, a further difficulty arises from what might be called the civilization quotient or the "moral" connotations of oral traditions (and consequently of the novel).

Let us consider two opposing attitudes toward orality and, by implication, oral societies and art. Each interferes with our ability to apprehend the relationship of oral and written texts to each other. The first attitude— of which we are quite conscious and which we challenge strenuously—

holds oral societies (and traditions) to be impoverished. The second—to which we may be less sensitive or to which we may unconsciously adhere—holds them to be exemplary. In other words, at certain moments in Western social and intellectual history and depending on the biases of the observer, the same phenomena are seen as evidence of either the superiority or decadence of European civilization and, concomittantly, of the inferiority or wholesomeness of non-European civilizations. The reversibility of this assessment is a remarkable example of the impact of the observer's intentions and presence on what he or she is able to observe and on the conclusions that might be drawn from those observations. The important point, however, is that these biases are often at work in our perception of African literature and that they skew the questions we ask and the conclusions we draw.

According to Ruth Finnegan and Honorat Aguessy, European awareness of African oral literature began with the publication in 1828 of Le Baron J. F. Roger's retelling of Wolof tales, *Fables sénégalaises recueillies de l'ouolof et imitées en vers français* (Finnegan 27, Aguessy 183). By midcentury there was growing interest in African languages among European scholars of comparative linguistics and among Christian missionaries, anxious to translate the Bible and to communicate in African languages. Collections of African narratives, proverbs, poems, riddles, and other genres became more common, and Europeans began to ponder the literary activity of Africans.

To understand how these works were received, we must recall that it was anthropology, more than history or political science or other disciplines, that dominated the study of African cultures. Thus anthropological assumptions and paradigms led the way in the European appraisal of African life and art.[4] Evolutionist theories—whose origins, as Lévi-Strauss tells us, can be found in Greek antiquity, Pascal and especially the philosophers of the eighteenth century (*Race et Histoire* 14–15)—formed the premise of studies such as Lévy-Bruhl's *La Mentalité primitive* and Tylor's *Primitive Culture*. If we read intellectual history as Edward Said has done, we can see why such theories took on new relevance and force in the imperialist nineteenth century. Contemporary Europe exemplified the adult stage of civilization, while non-European cultures (and the European peasantry) were seen as instances of the elementary stage—the historical "childhood" through which Europe had previously passed. Africa was without Culture. Thus Hegel could write: "The Negro exhibits the natural man in his completely wild and untamed state. . . . What we properly understand by Africa is the unhistorical, undeveloped spirit, involved in the conditions of mere nature, and [only] on the threshold of the World's History" (93, 99).

Viewed through the prism of evolutionist theories, then, oral traditions were considered primitive, and British folklorists, for example, studied the oral songs and poetry of contemporary British society as "survivals" of an earlier cultural stage, indices of the distance from which high culture had come.[5] Indeed the concept of folklore was developed in response to such forms, recognized as having little or no aesthetic value, and treated like literary stepchildren. With regard to African oral traditions, Finnegan hypothesizes that evolutionist biases manifested themselves in the very selection of oral materials made by collectors, in the kinds of thematic interpretations that poems and tales were given, in the lack of attention to literary qualities and effectiveness, and in the preoccupation with "traditional" tales as opposed to "new," innovative, or idiosyncratic ones that would have challenged the view of oral art as communally created. Written literature was an implicit norm against which oral literature was judged. The latter was seen as simple, uncrafted, and generally the product of the communal mind,[6] whereas written literature, especially the novel, was held to be at the opposite and final end of the developmental process: it was complex, deliberate, and the work of a single author. A related assumption undergirding many anthropological studies was that African institutions and artifacts were purely functional and served to maintain a social order (Finnegan 38). Unlike its counterpart in societies deemed advanced, oral literature was therefore devoid of aesthetic principles and concerns (Finnegan 26–47). H. L. Gates has referred to these assumptions, which plague studies of African and African-American literature and art, as the "collective and functional" fallacies.

Simplistic views such as these and their evolutionist underpinnings are, of course, no longer tenable. The pendulum has swung, and we sometimes now encounter a more subtle, equally troubling attitude in exaggerated claims for oral literature. Whether in an attempt to rectify prejudiced views of oral traditions or for other reasons, what was once deemed the primitive nature of oral literature and viewed as deficient is now proclaimed as pure and virtuous, as in the following passage from Paul Zumthor's broad and provocative study, *Introduction à la poésie orale*:

> Depuis le XVII siècle, l'Europe s'est répandue sur le monde comme un cancer: subrepticement d'abord, mais voilà beau temps qu'il galope, ravage aujourd'hui dément de formes de vie, animaux, plantes, paysages, langues. A chaque jour qui passe, plusieurs langues au monde disparaissent: reniées, étouffées, mortes avec le dernier vieillard, voix vierges d'écriture, pure mémoire sans défense, fenêtres jadis grandes ouvertes sur le réel. L'un des symptômes du mal fut sans doute, dès l'origine, ce que nous nommons littérature: et la littérature a pris consistance, prospéré, est devenue ce qu'elle est—l'une des plus vastes dimensions de l'homme—en récusant la voix. . . . Il s'agit de renoncer . . . à privilégier l'écriture. . . . Peut-être la grande et malheureuse Afrique, clochardisée par notre impérialisme politico-industriel, se trouve-t-elle plus que d'autres continents près du but: parce que moins gravement touchée par l'écriture. (282–84)

> [Since the seventeenth century, Europe has spread itself across the world like a cancer; stealthily at first, but now for some time it has run wild, ravaging today all sorts of forms of life, animals, plants, countrysides, languages. With each passing day, several languages of the world disap-

pear: repudiated, choked out, dead with the last old man, voices virgin to writing, pure memory without natural defenses, windows once wide open to the real. One of the symptoms of this plague was from the beginning, without doubt, what we call literature: and literature has gained ground, prospered, and become what it is—one of the vastest dimensions of man—by denying voice. We must stop . . . privileging writing. . . . Perhaps the great and unfortunate Africa, pauperized by our political industrial imperialism, will find herself closer to the goal than the rest of the continents, because she is less seriously touched by writing.]

Zumthor's claim is unquestionable, of course: for innumerable reasons (written) literature established itself in the West as *the* mode of verbal art, thereby devaluing oral forms to such a degree that their potential for aesthetic expression was, until recently, virtually ignored (see Eagleton and Davis). Indeed, Eric Havelock hypothesizes that it was above all the presumed superiority of writing, its presumed correlation to civilization, learning and intelligence, and the stigma associated with illiteracy that blinded classicists, in their reverence for Homer, to the oral mode of Homeric composition. This discovery, Havelock argues, required someone with fewer preconceptions, an American: Milman Parry.

Thus Zumthor's book is a significant contribution to the process of reevaluating oral art. But it is Zumthor's passion, in this excerpt as elsewhere, that catches one's attention, for he idealizes orality, exalts it above writing. He mythologizes and mystifies it as do other scholars. Orality/ Africa (passive and female) is the victim of writing/Europe (virile, aggressive, and male). Zumthor thus bemoans the plight of orality: suffocated virgin voices, pure defenseless memory, suppressed by literature that has prospered at orality's expense. It is perhaps not surprising that Zumthor— in a remarkable echo of Senghor—hopes for Africa's "oral" redemption of Europe. In *Le Modèle nègre* Jean-Claude Blachère demonstrates how this same hope characterizes the pre-Surrealist writings of Cendrars and Tzara.

The old interpretation that held oral literature to be impoverished is, as we have seen, well known and ably refuted. The second, manifest in Zumthor's remarks and often in African literary criticism, assumes or implies it to be morally superior to writing, good, even glorious. This interpretation goes unremarked or unquestioned and is, of course, equally inaccurate and obfuscating. It is important to understand arguments that are made to this effect.

In *Soundjata ou l'épopée mandingue*, D. T. Niane retells the Sundiata epic as told to him by the griot Mamadou Kouyaté. At an interesting textual juncture between the moment in which Soumaoro, enchanted by Balla Fasseké's playing of the balafong, decides to steal the griot and that moment in which Sundiata's kingly destiny becomes manifest, Kouyaté digresses to comment on kings, history, and griots. He eventually offers this view of speech and writing:

D'autres peuples se servent de l'écriture pour fixer le passé; mais cette invention a tué la mémoire chez eux; ils ne sentent plus le passé car l'écriture n'a pas la chaleur de la voix humaine. Chez eux tout le monde croit connaître alors que le savoir doit être un secret . . . ; les prophètes n'ont pas écrit et leur parole n'en a été que plus vivante. Quelle piètre connaissance que la connaissance qui est figée dans les livres muets. (78–79)

[Other peoples use writing to record the past, but this invention has killed the faculty of memory among them. They do not feel the past anymore, for writing lacks the warmth of the human voice. With them everybody thinks he knows, whereas learning should be a secret. The prophets did not write and their words have been all the more vivid as a result. What paltry learning is that which is congealed in dumb books! (*Sundiata* 41)]

Given his life, work, and family history, Kouyaté views speech and writing as antithetical modes of language and vehicles of learning. There is nothing surprising in Kouyaté's antagonism toward writing.[7] Kouyaté insists with passion and eloquence that speech—as opposed to writing— can be filled with the warmth of voice; it is more vivid, it requires and therefore encourages memory, it assures the exclusivity of knowledge and brings with it, as he tells us elsewhere, a guarantee of truth from the one who speaks.

We may be tempted for many reasons to agree with Kouyaté's description of speech, and it may be on the basis of some of the attributes he outlines that we revere oral traditions and hold them to be more beautiful and virtuous than written literature. But it is a futile exercise to insist on establishing a hierarchy between orality and literacy, based on their "intrinsic" qualities, because these categories are imbued with cultural biases. All of the admirable claims for speech can be met by equally admirable claims for writing and print. Speech and writing are often similar in their capacities and consequences, and they are often dissimilar. The prophets' words, which Kouyaté finds forceful and eloquent because they are delivered by the human voice, were nonetheless transmitted to Manding society and West Africa in general through written texts, and they are still learned in many areas with the assistance of tablets in Koranic schools.

There is another point worth emphasizing in this regard: we tend to think of oral traditions as universally egalitarian because every human being is endowed with voice and because writing and print are technologies that require special training and resources, but, in fact, as Kouyaté himself points out, the griot is in a position of power ("le savoir doit être un secret" ["knowledge must be secret"]). His message is proffered when and to whom he wishes to proffer it and is designed to suit the needs of the authority he serves (see Koné 62). Not everyone will or can be heard.

Neither voice nor print, then, is exempt from political persuasion a pressure.

Thus if Kouyaté privileges orality, it is because of cultural traditions that he embodies and that confer on him a certain authority. Many of us may tend to mystify orality for other reasons, however. At one point in his career, for example, Lévi-Strauss ranks orality and writing on the basis of the "authenticity" of the societies in which they occur. He defines authenticity by "le caractère concret de la connaissance que les individus ont les uns des autres" (Charbonnier 64) ["the firsthand nature of people's knowledge of one another"]. Elsewhere he elaborates on this point:

Or . . . ce sont les sociétés de l'homme moderne qui devraient plutôt être définies par un caractère privatif. Nos relations avec autrui ne sont plus, que de façon occasionnelle et fragmentaire, fondées sur cette expérience globale, cette appréhension concrète d'un sujet par un autre. Elles résultent, pour une large part, de reconstructions indirectes, à travers des documents écrits. Nous sommes reliés à notre passé, non plus par une tradition orale qui implique un contact vécu avec des personnes—conteurs, prêtres, sages ou anciens—mais par des livres entassés dans des bibliothèques et à travers lesquels la critique s'évertue—avec quelles difficultés—à reconstituer le visage de leurs auteurs. Et sur le plan du présent, nous communiquons avec l'immense majorité de nos contemporains par toutes sortes d'intermédiaires—documents écrits ou mécanismes administratifs—qui élargissent sans doute immensément nos contacts, mais leur confèrent en même temps un caractère d'inauthenticité. . . . Il est indispensable de se rendre compte [that the invention of writing] a retiré à l'humanité quelque chose d'essentiel, en même temps qu'elle lui apportait tant de bienfaits. (*Anthropologie structurale* 425–26)

[it is, rather, modern societies that should be defined in negative terms. Our relations with one another are now only occasionally and fragmentarily based upon global experience, the concrete "apprehension" of one person by another. They are largely the result of a process of indirect reconstruction, through written documents. We are no longer linked to our past by an oral tradition which implies direct contact with others (storytellers, priests, wise men, or elders), but by books amassed in libraries, books from which we endeavor—with extreme difficulty—to form a picture of their authors. And we communicate with the immense majority of our contemporaries by all kinds of intermediaries—written documents or administrative machinery—which undoubtedly vastly extend our contacts but at the same time make those contacts somewhat "unauthentic." . . . We should like to avoid describing negatively the tremendous revolution brought about by the invention of writing. But it is essential to realize that writing, while it conferred vast benefits on humanity, did in fact deprive it of something fundamental. (*Structural Anthropology* 363–64)]

Lévi-Strauss thus sees a correlation between orality and authentic living and goes on to say that there are pockets of authenticity within the larger inauthentic culture in which the West lives today. His interpretation represents a position of cultural relativity in anthropology characteristic of the period between the two world wars:

> The idea of Western culture as a universal norm began to be abandoned by those anthropologists whose direct experience of other cultures had impressed them with the range of possibilities of human adaptation to the natural environment and of human potential for cultural creation. . . . [A]nthropology now offered a new and positive evaluation of non-Western cultures. (Irele 14)

I have cited Lévi-Strauss because he articulates what is surely a common intuition in the West. The view that something is lost when we move from small communities to larger ones is widespread, Zumthor tells us. He finds (as does Marshall McLuhan) that "depuis la diffusion de l'imprimerie, l'Occidental semble habité par le regret d'un monde du toucher et de l'ouïe—celui même que lui faisait perdre la pure visualité abstraite de l'écriture" (284) ["since the spread of printing, Western man seems filled with longing for a world of touch and sound—the very one which the pure abstract visual nature of writing made him lose"]. In this regard Fredric Jameson signals the socioeconomic roots of such "longing" when he explains the persistence of romance as a narrative genre: "the oral tales of tribal society, the fairy tales that are the irrepressible voice and expression of the underclasses of the great systems of domination, adventure stories and melodrama, and the popular or mass culture of our own time are all syllables and broken fragments of some single immense story" (105). (Clearly, the oral tradition of Kouyaté is not the same one that Jameson conjures up.) It is surely a common view that Western metropolises may have something to learn from people who live far away from daily technological and media intrusions. Those who do not live in almost exclusively "oral," pastoral communities mourn the loss of a lifestyle they assume to be characterized by intimacy, harmony, and equality or perhaps homogeneity.

Lévi-Strauss's assessment of orality and writing is, we infer, born out of a certain disillusionment. He writes that "si l'Occident a produit des ethnographes, c'est qu'un bien puissant remords devait le tourmenter, l'obligeant à confronter son image à celle de sociétés différentes dans l'espoir qu'elles réfléchiront les mêmes tares ou l'aideront à expliquer comment les siennes se sont développées dans son sein" (*Tristes Tropiques* 466) ["Western Europe may have produced anthropologists precisely because it was a prey to strong feelings of remorse, which forced it to compare its image with those of different societies in the hope that they would show the same defects or would help to explain how its own defects had developed within it" (*Tristes Tropiques* 389)]. It is precisely for reasons such as these—Lévi-Strauss's equating of oral cultures with "authentic" living and his simultaneous admission of the self-interested origins of anthropology in Western remorse—that Jacques Derrida takes him to task. Non-European peoples, Derrida writes, are studied "comme l'index d'une bonne nature enfouie, d'un sol recouvert, d'un 'degré zéro' par rapport auquel on pourrait dessiner la structure, le devenir et surtout la dégradation de notre société et de notre culture" (*De la grammatologie* 168) ["as the index to a hidden good Nature, as a native soil recovered, of a 'zero degree' with reference to which one could outline the structure, the growth, and above all the degradation of our society and our culture" (*Of Grammatology* 115)]. Derrida traces a thread of "logocentricity" in European intellectual history from Rousseau's disenchantment with modern European civilization through Husserl and Saussure to Lévi-Strauss: the equating of voice with purity, the natural, and the good.

Lévi-Strauss is second to none, however, in his awareness of the tendency to exaggerate the goodness (or ugliness) of societies other than one's own and the dangers inherent in such exaggeration. No society, he states in *Tristes Tropiques*, is all good or all bad. In addition, the perspective from which one makes such judgments is, of course, not neutral, as he warns in his earlier *Race et Histoire*:

> la dimension et la vitesse de déplacement des corps ne sont pas des valeurs absolues, mais des fonctions de la position de l'observateur. . . . [P]our un voyageur assis à la fenêtre d'un train, la vitesse et la longueur des autres trains varient selon que ceux-ci se déplacent dans le même sens ou dans un sens opposé. Or tout membre d'une culture en est aussi étroitement solidaire que ce voyageur idéal l'est de son train. Car, dès notre naissance, l'entourage fait pénétrer en nous, par mille démarches conscientes et inconscientes, un système complexe de référence consistant en jugements de valeur, motivations, centres d'intérêt, y compris la vue réflexive que l'éducation nous impose du devenir historique de notre civilisation, sans laquelle celle-ci deviendrait impensable, ou apparaîtrait en contradiction avec les conduites réelles. Nous nous déplaçons littéralement avec ce système de références, et les réalités culturelles du dehors ne sont observables qu'à travers les déformations qu'il leur impose, quand il ne va pas jusqu'à nous mettre dans l'impossibilité d'en apercevoir quoi que ce soit. (43–44)

> [the dimensions and the speed of displacement of a body are not absolute values but depend on the position of the observer. . . . [T]o a traveller sitting at the window of a train, the speed and length of other trains vary according to whether they are moving in the same or the contrary direction. Any member of a civilization is as closely associated with it as this hypothetical traveller is with his train for, from birth onwards, a thousand conscious and unconscious influences in our environment instill into us a complex system of criteria, consisting in value judgments,

motivations and centres of interest, and including the conscious reflexion upon the historical development of our civilization which our education imposes and without which our civilization would be inconceivable or would seem contrary to actual behaviour. Wherever we go, we are bound to carry this system of criteria with us, and external cultural phenomena can be observed only through the distorting glass it interposes, even when it does not prevent us from seeing anything at all. (*Race and History* 25)]

Even when we judge another culture to be good or superior in a certain domain, our position as observer is present in that judgment. The question, then, is how do we understand and evaluate superlative judgments of oral traditions, such as Lévi-Strauss's and Zumthor's, when our own prejudices are operative? To what extent do we exaggerate this degree of intimacy? What measures do we have (those likely to read this book or those of Lévi-Strauss) of *how good* people thought (or think) their lives to be down on the farm, in the country, or in the past? For one who is highly literate and probably quite prosperous in an affluent society, the view that "pure" orality is more wholesome than writing (or mass media) is self-indulgent, born out of our "remorse." It is, at the very least, paradoxical, for we know that in the current global context, those who write are more nearly masters of their environment and are perceived as such. The individuals or groups who are "illiterate" or "nonliterate" are disenfranchised.[8] Even were the issues of alterity and perspective resolved, there would remain the question of whether oral and written modes of language are mere correlatives of "intimacy" and "fragmentation" or factors thereof. Despite a history of study, this question still has no entirely acceptable responses.[9]

If Kouyaté's glorification of oral language is comprehensible and if the mystification of orality in European discourse originates, as Derrida says, in the desire to find "the hidden good Nature," we cannot fail to ask whence comes its appeal to African writers and to readers of African literature. Why have many writers and critics mystified orality as the metonymy of a happy, or at least unstained, time? A plausible hypothesis is that to subscribe to this view is to assert a certain authenticity for African culture vis-à-vis European culture. It is no coincidence that a particular reverence for the "oral character" of Africa should mark the writings of the négritude writers and other pan-Africanists who have looked to cultural origins as a way of differentiating and shoring up the identity of Africa vis-à-vis Europe. Thus adherence to a view of orality as distinctively African complements the tenets of négritude. Senghor and Zumthor share the view that emotion, spontaneity, nature (and orality) will serve "to leaven" rationality, artifice, culture (and writing). Senghor presents this argument not only in rational discourse and essay but also in poetry, a far more powerful instrument of mythmaking and one that is still more impervious to debate:

Que nous répondions présents à la renaissance du Monde
Ainsi le levain qui est nécessaire à la farine blanche.
Car qui apprendrait le *rythme* au monde défunt des machines et des
  canons?
Qui pousserait le *cri de joie* pour réveiller morts et orphelins à
  l'aurore?
Dites, qui rendrait la *mémoire de vie* à l'homme aux espoirs
  éventrés.
Ils nous disent les hommes du coton du café de l'huile
Ils nous disent les hommes de la mort.
Nous sommes les hommes de la *danse*, dont les pieds reprennent
  vigueur en frappant le sol dur. (21–22, emphasis added)

[Let us answer "present" at the rebirth of the World
As white flour cannot rise without the leaven.
Who else will teach *rhythm* to the world
Deadened by machines and cannons?
Who will sound the *shout of joy* at daybreak to wake orphans and
  the dead?
Tell me, who will give back the *memory of life* to the man of
  gutted hopes?
They call us men of cotton, coffee, oil
They call us men of death.
But we are men of *dance*, whose feet get stronger
As we pound upon firm ground. (*Poems*, emphasis added)]

The terms of definition of *négritude* are, as Cheikh Anta Diop has
remarked, precisely those of Gobineau, with this difference that they are
now seen as positive and essential to world humanism (*Nations nègres*
1: 54–57; see also Hountondji 224). Similarly, as apostles and detractors
of négritude have pointed out, precolonial Africa is in this view a happy
world, a better world, a world of a priori goodness and harmony, Senghor's
"kingdom of childhood," where the black man lived presumably with no
alienation, happy in his village, out of contact with whites. Thus Senghor's
poems are studded with symbols of that world. "Orality" and "sound"
are a preeminent sign among them, as in the many poems that allude
to "koras and balafongs" or as in "Nuit de Sine":

Qu'il nous berce, le silence rythmé.
Ecoutons son chant, écoutons battre notre sang sombre, écoutons
Battre le pouls profond de l'Afrique dans la brume des villages
  perdus.
. . . .
Voici que s'assoupissent les éclats de rire, que les conteurs eux-
  mêmes
Dodelinent de la tête comme l'enfant sur le dos de sa mère
Voici que les pieds des danseurs s'alourdissent, que s'alourdit la
  langue des choeurs alternés.
. . . .

Femme, allume la lampe au beurre clair, que causent autour les
  ancêtres comme les parents, les enfants au lit.
Ecoutons la voix des Anciens d'Elissa. Comme nous exilés
Ils n'ont pas voulu mourir, que se perdît par les sables leur
  torrent séminal.
Que j'écoute, dans la case enfumée que visite un reflet d'âmes
  propices
Ma tête sur ton sein chaud comme un dang au sortir du feu et
  fumant
Que je respire l'odeur de nos Morts, que je recueille et redise
  leur voix vivante, que j'apprenne à
Vivre avant de descendre, au delà du plongeur, dans les hautes
  profondeurs du sommeil. (*Poèmes* 12–13)

[Let the rhythmic silence cradle us.
Listen to its song. Hear the beat of our dark blood,
Hear the deep pulse of Africa in the mist of lost villages.
. . . .
Now the bursts of laughter quiet down, and even the story-teller
Nods his head like a child on his mother's back
The dancers' feet grow heavy, and heavy, too,
Come the alternating voices of singers.
. . . .
Woman, light the clear-oil lamp. Let the Ancestors
Speak around us as parents do when the children are in bed.
Let us listen to the voices of the Elissa Elders. Exiled like us
They did not want to die, or lose the flow of their semen in the
  sands.
Let me hear, a gleam of friendly souls visits the smoke-filled
  hut,
My head upon your breast as warm as tasty *dang* steaming from the
  fire,
Let me breathe the odor of our Dead, let me gather
And speak with their living voices, let me learn to live
Before plunging deeper than the diver
Into the great depths of sleep. (*Poems*)]

In this sumptuous and soothing poem, Senghor evokes and highlights
the oral nature of the traditional world. The point is not, of course, that
Senghor is wrong to depict this particular characteristic. It is rather that
this characteristic becomes identified in discourse with the supposedly
idyllic, true, pure nature of African life before the stain of colonialism.
Thus Hountondji refers to the complicity in the 1930s and 1940s "between
Third World nationalists and 'progressive' Western anthropologists. For
years they will assist each other, the former using the latter in support
of their cultural claims, the latter using the former to buttress their pluralis-
tic theses" (159).

Orality is a complement to the vision of négritude; it is a thematic and stylistic object of négritude's literary texts, which seek to evoke it as in "Nuit de Sine" and to imitate its "breath and rhythms" in verse length and structure. Orality is a sign for original Africa. It is useful to grasp the ramifications of such usage.

Tine writes of "feigned orality," but in my view it has become in many instances "orality on display," a troubled sign. In poems in which Senghor names the oral origins of his poems—"Pour kora et balafongs," for example—there is an *écart* [gap] between the claimed orality, announced in the title (or directions), and the textual fabric of the poem, which does not and cannot demonstrate the requisite orality except at the price of too much calculation and thus awkwardness. Titles or directions ("for koras and balaphon") are, as we saw earlier, expressions of the poet's desire to situate his text in a certain tradition. They are less useful as guides to the stylistic particularity of the poem to ensue. Given the distance between poetic fabric (intrinsic quality) and the poet's will to situate his poem, the term *orality*, which we associate with the poem, becomes gratuitous and thus "on display." In addition, there are sometimes problems apart from the textual *énoncé* [enunciation] that lies on the page: orality becomes an overworked, and therefore devalued, sign made to stand virtually alone as a measure of authenticity in contexts where little else seems to emanate from traditional culture.

Orality "in Retrospect"

Even when evolutionist theories per se are put to rest, comparative studies of oral and written texts are still plagued by notions of progress and by linear thinking. Orality and writing are seen not only as exclusive domains but as successive moments—whether stated explicitly or implicitly, whether the advent of literacy and written literature is hailed or decried. Thus there often persists a view of two opposing worlds in struggle as in the passage from Zumthor: the "first" and frequently "naive" oral world, meeting defeat from the "later" and "sophisticated" world of writing. J. Chevrier brings to his assessment none of the passion of Zumthor nor the condescension of Roscoe, but he suggests nonetheless a conflict between monolithic, closed domains: "A une civilisation de l'oralité se substitue donc progressivement une civilisation de l'écriture dont l'émergence est attestée par l'apparition d'une littérature négro-africaine en langue française" (7) ["To a civilization of orality, a civilization of writing gradually substitutes itself; its emergence is affirmed by the apparition of a French language Negro-African literature"]. Chevrier's statement is typical of the premises operative in many comparative studies. Innocuous as it may appear, it contains a great many false emphases: the presumption of an old civilization and then a new one, of a given, necessary sequentiality, and of the role that French language is assumed to play. We are right back in the old dichotomy that sees Africa as essentially oral and writing as essentially European. The paradigm of *rupture* ignores the lessons of history and of cultural syncretism; it accords to Europe too much importance and to Africa too little strength.

Abdul JanMohamed, whose Marxist reading of African texts distinguishes it in significant ways from most African literary criticism, also adheres, it would seem, to this view of progressive civilizations. He maintains that "the origin of the African novel lies in the transformation of indigenous oral cultures into literate ones" (2). He welcomes "the development of historical consciousness" which is said to develop with writing[10] and which, by many accounts, favors the rise of the novel (9, 280–83).

We have already examined the assumptions that writing is not indigenous and that it is therefore foreign, that "indigenous oral cultures" have been uprooted and supplanted by new systems. On the contrary, the evidence suggests that cultures are neither entirely and exclusively oral nor singularly literate. Terms such as *transformation* and *substitution*, even more than *transition* and *passage*, tend to obscure the coexistence and reciprocity of oral and written languages that characterize most societies, regardless of their degree of technology.

It is obvious, too, that in Africa as elsewhere printing, reading, and writing were material preconditions to the novel, but the rise of the novel can hardly be considered a consequence of literacy. I infer from the rather concise manner in which he outlines this argument that JanMohamed may in fact have questions about it. Literacy is an imprecise characterization of cultures where the majority of people were not literate and where the novel was the product of and for a minority of individuals who from a very early age were immersed in written traditions in their British or French colonial schools. The cultures that formed the context of production of these novels and that were their subject unquestionably were undergoing change in which new media of communication played a part, but at best this is a superficial explanation. Can aesthetic forms be accounted for merely because we have the technology to produce them?

Moreover, JanMohamed's view of the transformation of civilizations and, consequently, of narrative forms implies that the novel is an inherently superior form, another problematic assumption that is nearly inevitable whenever oral cultures are said to be transformed into literate ones and verbal art is said to pass necessarily from orality to writing. Orality is then viewed as a precious good threatened by writing, but one that nonetheless will be or must be distilled and preserved inside it.

From Definition to Prescription

If we have been made aware of the way in which early definitions of "African" were less a matter of self-definition than definition as Europe's opposite, then the orality/writing–literacy antithesis is another facet of that definition by contrast, which we have perhaps ignored. It is precisely to this habit of thought—which defines what is African in opposition to what is given as European—that Valentin Mudimbe refers when he warns African thinkers that

> échapper réellement à l'Occident suppose d'apprécier exactement ce qu'il en coûte de se détacher de lui; cela suppose de savoir jusqu'où l'Occident, insidieusement peut-être, s'est approché de nous; cela suppose de savoir, dans ce qui nous permet de penser contre l'Occident ce qui est encore occidental; et de mesurer en quoi notre recours contre lui est encore peut-être une ruse qu'il nous oppose et au terme de laquelle il nous attend, immobile et ailleurs. (44)
>
> [to truly escape the West presupposes that we understand exactly what it will cost to detach ourselves from it; it presupposes that we know just where the West may, perhaps insidiously, have drawn close to us; it presupposes that we know what remains Western in our very ability to think against the West and that we measure to what extent our rebuttal against it is perhaps yet another trap it uses against us and at the end of which it awaits us, quietly and elsewhere.]

To exalt orality and oral traditions, then, is ultimately as sterile and as blinding as to malign them. The exaggerated dichotomy between the orality of Africa and the writing of Europe took in the past a different form (orality as primitive/writing as evolved) which we have long dismissed. But it nonetheless reproduces itself as the object of literary criticism in the propensity to elevate the oral mode and world above the literate/technological one.

Peter I. Okeh, for example, begins his "Les origines et le développement de la littérature négro-africaine: un regard critique" with the entirely acceptable view that "la littérature écrite . . . marque le développement d'une littérature et non sa naissance" ["written literature . . . signals the evolution of a literature, not its beginnings"], but he goes on to privilege orality:

> La littérature africaine, à mon sens, sera par l'oralité ou elle ne sera pas. C'est bien de vouloir la recueillir à l'aide de magnétophones afin de la transcrire en documents écrits; c'est bien de la transposer en romans, en pièces de théâtre et en poésie; c'est bien de la rendre accessible au monde extérieur en anglais, en français . . . mais cela ne devrait jamais remplacer son oralité. (413)
>
> [African literature, in my opinion, will exist through orality or it will not exist. It is good to want to collect it with the help of tape recorders in order to transpose it into novels, into plays and into poetry; it is good to make it accessible to the outside world in English, in French . . . but that should never replace its orality.]

If Okeh's remarks are meant to remind us of the discrepancy between the quality of performance and the quality of the tapes and transcriptions of oral narratives and poetry that bring them to readers or distant audiences, then his comments help keep us on course. But his remarks do not seem to stress the need for greater respect for the context and art of oral performance. Okeh seems rather to valorize "the oral" in and of itself, as though its value were somehow primordial and self-evident. The danger here lies in Okeh's future and conditional tenses, his predictions and pre- scriptions for what African literature will or should be. It is the danger inherent in any definition—Tine's argument that "oralité feinte" is the dis- tinguishing characteristic of African literature and Kane's proposition that the originality of the African novel must be sought in its relationship to forms of oral literature.

Several conclusions may be drawn at this point. First, the oral tradi- tions of Africa are vigorous aesthetic and social acts, but there is nothing more essentially African about orality nor more essentially oral about Afri- cans. Second, to say this is not to question an African predilection for words well expressed. Camara Laye tells us that "le goût des palabres et du dialogue, le rythme dans la parole, le goût qui peut faire demeurer les vieillards tout un mois durant, sous l'arbre à palabres, pour trancher un litige, c'est bien cela qui caractérise les peuples africains" (*Le Maître de la parole* 22) ["the appetite for palavers and dialogue, for the rhythm of words, this appetite that can pin down old men for the duration of a month, beneath the palaver tree, to settle a dispute, it is this, indeed, that characterizes the people of Africa"]. What must be recognized, it seems to me, is that speech/listening is a mode of language as is writing/ reading. The art of speaking is highly developed and esteemed in Africa for the very material reasons that voice has been and continues to be the more available medium of expression, that people spend a good deal of time with one another, talking, debating, entertaining. For these very rea- sons, there is also respect for speech and for writing as communicative and powerful social acts.

Our objective, then, as readers and critics should not be to isolate orality, to see it as singular, as inherently "first" or "other" in opposition to writing. Neither medium is "the good guy" or "the bad guy." Neither should serve as metonymies for African or for European. Speech and writ- ing are modes of language, and both modes are ours when we have the means to produce them. When we look at their interaction in literary gen- res, it therefore should not be in an effort to prove or disprove cultural authenticity but rather to appreciate literature as a social and aesthetic act.

Second, there must not be and cannot be prescriptions for authentic- ity. As M. Z. Rosaldo explains, the search for origins is a dubious quest:

> To look for origins is, in the end, to think that what we are today is
> . . . primordial, transhistorical, and essentially unchanging. . . . Quests
> for origins sustain (since they are predicated upon) a discourse cast in
> universal terms; and universalism permits us all too quickly to assume
> . . . the *sociological* significance of what individual people *do* or even
> worse, of what, in biological terms, they are.

Stated otherwise, our search for origins reveals a faith in ultimate and essential truths. (392–93)

That there is a continuity in African verbal arts is obvious. The artists in question are creatures of culture, their traditions are in them and inform their works. To designate orality as the locus of originality and thus the source of continuity mystifies and disregards, then, the tradition that evolves within. It is surely to the Eurocentric reception of African literature that we owe the current orientation in studies of oral traditions and literature. If there had not been the Eurocentric annexing of African texts, the issue of continuity might never have arisen as it did—with its urgency and emphasis on the "Africanness" of literary texts. The exploration of links between oral and written art forms might then have taken a less ideologically motivated course, and studies of orality and literature might have examined the two, not in their supposedly essential nature as African and European, but in the interplay of aesthetics and social context that they imply.

2

An Impoverished Paradigm

We refer to the continuous dialogue of works of literature among themselves as *intertextuality*: texts comment and expand upon their predecessors or break with them entirely, as their situation in specific social and historical contexts shapes them. Far from being a closed unit, "tout texte est absorption et transformation d'une multiplicité d'autres textes" (Ducrot and Todorov 446) ["each text is an absorption and transformation of a multitude of other texts"]. The exchanges, allusions, and self-reference that we take for granted among written texts exist across modes of language and narrative art as well; such is in fact the topic of the many studies that inquire into the *oral* nature of African novels.

Yet the term *orality* is used to refer to several types of phenomena that may overlap in any instance; hence, the objective of such studies is variable. There are, first of all, those written narratives that retell narratives of the oral tradition (A. Tutuola's *Palm-Wine Drinkard,* D. T. Niane's *Soundjata*). Because the new context of enunciation implies shifts in audience and message, such written texts are, of course, never transparent or equivalent copies of oral stories, but studies of such narratives usually compare oral and written versions for similarities of plot or of language that is characterized by parallel phrasing, repetition, antitheses—attributes that are considered traces of oral transmission or performance.

Questions of a different sort are raised by studies devoted to those written texts which do not represent oral texts outright. For many, the oral nature of African novels refers to the representation of everyday conversation, or the inclusion of proverbs, tales, riddles, praises, and other oral genres, which Alioune Tine has called the *ethno-text* (105–6), a term that reveals an interesting set of premises.

For still others, the oral nature of the novel is especially a question of narrative form, the adaptation of principles of oral narrative genres. Mohamadou Kane thus refers to the structure of novels, their characterization, the "presence" of the narrator; Harold Scheub refers to cyclical time, to heroes who transgress societal rules or transform them.

We may define yet another type of "oral presence" in novels if we are in agreement with those scholars who hold that modes of language are an important factor in the determination of cultural values. Kane claims, for example, that the narrator in many novels is a *formal* device that manifests a *cultural* privileging of rapport between addressor and addressee.

In this chapter we shall consider a series of problems that recur in studies of the oral nature of African novels. The discussion that follows shall focus primarily on the question of narrative form, the incorporation into the novel's architecture of narrative principles particular to oral storytelling.

The Trouble with Difference

The issue for scholars who engage in such studies has been to determine, first, what constitutes the "oral" nature of oral texts—their form and content as determined by their oral mode of transmission, genre, and cultural values—and, second, what traces of oral traditions might "appear" in writing. Needless to say, folklorists and literary critics, including Finnegan, Havelock, Johnson, Lord, Obiechina, Parry, and Scheub, have devoted reams to this controversial issue. What is oral narrative? What is written narrative? How does the one differ from the other? Can one contain the other? How can we recognize the signs of one "inside" the other?

The initial question—What is oral narrative?—is of itself complex and difficult for those who study oral traditions. We have come to recognize that speech and oral traditions cannot be grasped adequately from paper representations. Thus it is not simply a matter of "collecting stories" but, ideally, of understanding performances as do their participants. Such studies will still be subject to preconceptions and misconceptions, of course, but they will not be skewed at least—as in the case of those who study the "oral" nature of written texts—by the continuous need to distinguish what is seen in performance from another art form.

In the case of observing oral narrative at work "inside" written narrative, hard and fast distinctions seem absolutely necessary, since it is presumably the gap between oral and written narrative which makes for our perception of difference and thus "orality in the novel." For some, a vestige of oral narrative in written narrative is ample use of dialogue and "scenes" (Dehon); for others, it is a lack of "good" dialogue (Larson). For some, plots are linear (Kane); for others, they are cyclical (Scheub) and digressive. Not surprisingly, there is a profusion (and sometimes confusion) of terminology, partly because such judgments are made with regard to narratives from all over the continent and partly because oral narratives are highly varied.

I do not pretend to resolve these perennial riddles here. While some distinctions may be possible, it is important to understand the trouble that arises with definitions based on *difference*. Even when we are most conscious of the importance of correctly apprehending oral narrative, it is almost always seen as an *écart* [divergence] from the novel, and the distinctions we make are often neither real, absolute, nor necessary. We will see further on precisely how this process operates, but let us note that in discussions of written literature and literary merit, the binary opposition between "orality" and "writing," between oral narrative and novel, may tend to obscure more than it illuminates.

Still more important is the fact that the question of the oral nature of the African novel almost always has a double: *Is the novel European?* It is an idealist question which assumes the existence of aesthetics apart from sociohistorical context, and it saps precious energy and confounds us. The issue of the oral nature of the African novel is always conflated with that of the Africanness or Europeanness of the novel as a genre. Thus no matter a critic's stance on oral and written narrative, no matter the insights and nuances of his or her argument, these are always distorted by the hidden question. The important and exciting issue implicit in such studies is the elasticity of art forms, the mechanisms by which they adapt to historical periods and cultural contexts different from those of their origin. But this issue is rarely raised because discussion is always sidetracked by the need to differentiate the African from the European.

Let us consider the introduction of Eustace Palmer's *The Growth of the African Novel*, in which the author takes up the question of which critical standards should apply to the African novel. The debate brings him, of course, to the origin of the novel in Africa: "If it could be proved . . . that the African novel emerged from traditional African sources quite independent of western influences, then there might be some justification for the use of purely African critical terms of reference in keeping with the sources and the indigenous development of African fiction" (4). Most of us would probably not want to limit ourselves to a single set of critical terms in any event, but more problematic is the assumption that a literary form's ancestry, its origins (in this case, emergence from traditional African sources), should justify or determine particular standards. If indeed a specific set of critical terms of reference pertains, it is not because the literary genre in question is *descended* from a previous genre.

As for the origins of the novel, Palmer states, "A number of African novelists incorporate elements of the oral tradition into their novels, but these are not therefore outgrowths of the oral tale. Much as we would like to think so for nationalistic and other reasons, the novel, unlike poetry and drama, is not an indigenous African genre" (5). With regard to its aesthetic design, Palmer concludes that "the African novel grew out of the western novel, but . . . African novelists have modified the genre largely in the direction of themes, language, setting, and point of view" (5–6). Here it becomes obvious that the question of the oral "heritage" of the African novel is another way of asking whether the novel is African or European.

The ideological nature of this issue is also underscored in Harold Scheub's "Review of African Oral Traditions and Literature," a compelling response to the compartmentalization in African literary criticism. Scheub both offers his account of the historical development of the novel as a genre in Africa and considers ways in which individual contemporary novelists adapt motifs and images of the oral tradition in their works. Unlike Palmer, Scheub argues—in a fashion reminiscent of Scholes and Kellogg's chapter on the oral heritage of Western literature in *The Nature of Narrative* and Georg Lukacs's *Theory of the Novel*—that the novel in Africa evolved from the epic of oral tradition. "The assumption that the novel form evolved in the West and was transported to the rest of the world is as blind as it is arrogant . . . the novel was vibrant some three or four thousand years before workers went to factories in Europe" (74). He cites as evidence Egyptian texts such as "The Story of Sinuhe," which Miriam Lichtheim dates from the Middle Kingdom, and "The Report of Wenamun," composed during the New Kingdom (*Ancient Egyptian Literature* 1: 222–35, 2: 224–30). Scheub concurs with Lichtheim that these narratives depict in realistic fashion human characters, relationships, and feelings and thus demonstrate the interest in human psychology and in individual experience that we associate with the novel.

Scheub's argument is important in the context of the current work, for it exposes several fundamental issues: first, the problem of defining the term *novel*. In this regard, if we subscribe to Bakhtin's point of view, for example, that the novel is a tendency toward parody and desacralization, the conclusion that novels existed as far back as the ancient Egyptians has nothing shocking about it. On the other hand, for those who hold the view that the novel that Scheub describes (human psychology, individual experience) is the narrative form that corresponds to the rise of European bourgeois culture in the seventeenth, eighteenth, and nineteenth centuries, Scheub's claim is problematic, for the novel could not possibly have existed in ancient Egypt.[1]

Clearly, Scheub's argument highlights and attempts to redress the ethnocentric bias of which we are all aware in African literary criticism: the term *novel* is often used as a transhistorical, transcultural literary category, but, as we know, in actuality its "platonic" features just happen to be those of certain European narratives. Yet his claim does not succeed in rectifying this literary and cultural imperialism; on the contrary, it would seem to contribute to the problem by acquiescing to the view that the novel, so typically European, is a superior form of narrative and that there is *one* novel. These assumptions alone give a desperate quality to arguments about the origin or merit of novels in Africa. One senses an urgency to escape the stigma that Césaire suggests in *Le Cahier* when he describes black people as "ceux qui n'ont jamais rien inventé . . . rien exploré . . . rien dompté" (117) ["those who never invented anything . . . explored anything . . . tamed anything"]. Scheub's argument with regard to the novel is sensational, because it claims the esteemed novel as African in the first place. Scheub's theory of the evolution of heroes and narrative forms may pertain to the development of the Egyptian narratives mentioned above, but it seems less relevant to the development of the novel in sub-Saharan Africa, which did not evolve gradually. The important point, however, is that it matters little for gaining an understanding of the efficacy and workings of African novels, on which horizon the novel genre first appeared. I am reminded in this regard of Lévi-Strauss's comment on the industrial revolution:

> Soyons donc assurés que, si la révolution industrielle n'était pas apparue d'abord en Europe occidentale et septentrionale, elle se serait manifestée un jour sur un autre point du globe. Et si, comme il est vraisemblable, elle doit s'étendre à l'ensemble de la terre habitée, chaque culture y introduira tant de contributions particulières que l'historien des futurs millénaires considérera légitimement comme futile la question de savoir qui peut, d'un ou de deux siècles, réclamer la priorité pour l'ensemble. (*Race et histoire* 65)

> [if the industrial revolution had not begun in North-Western Europe, it would have come about at some other time in a different part of the world. And if, as seems probable, it is to extend to cover the whole of the inhabited globe, every culture will introduce into it so many contributions of its own that future historians, thousands of years hence, will quite rightly think it pointless to discuss the question of which culture can claim to have led the rest 100 or 200 years. (*Race and History* 38–39)]

The issue, then, is neither the novel's origin in historical time and continental space nor from which other genres it descended. It is precisely when he is no longer entangled in the contradictions of this issue that Scheub goes on to do an important comparative study of tale, epic, and novel heroes. It is the assumption of continuity that permits this analysis, and it is ultimately the assumption of continuity (rather than a struggle to prove it) that is most compelling.

Other prominent studies devoted to these questions are Mohamadou Kane's "Sur les formes traditionnelles du roman africain" and *Roman africain et tradition*. Like Eustace Palmer, Albert Gérard, and others, Kane concedes that the novel is a European import in Africa, but he argues that African literature (written in European languages) must be understood not as an appendage to European literary traditions but within an African aesthetic lineage. He claims that African writers are heirs of two distinct artistic traditions. He brilliantly exposes the weaknesses of earlier criticism, with its exclusive focus on themes and language, and concludes that the African novel has been misunderstood by readers and critics who have no familiarity with the oral traditions of Africa, for its structure and many of its "peculiar" qualities are explained when we refer to oral storytelling.

Kane: see thru lens of novel; debate OT traits in novel that aren't justified

For Kane this continuity is a matter of formal structural transfers between oral and written texts.

Kane's analysis is essentially synchronic (rather than historical) and is a compendium of traits he considers to be characteristic of or derived from oral tales and that occur in most francophone novels. Kane makes astute observations and argues compellingly, but the traits that he ascribes to oral tradition and (by implication) to the novel are, of course, both mutually exclusive and highly debatable. This is a case, I believe, of seeing the oral tradition through the lens of the novel, which means seeing it not disinterestedly, but seeing it distortedly. That vision then reciprocally distorts the sense of the novel. The important point to be made, it seems to me, is that studies of oral narratives do not seem to justify the traits that Kane outlines; it is rather the juxtaposition of tale to novel that necessitates them: the assumption that the novel is already one thing, that the oral tale is therefore already its opposite—two tautological and reciprocally affirming assumptions.

The foremost trait of the oral tale in Kane's study, then, is unity of #1 action or "linearity," "a single action," reflecting the storyteller's obligation to eliminate everything that prompts even the least confusion ("Sur les formes" 553). Related to unity of action are a single dominant character #2 who often serves as a pretext for (the narrator's or author's) observations and commentary, the motif of the journey (frequently in three stages: #3 home, away from home, home once again), and the inclusion of several #4 genres (proverb, riddle, tale) within a text.

If the tale of oral narrative has its rules, the written form or novel (or at least the ideal novel, which Kane feels is the one African writers should have aimed for) is presumed to have quite different rules. Indeed this ideal novel is so much the norm that he never states exactly what its rules are. We infer them from the following passage:

> Pourquoi dans des romans où l'on voulait présenter les divers aspects d'une société donnée, les multiples problèmes suscités au sein de cette société par la situation coloniale, l'exigence de progrès, la nécessité d'une rapide adaptation au monde moderne, n'a-t-on pas, à l'exemple des Balzac, Zola . . . , diversifié l'action et par là même conféré une plus grande autonomie, une psychologie plus profonde, aux personnages. Pourtant ces romanciers ont reçu souvent une excellente formation. Parfaitement au courant des problèmes de l'esthétique romanesque, ils en sont souvent restés dans leurs oeuvres à des techniques que l'on n'a pas hésité à qualifier de primaires. ("Sur les formes" 553)

> [Why is it that in these novels which aim to portray the various facets of a given society, the many problems sparked within this society by colonialism, the demands of progress, the need for a rapid adaptation to the modern world, has one not, following the example of a Balzac or a Zola . . . , diversified the action in order to accord a greater autonomy and deeper psychology to the characters? Nevertheless, these novelists

have often received an excellent education. Being perfectly aware of the problems of the novel's esthetic, they have often relied in their own works on techniques readily characterized as elementary.]

Let us leave aside, for the moment at least, the idealist nature of this definition of the novel and the fact that aesthetic judgments are not independent of social and historical context. We note, then, that Kane seems to say that in place of a unified plot and a single important protagonist, the African novelist might have elected to follow the Balzatian (a more "novelistic") model: a multilayered plot and a larger cast of characters whose motives and psychology might have been more prominent. (Only a few African novelists—Hazoumé, Sembène, Ouologuem, Ngūgī, Labou Tansi, for example—have written in this way.) Yet why assume the mutual exclusivity of the characteristics that he identifies as proper to the tale and those proper to the novel?

"Unity of action" is a problematic criterion if it is held to be typical of the oral tale (and it is similarly problematic if it is held to be atypical of the novel). Despite the claim for unity of action, studies of African oral narrative syntax and structure with which I am familiar have not shown this feature to be especially characteristic. In "Morphologie du conte africain," Denise Paulme describes the basic syntax of West African tales as follows: "un grand nombre de contes africains peuvent être considérés comme la progression d'un récit qui part d'une situation initiale de manque (causé par la pauvreté, la famine, la solitude ou une calamité quelconque) pour aboutir à la négation de ce manque en passant par des améliorations successives" ["a large number of African tales can be thought of as the development of a story that begins with an initial situation of want (caused by poverty, famine, solitude or some sort of misfortune) and ends with the negation of this want, achieved by successive improvements"]. She adds that the opposite movement (from equilibrium to disequilibrium) is also possible although much less frequent and then explains that this format is the basis of more and more elaborate stories: "A partir de ces formes simples: *ascendante, descendante, cyclique* (retour à l'état initial, bon ou mauvais), on peut concevoir des formes plus complexes . . . [des récits en] *spirale, miroir, sablier*" (135–36) ["On the basis of these elementary forms: *ascending, descending, cyclical* (the return to an initial state, whether good or bad), one can construct more complex forms . . . *spiral, virtual,* or *hourglass*"].

Narratives are composed of repeated sequences, capable of ever greater development, which together complicate and prolong a narrative. Others lend themselves to embedding or linkage. In this regard Birago Diop comments, "Sortir de son propos—souvent à peine y être entré—pour mieux y revenir, tel faisait à l'accoutumée Amadou Koumba" (*Contes d'Amadou Koumba* 13) ["It was a matter of habit for Amadou Koumba to leave his subject aside—often when he'd barely begun—to come back to it all the better"]. Could it be that unity of action is in this instance a paper concept: that which we perceive of narrative structure when performance has been taken away?

Harold Scheub, who has done extensive research on southern African narratives, also describes oral traditions as having a "predisposition for complexity": "it is what enables the riddle to become lyric, the lyric to become heroic poetry, heroic poetry and the tale to become epic" (24). This tendency of genres to mutate and expand in new ways has its parallel within a single narrative. Scheub indicates this property in a number of studies when he writes of the "expansible image."[2]

At best, it may be that what is meant by "unity of action" in the tale is the deliberateness and rapidity with which the conflict of any single sequence resolves itself. But my concern here is less for the accuracy of criteria than for an awareness of the assumption which leads us to determine that "unity of action" is characteristic of the tale. We make this determination perhaps because we assume that complexity of action is characteristic of the novel and that the two genres are mutually exclusive.[3]

It is similarly difficult to accept without reservation the proposition that traditional narratives, as a rule, focus on the adventures of a single protagonist. In my reading of a wide collection of traditional West African narratives including Birago Diop's *Contes d'Amadou Koumba,* as well as *Contes wolof du Baol* and more serious long narratives such as *Kaïdara* and *Silâmaka et Poullori,* which are popular in the regions of Senegambia, Mali, and Guinea, it is not clear that single protagonists are the rule. While there is no question that the trickster (Leuck the hare or Anansi the spider) is a lone protagonist who undergoes or triggers a series of adventures, many tales create a dialectic between the behavior of two or more characters (Paulme's "virtual" or "hourglass" narratives): the virtuous and the villainous, the generous and the selfish, the wise and the foolish. These tales rely on "doubles" to make their lesson obvious. So it cannot be assumed that a single protagonist is basic to the oral tale and that its presence in the African novel necessarily derives from the oral tradition. In fact, could it be that Kane and we perceive the single protagonist as somehow particular to the tale because it seems, given the Balzatian model, anomalous in the written novel?

If we consider such a definition of the novel, it is even more questionable than the aforementioned definition of the tale. Kane chooses as his model the fiction of Balzac and Zola with their multiple events and characters, but there are any number of twentieth-century French and English novels—to mention the most obvious—which do not fit this model and which also rely, to varying degrees, on "unity of action" as described above and a single protagonist: *La Nausée, L'Etranger, Voyage au bout de la nuit, L'Immoraliste, Heart of Darkness, Molloy.* The argument is thus weakened by its assumption that the novel is an ideal, transhistorical category. It is hard, then, to qualify narrative as "oral" or "written," tale or novel, using such criteria. Neither the oral nor the written mode of narrative is restricted to the simple or the complex, and so simplicity or complexity cannot be considered indices of the origin of narrative structure in African novels.

The contradictions in such arguments are highlighted once more in Kane's discussion of African autobiography. Given the more or less ubiquitous attributes of unity of action and the single protagonist in autobiographies (or pseudoautobiographies), Kane nonetheless finds the preponderance of such texts among the earlier African novels anomalous. The presence and number of autobiographies work against his model of the passage from oral to written forms, he tells us, because this form has no equivalent in the oral tradition where storytellers do not speak undisguisedly of personal experiences and where all stories are told in the third person. Here then are texts which exhibit the very qualities of his oral narrative model and which do not, by his reckoning, meet the criteria for oral narrative. This would seem to be an admission that the cluster of traits in question—unity of action, single protagonist, and even voyage—is not decisively and exclusively "oral."

A final irony in the discussion of autobiography is Kane's conclusion that African writers are self-indulgent and abusive of the freedom granted by writing when they follow their penchant for this form! Why, in this instance, elevate the "oral" rules above those of "writing" through an accusation of self-indulgence when elsewhere it is the written (Balzatian) novel which is elevated above the oral tale?

The Trouble with Sameness

The third and final major trait of the oral tale that recurs in African novels, according to Kane, is the journey: "on voyage inlassablement" ("Sur les formes" 557) ["heroes travel untiringly"]. Harold Scheub concurs with this judgment. Referring to Pita Nwana's *Omenuko* and later to *Things Fall Apart*, Scheub states that "the structure of the story is taken from the oral tradition, centering on a person who, because of a flaw in his character, absents himself from home, and while in exile undergoes a change" (62). Indeed, in a great many novels, from Laye's Clarence to Salih's Mustafa, protagonists move around endlessly. Here, the problem, as I see it, is of a different nature, for if heroes do travel, how can we know that the voyage is everywhere necessarily reminiscent of an oral tradition? How best to respond to Céline's Ferdinand, Gide's Michel, and Conrad's Kurtz than with a wandering protagonist? To what extent, then, can we claim that this cluster of features is derived from oral traditions? My reading of texts by women novelists does not reveal the same patterns and suggests therefore that gender, too, may play a role in choice of genre and narrative form. The choice of the single protagonist, "unity of action," and the voyage may be dictated by other circumstances or intentions, regardless of the writer's familiarity with oral traditions. Why might they not be equally "derived" from those European novels to which many early African novels were, in large measure, a reply? Why might they not be a function of the reading audience's expectations? Or of publishers' influence? Or of the fact that those likely to write in European languages and to be published were most likely to have journeyed themselves from village to city, from Africa to Europe?

My point is not that we must prove the absence of these elements in European novels in order to say they are derived from African oral narratives. Those elements in African novels—even if they are present in the literatures of other cultures—may well derive from African oral traditions. But then we must ask ourselves, What is the usefulness of this judgment, standing on its own? When such elements exist in texts from elsewhere (and even when they do not), what do we know once we have learned (if we could learn) that this text derives from an oral tale? I hazard two responses. First, we may perhaps "prove" the continuity with an indigenous form—a narrow harvest, it seems to me, in the 1990s. Second, we explain what seems "anomalous"—a risky venture, which we shall consider below.

To conclude, several of Kane's criteria are debatable—a situation that is typical and healthy in intellectual activity. What is significant, however, is that the criteria may have been perceived by him as characteristic of the tale because of his sense of the novel's rules and because of what he considered all along, perhaps intuitively and unconsciously, as weak points in the novels he considered.

From Difference to Deficiency

Taken to its limit, the division of narrative into the "unity of action," "single protagonist," and voyage of the oral tale, on the one hand, and, on the other, the Balzatian multiplicity of characters and events in the novel, leads once again to the deficiency of the oral tradition and of the African novel. Or, as I have been arguing, it may be the opposite that is true: leaving aside the issue of the (ideological) contexts in which aesthetic judgments are formed, oral traditions are examined in analyses such as this through the lens of the presumed deficiency of the novel. They are perceived as the cause of that deficiency and thus likely to be misperceived and misdefined because of the optic under which they are seen (or the burden that they are asked to bear) in this context. Kane, like many of us, is caught between wanting to explain seemingly odd traits of the novel (which, in fact, he will eventually call "weaknesses") and claiming an a priori Africanness in them because of the oral tradition—a bind, a double agenda that makes it difficult to perceive and judge the literature. Let us begin with the last of Kane's remarks, cited above:

> Pourtant ces romanciers ont reçu souvent une excellente formation. Parfaitement au courant des problèmes de l'esthétique romanesque, ils en sont souvent restés dans leurs oeuvres à des techniques que l'on n'a pas hésité à qualifier de *primaires*.

On peut certes arguer de *l'insuffisance* de la maîtrise des techniques de création chez bien des romanciers. Cependant la véritable explication de cette situation que l'on s'est presque toujours borné à constater, ne peut être trouvée qu'en référence, à la littérature traditionnelle. ("Sur les formes" 553, emphasis added)

[Nevertheless, these novelists have often received an excellent education. Being perfectly aware of the problems of the novel's esthetic, they have often relied in their own works on techniques readily characterized as *elementary*.

One can argue, of course, that many novelists have *insufficient mastery* of creative techniques. However, the real explanation of this situation, which we rarely go beyond mentioning, can be found only in reference to traditional literature.]

Kane chooses the fiction of Balzac and Zola perhaps because of the importance of realism in their work as in that of the African novelists and also because of the vagaries of the social contract under consideration in each case. Contrasting Balzatian or Zolaesque fiction with oral stories in the initial article, "Sur les formes traditionnelles," he finds that African writers have attempted to reconcile two conflicting sets of rules for narrative art and that their novels are something of a mixed breed. But it is also clear that Kane is not merely describing the pedigree of African novels: he is also expressing criticism, albeit in mild form.

In his later *Roman africain et tradition,* however, he takes a more prescriptive attitude toward African novelists, as many others have done. He almost berates them for having relied on the motif of the journey and on the hero-witness rather than on multiple "well-developed" characters whose experiences, in Balzatian fashion, would have represented many aspects of reality: "Issu de la littérature traditionnelle, le voyage, pour ne pas dire la technique picaresque, est responsable du recours à des formes de simplification abusive qui s'harmoniserait, jadis, avec le contexte de l'oralite (*Roman* 205) ["Arising from traditional literature, the journey— or, rather, the picaresque technique—is responsible for the recourse to oversimplified forms which, in the past, would have harmonized with the context of orality"]. Nothing is made of any possible correlation of this vision on the part of African novelists to specific conditions of colonial Africa. Kane states with no reference to historical context that the African protagonists are energyless:

Rien ne rappelle l'intelligence, la volonté, la force de caractère d'un Julien Sorel ni les facilités d'adaptation de la plupart des héros balzaciens montés de leur campagne natale à la conquête de Paris. Dans le roman africain, le personnage se présente moins sous les traits d'un homme d'action que sous ceux d'un témoin promis au statut de victime. (*Roman* 218)

[Nothing brings to mind the intelligence, the will, the strength of character of a Julien Sorel, nor the capacity for adaptation of most Balzatian heroes, headed from their home in the countryside to conquer Paris. In the African novel, the characters appear less as men of action than as witnesses destined to become victims.]

Referring more specifically to Oyono's Toundi as the prototypical African protagonist, Kane says, "On ne peut mettre à son actif aucune initiative conséquente" (*Roman* 218) ["One cannot credit him with a single action of any importance"]. Kane's observations are, of course, accurate with regard to many first-generation West African novels. Were they simply comparative, evaluative rather than normative, they would provide an important starting point for analysis: might not this particular pattern of the African novels (the passivity of their protagonists) be a part of their *meaning*, the equivalent of a sense of impasse under colonialism? Perhaps what is lost by forgoing the Balzatian character is gained, for author and readers, in the sense of self-questioning, alienation, disillusionment that surfaces in some texts. Dakar, Abidjan, and Yaoundé in the 1940s, 1950s, and even 1960s were not, after all, the equivalent of early nineteenth-century Paris and French provincial towns. Furthermore, there are examples of metropolitan heroes who also "subissent le monde nouveau plus qu'ils n'agissent sur lui" (*Roman* 217) ["endure the new world more than they act on it"]: Candide and Uzbek, whose authors, we might note in passing, were also engaged in treatments of social and political life. It is a common practice in social and political satire to send a young innocent on his way to discover the perils of social existence.

Kane's references to Victor Bol's remarks on this issue thus disguise the fact that the "psychological development" of characters is an attribute that has no *inherent* literary value. If it is a matter of discerning effective from ineffective books, all that can be asked is that characters fit the overall conception of the work in which they appear. But African novels are generically stigmatized by Bol for

la ténuité de l'affabulation . . . peu de complexité psychologique, pas ou guère de caractères dont on pressente la richesse intérieure . . . Les événements s'y présentent souvent comme le fruit du hasard ou plutôt de l'arbitraire, dans un déroulement chronologique à peine organisé, ou encore, des antagonismes sont indiqués entre les personnages et l'auteur ne se préoccupe pas de les amener à l'affrontement et au conflit . . . Ils [the novelists] semblent n'avoir éprouvé aucun besoin de dramatisation et n'avoir pris que peu de souci de l'objectivation romanesque. (*Roman* 212)

[thinness of plot . . . lack of psychological complexity, few or no characters whose inner depth is intimated. . . . The action here often appears to be either arbitrary or attributable to chance, within a chronological development that is barely organized. Or, still more, antagonisms between characters are hinted at but the author fails to bring them to confrontation and conflict. . . . [The novelists] seem to feel no need for dramatization and to pay but little attention to novelistic objectification.]

In his earlier article, "Sur les formes traditionnelles," Kane had examined this aspect of the fiction described above by Bol; authorial intrusion, he argued, reflected a desire on the part of the novelists to be in contact (as is a storyteller) with their audience. But what begins as a statement of observation and explanation in "Sur les formes traditionnelles" has become in the later *Roman africain et tradition* an accusation of deficiency. And yet when Bol's observation might be made of certain "characters" in the *nouveau roman*, why is that observation held to be a sign of weakness—poor mastery of form—in the context of the *African* novel? Moreover, why is "weakness"—if weakness there is—attributed not to the novelists themselves but *generically* to familiarity with oral traditions? Oral traditions are thus held to be the cause of weak qualities in certain narratives, as in the case of *Une vie de boy,* and of exemplary qualities in others, such as Paul Hazoumé's *Doguicimi.* Thus Kane writes of Hazoumé:

> Il concilie sa volonté de réhabiliter les civilisations africaines, de *rester fidèle aux formes du discours traditionnel* et de restituer la mentalité de ces peuples que l'Europe avait jugés et qu'elle avait souvent condamnés à une remarquable assimilation de l'art littéraire européen. Une réussite semblable est restée unique dans les annales littéraires africaines. ("Sur les formes" 550, emphasis added)

> [He reconciles his will to rehabilitate African civilizations, *to remain true to the forms of traditional discourse,* and to restore the mentality of the peoples whom Europe had judged and often dismissed with an extraordinary mastery of European literary art. This tour de force is unique in the annals of African literature.]

It is almost always true that in comparative studies of oral "sources" and written texts, the oral tradition is held to be the cause of the novel's success or failure or becomes itself the target of blame or praise. Oyekan Owomoyela, for example, makes an astute observation with respect to the reception accorded African poetry and drama, on the one hand, and novels, on the other: "residual cultural influences in modern African poetry (and drama) are accepted because these forms are supposedly integral parts of the African heritage, while corresponding influences in the novel are seen merely as a result of the imperfect assimilation of a totally strange import" (79). But he does not sufficiently explore this and other contradictions which he himself signals. He follows Adrian Roscoe's lead in arguing that the problem with the novel (for example, the absence of psychological development of characters, bad management of dialogue) is the tale and that novelists are "actually short-story writers trying to write novels" (78). Ali Mazrui also privileges the novel and attributes the weak individuality and characterization of African novels to the oral tradition (169–80).

If for these writers the oral tradition menaces the novel, for Scheub, "oral" written works seem better. He, too, resorts at moments to definitions of oral texts ("extreme emotion") and written texts ("linear use of language") that are vague and questionable. The problem is exacerbated because Scheub perceives orality in so many varied written texts. Moreover, in his enthusiasm for oral art, Scheub, unlike the others I have cited, overvalorizes orality. He makes a useful distinction between those written texts which, on the one hand, simply write down oral stories and are therefore dead ends ("mimicry") and those which, on the other, truly evoke, reinvent, and transform them ("organic growth"). His preference is, of course, for the latter, which are for him "most oral," a confusing designation since, as Scheub states, it is the author's mastery of the written medium that makes possible an effective simulation or mediation of orality. Thus Scheub makes these judgments: in Tutuola's works, "the original oral tale has lost most of its orality, so that the reader becomes despairingly conscious of repetition" (56). Cyprian Ekwensi's *People of the City* and *Jagua Nana* "are at their best when they are most oral, but Ekwensi is unable to sustain this, and his works suffer as literature" (57).

Determinism

If it could be said at one time that readers and critics often misread and misperceived African literature because they failed to take the writer's background into account, we have now come to a point where we misperceive because we overestimate the importance of the writers' background and of the narrative predecessors of the African novel. Apart from the problems implicit in the formal models of oral story and written novel, and yet related to them, another assumption informs the judgments of Owomoyela, Mazrui, Kane, and others. Kane, for example, writes of the African novelist:

> Quel que puisse être, par la suite, son degré d'adaptation à la culture française, il sera toujours impossible d'expliquer ses oeuvres en faisant abstraction de son origine. C'est en cela d'ailleurs que réside la différence entre le romancier africain et le romancier étranger qui écrit sur l'Afrique. ("Sur les formes" 549)

> [Whatever degree of adaptation to French culture he may subsequently attain, it will always be impossible to explain his works if we leave out his origins. It is here, moreover, where lies the difference between an African novelist and any other novelist who writes about Africa.]

Kane's statement is actually tautological and is true of any writer in any culture. So what is the sense of such a statement? The implication seems to be that the African writers' origins are manifest in the oral form of their writing. Yet Kane's statement carries its own criticism. His perspective is not expressed in an identifiably "oral" style or structure, and yet it echoes Birago Diop's "Les Mauvaises Compagnies" and other such tales in which the lesson is that "one should always stick to one's own kind"— the assumption being that one's origins are absolute.

The fact that one's origins are fixed does not warrant the conclusion that one's identity is finalized at birth and must manifest itself in certain ways. V. Y. Mudimbe takes a more satisfying view in my opinion. He agrees with Kane that one's origins stay with one: "la tradition comme le passé, c'est en nous qu'ils sont et non derrière nous. Ma tradition comme mon passé sont dans ma parole présente" (193) ["tradition, like the past, is within us, not behind us. The traditions and past from which I come are in my words each and every day"]. Mudimbe then insists that we therefore need not—in fact, must not—objectify or brandish our origins. "[L]es discours qui prétendent le traduire comportent régulièrement une part de mystification" (193) ["As a rule, discourses which claim to translate [one's origins] engage in mystification"]. Kane, like Palmer and many others, strongly feels the need to identify one's origins in order to know what one (or what one's writing) is. Mudimbe argues, on the other hand, that our origins take care of themselves and that we need not go proclaiming them.

The mystification of "the past" or of origins contributes to the concept of an atemporal African essence, which then can become something of a requirement of authenticity. Origins become the object of our quest, a sufficient explanation of literature, a self-fulfilling prophecy.

There are two important conclusions to be drawn. First, the question of origins leads many of us to see the novel as a battleground in which African elements vie with a recalcitrant, if not intractable, Europeanness. This is a red herring to which we might apply Paulin Hountondji's comments on philosophy, technology, and science. His view is similar to that of Lévi-Strauss, cited above:

> un lien historique n'est pas un lien essentiel. C'est un lien de fait qui n'est pas un lien de droit. . . . la technologie moderne, la science moderne au sens le plus étroit du mot, se sont davantage développées dans la culture occidentale, que dans les autres cultures. Mais de là à prétendre que l'Afrique, la Chine, l'Inde sont en train de s'occidentaliser parce qu'elles s'efforcent de produire, de développer, à leur tour, la science et la technologie au sens le plus moderne du mot, il y a aussi un énorme saut. ("Table ronde" 6–7)

> [an historical bond is not an essential bond. It is a *de facto* bond which is not a matter of principle. . . . [M]odern technology, modern science, in the strictest sense of the word, developed more fully within Western culture than in other cultures. But to pretend, on that basis, that Africa, China, and India are becoming Westernized because they, in turn, are striving to produce and develop science and technology in the most modern sense of the word requires an enormous mental leap.]

Oral elements may well be a vestige of oral narrative traditions and will therefore be experienced as aesthetically African, but a work that does not contain, or that transforms, such elements is not necessarily less African. To fail to make use of oral traditions is not to forgo Africanness.

demystification
Ls anyone
Can write " African "

The corollary is that African novelists may choose (as much as any writer can be said to choose) to reproduce the formal qualities of the oral genres but that they will not necessarily do so because they are African, nor should they be expected to do so. Their cultural heritage is in them, whether or not they follow in their writing the principles of oral narrative performance. An Irishman, too, with sufficient exposure and practice, could undoubtedly write about Africa in an oral style, typical of African oral traditions. So could I. A comment of Larry Neal comes to mind: a style is an idiom, a language that can be learned and reproduced, as is jazz, by any—be they African or Japanese—who care to learn.

Second, references to oral speech, oral genres, and oral performance in African novels, whether they be explicit or implicit, are neither necessary nor generic, but are rather arbitrary and specific. The model that ties orality to origins sees the writer as helpless and prey to the past: he or she cannot but write this way. This model is seductive because it fits the evidence superficially, but it is, in fact, reductive. It offers a quick and easy answer, which eliminates a great many questions. My term *arbitrary* means, then, that writers do not evoke and are not bound to evoke "orality" because they are African (where Africanness claims, as a transhistorical feature, an "oral upbringing" that has permanently fixed one's sense of character, plot, etc.). We have already examined in Chapter 1 the problematic discourse that ties orality to Africanness. Obviously, African novelists have been as marked by reading as they have by listening. If we accept the premise that participation in oral performance has been, by and large, a significant aspect of the education and aesthetic life of many African novelists, we know also that many such young listeners were also young readers of novels in colonial and national schools. They were participants in several modes and genres of narrative and may call upon all these aesthetic experiences in their writing. Their work may be rich, indeed, precisely because these novelists have such a varied range of experiences upon which to draw, but writers are not bound to call upon any single one.

Moreover, references to orality in African novels are not generic (ubiquitous and universal) but are *specific*. All novels do not seem to be marked by orality, and those that are do not manifest the same characteristics. The application of oral narrative rules and solutions to African novels is not naive and a function of the writer's origins; it is as conscious for the African writer as is the use of specific techniques for any writer. An African writer whose novel takes oral texts as its intertexts is as conscious and crafty as is William Faulkner.

This is obvious, of course, in the case of a writer like Birago Diop or Camara Laye. No one would doubt for an instant the deliberateness of these writers as they composed *Les Contes d'Amadou Koumba* and *Maître de la parole*. Here the writers' aim is to "reproduce" texts of the oral tradition, and they bring to bear all of their skill as writers to evoke a universe of oral storytelling and orality, including the elaboration of all-knowing, fully credible narrators who furnish appropriate detail for a heterogeneous (and presumably less informed) audience.

Yambo Ouologuem and Ahmadou Kourouma are surely just as deliberate in their evocation of the cadences and energy of speech. Ouologuem's *Le Devoir de violence* articulates its anti-epic in a griot's style and effectively slanders négritude's romantic vision of precolonial Africa. Kourouma's *Les Soleils des indépendances* strives to rework French into a medium commensurate with Yama's "postindependence" reality.

In these instances it is quite clear that writers are aware of oral speech and genres as objects of or major factors in their discourse.[4] In light of these arbitrary and specific (that is, deliberate and purposeful) uses of orality, it is surprising that generic hybrids—narratives that are deemed novels and that incorporate traits of the epic or initiation story, associated with oral traditions—are frequently assumed to have been created that way without the complicity or knowledge of the author. This is, in effect, the implication in accounts that place the oral component of this dual tradition not in the writers' minds and hands, but in their oral origins. Such typologies of orality and the novel make types not only of the texts but also of the writers.

PART II

The Arbitrariness and Specificity of Form

3

The Importance of Genre

There is perhaps general agreement that a writer may learn from a technique or procedure in one genre or medium (in this instance, the oral poem or narrative) and apply it to another (the novel), but once we forsake notions of orality as authenticity in the novel or of the passage from orality to writing, or of orality as strength or weakness, how do we study the adaptation of oral narrative procedures and genres in African novels?

It will be noted that all the aforementioned assumptions regarding this aesthetic issue tend to focus on what in the writers' *background* makes them choose oral techniques or forms. The question of the writers' background is, however, beside the point. If novels refer in either their stories or their form to oral narrative and performance, it is not because writers are unwitting puppets of their experiences (the implication in many arguments being that "this is the only way they know how to tell a story"). I suggest instead that it is because these references serve a purpose: they solve or help to solve a formal or aesthetic problem that the writer faces, and they suggest at the same time facets of a particular social situation. Thus, even though such appropriation may not be a calculated and articulated strategy on the part of the writer, these adaptations are neither natural nor gratuitous in the novel. We therefore must shift our attention from what in the writers' background impels them to what in the present (text and context) calls for this technique or element, the relationship it entertains with other elements of the work. The emphasis in the following analyses therefore is not on what aesthetic experiences in the writers' background are available to them but on what needs in the work (and in social reality) may make them turn to those experiences.

My objective, then, is neither to document the "influence" of an oral narrative upon a written one by establishing a list of similar elements, nor to blame or to praise. Rather, I will focus on what the novels in question do with certain elements and on the implications of similarities and differences in the texts. There is much to be gained in this shift in perspective, in my view, for when we abandon the search for influence, we cease to be guided by the misleading urge to prove continuity, the preservation of some authentic element from one mode to another. If it is the wholeness and unity of African cultures we wish to make manifest, we accomplish this less, it seems to me, in defensively trying to establish the derivation of one thing from another, than in asserting coequal terms, each to be illuminated by the other, both in what they share and how they differ.

My ultimate goal, then, is to examine ways in which the adaptation of genres associated with the oral tradition reveals not what has often been thought of as virtually blind adherence to the conventions of traditional art but rather narrative goals, social and ideological vision. I have chosen to focus on genre both because it is the most troubled aspect of this critical practice (oral traditions and the novel) and because in concentrating on specific forms, we dehomogenize orality, thereby discrediting a still widespread perception in novel criticism of universality and uniformity. Finally, I believe a study of genre has much to teach us.

Thus I distinguish between genre and the inclusion of proverbs, songs, tales, riddles and other forms of speech, as we find them in *Things Fall Apart*, *Les Bouts de bois de Dieu*, and a great many other novels.[1] Those forms, along with the characters and settings, establish the locus of action; I view them primarily as topographical rather than constitutive. An analogous distinction in the visual arts might be that between the *portrayal* of an African mask or statue in a contemporary painting and the *adaptation* of traditional aesthetic principles in such a painting. The former are present as an object of the novel (or painting) to which the work calls attention, but they do not reveal the rules or processes by which a work has been constructed.

Those rules and processes are delineated, as we shall see, when we consider genre (narrative structure and impulse). Such an approach may seem to ignore the performance aspect of oral forms—except to the degree that the medium is the message or, in other words, the extent to which performance has shaped the written texts that here serve as models.[2] Yet to study form is not to discount performance; on the contrary, a consideration of form in this instance presupposes an awareness of the conditions of production and reception.

Generic tendencies, I shall argue, are not the trace of authenticity but are more nearly a tool of social vision. In their patterns we can grasp the underlying assumptions of a work, its struggle to reconcile new historical situations with what we might call—following Fredric Jameson's lead—the "ideology of form." This premise, which offers rich possibilities for interpretation, informs the following analyses as do a number of other critical approaches. From a theoretical point of view, then, the current work surely draws on readings in materialist criticism, structuralism, deconstruction, and feminist criticism, many of which overlap. An important theoretician for this work is Mikhail Bakhtin, whose treatment of the novel and epic I cite often in the initial analyses and whose theory of language seems to me a useful model for the intertextuality which, I feel, binds oral genres and the novel. The history and contradictions of language (and literature) are present in my new act of speech (or writing), which—being particular to the historical moment and social circumstances in which I live—necessarily reconfigures language (textual signs) and its (their) meaning. The recombination of elements from other texts gives not the same elements with old meaning but new elements with new meaning. Semiotically speaking, repeating an utterance is not, in fact, to repeat it but is, rather, to speak in a new context and thus create a new utterance. So the elements of traditional oral genres repeated, as it were, in new forms mean something new, accomplish something different. An argument such as this is analogous to Jameson's concept of the "marbled" structure of the novel, which strives to accommodate heterogeneous and sometimes conflicting narrative paradigms (144).

The three narrative forms or genres, present in many oral traditions and reappropriated in the novels I will examine here, are the epic, the initiation story, and the fable. I focus this study on novels of French expression. In addition I include one novel in Gĩkũyũ (available in English) because it is an important commentary on the debate that is the subject of this research. I found no novels by women that adhered to the traditional models. This lacuna could be due to my own failure of perception, but I should like to advance another hypothesis: women writers, by and large, may not be drawn to the epic, initiation story, or fable in their traditional acceptations.

There may be little surprise in the absence of an epic tendency among women writers. This hierarchic form is tied to nationalistic agendas and military might, which have been and continue to be, for the most part, provinces of patriarchy.[3] The traditional initiation story, also a production of hierarchic culture and essentially a praise-song to established authority, is also absent in novels by women. Here I am distinguishing between the traditional initiation story and novels of growth, such as Ken Bugul's *Le Baobab fou* (1984), Buchi Emecheta's *Joys of Motherhood* (1979), and Mariama Bâ's *Une si longue lettre* (1979). (There are also novels of this type authored by men.) These are individual-centered narratives whose impulse is realist and developmental. As we shall see, they share little with the initiation stories proper, wherein the initiate, after an appropriate apprenticeship, enters a luminous, virtually beatific state of Truth. The nonofficial, nonformalized, and more realist novel thus may have particular appeal to women because it offers the opportunity to explore more personal experiences, to allow for desire that goes unarticulated, indeed, unvoiced in the other forms. The very act of writing for a woman, then, can be seen as transgressive against the order which the initiation story proper represents.[4]

Fable, as we shall see, is less well defined than either epic or initiation story.[5] I read it as a potentially subversive rather than ratifying form, premised on magical possibilities or the fantastic. Emecheta's *Rape of Shavi* (1985) might have been included in this category because it is allegorical, but the narrative limits itself to retelling (in another register) the story of the colonial encounter.

The issue of the relationship between gender and genre requires a study of its own, but reasons for differential reappropriation by women and men of certain genres may become clearer as we proceed.[6]

Epic

4

A Dubious Heroism: Epic Modalities in
L'Etrange Destin de Wangrin

> Qu'on ne cherche donc pas, dans les pages
> qui vont suivre, la moindre thèse, de quelque
> ordre que ce soit—politique, religieuse ou
> autre. Il s'agit simplement, ici, du récit de la
> vie d'un homme.
>
> (Amadou Hampâté Bâ,
> *L'Etrange Destin de Wangrin*)
> [It would be useless to look for any kind of
> thesis, be it political, religious or other, in
> these pages. This is no more than the story
> of a life.
>
> (*The Fortunes of Wangrin*)]

The literatures of Africa are replete with valiant and noble heroes—warriors, emperors, and kings like Chaka, Mwindo, Sundiata, and Silâmaka. The lives of heroes, it would seem, call for and fit quite naturally into the contours of epic. But, in fact, the opposite is true: a life and its events are amorphous, raw materials of which narrative proposes a story and forms a vision as great or heroic. Narrative form organizes a life *into* greatness, ushers it *into* heroism. Nowhere is this more obvious than in Amadou Hampâté Bâ's *L'Etrange Destin de Wangrin* (1973), which demonstrates very clearly that an ordinary man can be made into a legendary hero. Wangrin is an interpreter and subsequently a merchant in French West Africa (Mali) who uses his position and intelligence to foster his own strength and wealth and, as a result, to outdo the French. The novel thus discloses the usually undetected truth that the heroes of epic and of all narrative are made, not born.

In this chapter, then, we shall consider how and why Bâ's novel appropriates elements of oral epic traditions in order to elevate an ordinary individual into a legendary figure. The primary epic on which I base my discussion is that of Sundiata (Johnson, Laye, Niane). We shall consider certain features of *Wangrin* that are typical of epic (its treatment of time,

elaboration of the hero, episodic patterning, and forecasting), the occa-
sional awkwardness of these features, and the implications of that awkwardness. I do so not in an effort to catalogue similarities between the
novel and the oral tradition nor to document this novel's origins, but to
demonstrate the novel's complexity and originality.

Bâ is a Malian storyteller, author, and scholar, renowned for his work
in and on Pular oral traditions. *Kaïdara,* the Pular initiation story, is perhaps the best-known text of this body of work, one with which *Wangrin*
has several affinities, not the least of which is the grandeur of the hero.
Bâ may indeed have no special political or religious design in recounting
Wangrin's life, but his story is motivated by a particular narrative impulse
or desire, which does itself have designs. Thus while the reader is led to
identify with Wangrin, while the author insists on the truth of his story
and on his personal acquaintance with the subject—all standard features
of realistic novels—*Wangrin* nonetheless appropriates the structures of epic
and produces a hero of extraordinary proportions. There are no valueless
literary or narrative forms; given its historical and cultural context and
its particular structure, then, *Wangrin* fits into a particular ideological
niche. It is clearly not the content or facts of the story that beg epic form,
and so it is the impulse to organize Wangrin's story in that form that seems
significant. Thus the content of epic is not necessarily dictated by the
history of him who is its subject, although the form is surely dictated by
the situation of him who speaks or writes the story and by that of his
audience.

For this reason, an appropriate title for this study might have been
"The Curious Story of *Wangrin*": *curious* because the concept of destiny,
which Bâ cites as the organizing principle of Wangrin's life, clearly situates
the narrative in the epic tradition while the narrative proposes nonetheless
a landscape and cast of characters that hardly fit the standard world of
epic and that seem moreover to require more ambivalence in the telling
than *Wangrin*'s epic self can admit.

The Epic Self: Time

Of those features of *Wangrin* that derive from or draw on the epic tradition
and whose role and value we shall examine, one of the most significant
is time. The story is situated temporally in early to mid-twentieth century
in French colonial West Africa, then known as the "Soudan." This real
time is not so very far back from the recounting or writing of Bâ's story
(thirty to sixty years), but it assumes nonetheless near legendary status,
like time in true epics.

Bakhtin makes a distinction regarding time in Western epics that, in
my opinion, may be usefully applied in this discussion. The important
point, he writes, is "not that the past constitutes the content of the epic.
The formally constitutive feature of the epic as a genre is rather the trans-
ferral of a represented world into the past, . . . and the authorial position

immanent in the epic and constitutive for it (that is, the position of the one who utters the epic word) is the environment of a man speaking about a past that is to him inaccessible, the reverent point of view of a descendent" (*The Dialogic Imagination* 13). What is significant, then, is that listener/reader and speaker/writer share a "present" moment, while the events of epic narrative are projected into what Bakhtin calls—using Goethe's and Schiller's terminology—"the absolute past." For Bakhtin, this past is closed off from the present, which he characterizes as "developing, incomplete and therefore re-thinking and re-evaluating" (17), and it is valorized: "all the really good things . . . occur *only* in this past. The epic absolute past is the single source and beginning of everything good for all later times as well" (15).

Bakhtin's analysis would suggest in this context that for Bâ and his readers, Wangrin is a cultural hero whose successes seem altogether unlikely in the present. (We might conjecture that villainy in now independent Africa is a more ambiguous proposition, since an African bourgeoisie has replaced European colonizers, and the morass of bureaucratic procedure is a far more alienating and demoralizing state of affairs; it cannot be localized in a tangible and worthy potential adversary, but is rather structural, thus seemingly intangible.) Thus, although the life and adventures of Wangrin the person are situated not so far back in real time—as a boy, Bâ knew him—they nonetheless participate in Bakhtin's absolute past because their epic mold gives them a certain grandeur that seems beyond our reach today.

I have been arguing that the real time of colonialism and its aftermath matters greatly in determining the impulse for (and form of) Bâ's narrative. Inside the story colonialism matters insofar as it correlates to the presence of Wangrin's adversaries, the French colonial administrators, known more commonly and pertinently as "les dieux de la brousse" ["deities of the bush"]. The ironic nickname is simultaneously reverent and irreverent, suggesting that the French are fitting adversaries and dupes. The colonial presence is thus both significant and insignificant. It is significant in the sense that colonialism requires correction and therefore justifies Wangrin's excessive appetites, his determination and frequently extraordinary behavior. The quality of the colonial foe earns him sympathy and admiration. But colonialism is insignificant, on the other hand, because it is hardly the subject of Bâ's narrative. This is Wangrin's story, and one in which colonialism is merely Wangrin's foil. The narrative is historically situated, but history is a backdrop to Wangrin's prowess and heroism.

Elaboration of the Hero

Thus the narrator begins his narrative not with the notorious historical situation but precisely where stories of epic heroes always begin with the place, time, and mysterious circumstances of their birth:

Wangrin naquît dans un pays à la fois ancien et mystérieux. Un pays où les pluies et les vents, au service des dieux, croquèrent de leurs dents invisibles et inusables les murailles de montagnes, créant, pour les besoins de la cause, un relief plat en même temps que monotone.

Les quelques saillies granitiques ou latéritiques qui résistèrent surplombent encore la plaine, de loin en loin.

C'est au pied d'un de ces monts rebelles aux érosions que fut fondé un village prédestiné, lequel donnera son nom à tout le pays: Noubigou. (11)

[Wangrin was born in a country both ancient and mysterious, a country where rain and wind, in the service of the gods, gnashed the mountainside with their invisible and everlasting teeth, creating in the process a flat and monotonous surface. A few ledges of granite or laterite managed to survive. Now they jut out at well-spaced intervals over the plain.

At the foot of one of the eminences that had rebelled against erosion was founded the foredoomed village of Nubigu which would later give its name to the country that surrounds it. (4)]

The village in which Wangrin is born is itself predestined and is born out of hardiness and resistance to the elements, which we will encounter again in Wangrin's character.[1] The narrator enumerates the roles of the deities who rule over this region and then describes the moment of Wangrin's birth. The rhetoric of this sequence echoes the oral style characteristic of Birago Diop's tales and of Bâ's traditional narratives, both in its metaphor—the sun "fit bouillir comme une marmite la couche gazeuse qui enveloppait la terre" (13)—and its parallelisms:

Les hommes *buvaient à longs traits* et *suaient à grosses gouttes*.

Les poulets, ailes ouvertes à demi, respiraient avec *force* et *précipitation*. Les chiens, *langue tirée* et *flancs battants*, ne sachant plus où se mettre, haletaient en faisant la navette entre *le dessous des greniers à mil* et *les maigres abris construits devant les cases*. (13, emphasis added)

[Men drank in deep gulps, sweat poured from their bodies in large drops. Chickens, their wings slightly askew, breathed fast and loud. Dogs, with flopping tongues and palpitating sides, unable to find a comfortable spot, panted and shuttled to and fro between the underside of the millet granaries and the narrow awnings that had been set up in front of the huts. (6)]

The birth is likewise accompanied by a birthing song, sung by the midwife, which both encourages the mother and calls on the maternity goddess to assist. Thus Wangrin's arrival is graced by the narrator's poetic flight and by the suggestion of music and the presence of deity. In fact, Komo, the god of blacksmiths, announces on the evening of Wangrin's birth that the child will have an exceptional career. The attention and care given to Wangrin's birth are typical of the epic and are neither simply "formulaic" nor gratuitous, because Wangrin is to be a creature of destiny. The initial sequence draws attention to birth, which the narrator continually signals as justification for Wangrin's future behavior.

There is, however, the uncharacteristic absence of Wangrin's genealogy, which reveals the particularity of this story and its difference from its narrative forebears. Amadou Koné notes in *Du récit oral au roman écrit moderne* (1985) that oral tellers demonstrate their virtuosity in recalling a long chain of ancestors and that such detail anchors the epic hero to a concrete world (38). Bâ announces in the foreword to his narrative, however, that he will name his hero only by the pseudonym *Wangrin* in order to protect the latter's family from any possible embarrassment or notoriety. Thus Bâ's Wangrin is a curious mixture. He participates simultaneously in an "historical" world, documented in footnotes, and in a mysterious and ambiguous one, suggested in the origins of his land of birth, as the narrator presents them. Koné notes that the heroes of initiation narratives (unlike those of epic) have vague beginnings (37). Thus Wangrin's origins/ "nativity" in both the historical world and the more ambiguous atemporal one mark a shift from oral to written production, from an indigenous to a foreign adversary, from an indigenous, ethnic audience to an international, multicultural one. Wangrin's multifaceted nature is highlighted later in his choosing a number of pseudonyms, one of which is Gongoloma-Sooké, the name of a Bambara god of a mysterious and contradictory nature who will be Wangrin's patron and protector.

A real challenge in this narrative, then, is the negotiation between Wangrin's epic dimensions and his life as one of us, the novel hero with whom we wish to identify. It would not do were he truly a god; our interest hinges on his simultaneous ordinariness and extraordinariness. Wangrin is an epic hero because he is of noble rank and is destined to live a great life, and conversely, he is of noble rank and is destined to live a great life because he is an epic hero. "O Wangrin, ce n'est pas le fait d'avoir su lire et écrire de gauche à droite qui a fait de toi ce que tu es, mais c'est ta naissance. C'est le lait que tu as sucé de ta mère, c'est le sang vermeil de ton père. Tu es aujourd'hui, parce qu'hier tu fus" (80) ["O Wangrin, it is not merely because you have learnt to write from left to right that you are what you are. It is because of your birth. It is because of the milk you have sucked at your mother's breast, and because of your father's vermilion blood. You *are* today because yesterday you *were*" (47–48)]. The emphasis on birth and destiny suggests the importance of origins (essence) in determining life goals and possibilities. This predetermination recalls the distinction between the epic and the novel in Bakhtin's schema: in the epic there is no mutability, no sense of endless possibility, but rather a sense of life and its events as *already fixed*.

Thus the narrator continually assimilates Wangrin to grand heroes, such as Silâmaka and Poullori. He comments: "Ce sont les époques et les lieux qui mettent davantage les étalons en valeur. Certes, si tu étais venu plus tôt, tu aurais été roi, et plus que roi, tu serais un empereur, comme Tounka et Mannga" (81) ["Standards of value are established through time and place. It is certain that in former days you would have

been a king, or rather an emperor, as were Tunka and Mannga" (48)].
This passage offers a curious reflection on historical and narrative possibilities. The present time and place, the narrator implies, do not permit the
same show of (masculine) grandeur as in other times, and yet Bâ's narrative
seeks to assert that grandeur for Wangrin. If the grandeur is—historically
speaking—impossible, Bâ does not conclude that the epic form of narrative
is also impossible. There is furthermore an important slip into the *present*
conditional, "tu serais un empereur." *Wangrin*'s narrative vision of grandeur is a wish for an historical context it sees as inexistent or past.

In addition to the "chance" of his birth and thus his preordained aptness for heroism, Wangrin is accorded personal qualities that set him above
other men: he is exceptionally intelligent and cunning, and he respects
tradition. But these are not qualities for which Wangrin must strive in
the course of his life; they are not any more earned than is his birthright.
They, too, therefore seem "naturally" his, from the beginning. He is
pleased with his own intelligence, education, adaptability, and successes.
Needless to say, as befits an epic hero, Wangrin has no small measure
of pride.

Wangrin's exceptional qualities allow him to straddle both worlds, to
succeed in each. He will begin his career as the director of a school, an
appointment that reveals once again Wangrin's stature. Such a position
is an honor for a young man at this time and thus appropriately falls
to Wangrin the hero. It also indicates the particular niche that he will
fill, one for which his many talents will serve him well: mediating between
two cultures. Bâ's hero and the context in which he operates suggest a
dynamic society that is constantly readjusting and readapting to new situations.

The insistence on Wangrin's birth, nobility, and missed destiny emphatically places Wangrin in the lineage of epic heroes, and Wangrin embodies continuity and discontinuity, qualities which Scheub sees as characteristic of epic heroes:

> The epic carries with it images and experiences of the past, what the
> society has traditionally stood for, into the new world. The hero is a
> part of both realms; he would not be able to take his people with him
> if he were not identifiably a part of the cultural past. But he has a vision
> of the new world. If he dies in the process of realizing it, if his flaws
> are exposed, his vulnerability exploited, that is a part of change; and
> the atmosphere of yearning, regret, and loss are a part of the epic tradi-
> tion, because it involves leaving a familiar world, and a transition into
> an uncertain one. Epic embraces both worlds. To make the change, the
> hero moves to the boundaries of his community, necessarily so; and as
> he escorts his society into the new world, he becomes its original insider.
> (18)

Like the hero of epic, Wangrin is at the boundary of old and new.
The narrative recognizes the inexorable process of change and is nostalgic

[handwritten margin notes: "mixed epic hero trickster = trickster (cf. Haitian tales)"]

for the past. But Wangrin has still more of the trickster in him. Scheub contrasts these two heroes in this way:

> The culture hero always leaves a residue; in his activities, he transforms the earth or human society or the relations between humans and gods, between ruler and ruled. The trickster also recreates the world, through illusion and deception. The difference between the trickster and the culture hero lies here: the trickster's creations are evanescent; they die as quickly as he obtains the fulfillment of his desires. . . . But the culture hero's illusions are forever; they are the form of the mountains, the curbs on the rights of kings; they are, in the Fon culture hero's case, for example, the mediating of gods and mortals. (21-22)

We will consider the durability of the trickster's (Wangrin's) "creations" at a later point, but let us note that Wangrin always uses his intelligence and cunning, first of all, to further his own selfish ends. He is avowedly greedy for wealth and power, and it usually happens that what is good for Wangrin is good also for his African subordinates, who are being exploited by the French. Yet the changes wrought by Wangrin are, as Scheub proposes, minor, temporary, and individual. Wangrin is of mixed breed, and this modulation is significant, as we shall see later in this chapter and in the chapter on Ngũgĩ's *Devil on the Cross*.

[handwritten margin note: "not epic"]

Wangrin's tricks range from the comic to the grand. When he intimates to the French commandant that a new association of young people has been created, the commandant sends two cases of wine, puts in a personal appearance and presents the society with the French flag on behalf of the local government. "Ainsi, une association qui n'existait pas était-elle officiellement reconnue par l'Etat! C'était du Wangrin tout pur" (147) ["Thus, a nonexistent society came to be officially recognized by the government. It was pure Wangrin!" (90)].

The most notable trick on the French is perhaps the creation of new distribution networks for the farmers' harvest at Dioussola. Not surprisingly, the role of adaptor, of intermediary between two cultures, in this text as in others, falls to the one (that is, the African) who speaks languages, and it is a position that brings with it wealth, prestige, and power. The connection between language and wealth should not be overlooked. "C'est ainsi," says the narrator when Racoutié has been stripped of his functions, "que Wangrin mit pour la première fois le pied dans l'étrier d'or que constituaient les fonctions d'interprète" (58) ["So it happened that Wangrin became an interpreter, which in those days was equivalent to slipping one's foot into a gold stirrup" (33)]. It is no coincidence that Wangrin will occupy two roles in his life: interpreter and merchant. Wealth becomes the new means to power and thus the sign of the hero's grandeur and of his ability to rally the people around himself. Thus the measure of heroism has shifted.

The response of Wangrin's African subordinates to his enterprising nature and successful career is admiration—save when it is jealousy. Bâ seems to argue therefore, both through his characters and through the epic design of his narrative (that is, Wangrin's stature as hero), for an acceptance of change and the ability to adapt to it. The status of *assimilé* is double-edged, of course.[2] We shall have occasion to come back to the implications of Wangrin's wealth and his status as *assimilé*.

Despite Wangrin's cleverness and fundamental magnanimity, he does not always behave in a noble and generous fashion. He abuses in the most outrageous way the hospitality and friendship of Romo, who then becomes one of his archenemies. Romo's hospitality and display of wealth might be considered "naturally" provocative to someone of Wangrin's stature and nobility, but the text disabuses us of any inclination to rationalize and unify Wangrin's behavior, of any longing for coherence: "Wangrin oublia morale et bienséance, justice et reconnaissance" (120) ["Wangrin forgot all feelings of moral uprightness, decency, justice, and gratitude" (74)]. Likewise, in the "cattle affair," the first big scheme of his career, Wangrin takes advantage of his poorer compatriots, who are neither rich bourgeois nor collaborators. He uses his stepdaughter, Tenin, to drug and spy on (that is, become the mistress of) Chantalba. He deceives and belittles the unsuspecting Rammaye, wife of commandant Gordane.

There are comparable episodes in the Sundiata epic: Diata's wrath against the sorcerer king Mansa Konkon, spying by Nana Triban, Sundiata's sister, on the archvillain Soumaoro. But in all these instances, Sundiata himself is blameless. He is provoked by Mansa Konkon, and Nana Triban is taken hostage by Soumaoro. There is thus once again in *Wangrin* a readjustment downward in the external measures of heroic stature. Wangrin's more ordinary nature is obvious in this fall from the high stratosphere of grace in which Diata and his peers operate.

No mere Robin Hood, Wangrin is an early-day Ngũgĩ thief, who would never murder to achieve his ends (as would Ngũgĩ's contemporary "businessmen" in *Devil on the Cross*), but Wangrin understands nonetheless the value of violence and manipulation. If Ngũgĩ were telling this story, Wangrin would not be an epic hero but a villain—not because he has broken with traditional values per se, but because he participates in an exploitative economic system. The similarities between Wangrin and Ngũgĩ's thieves make it clear once again that narrative form is dictated not by the content of the story but by a particular vision.

In order to maintain Wangrin's stature as hero and our empathy for him, Bâ's text compensates for Wangrin's failings:

> Sa grande concupiscence naturelle, qu'il avouait hardiment et qu'il haïssait sincèrement sans pour autant pouvoir s'en corriger, ne l'empêchait nullement, en effet, d'avoir du coeur et d'être enclin à la charité. Certes, pour avoir de l'argent, il était prêt à jouer des tours pendables, mais toujours au détriment des colonisateurs ou des chefs de canton ou des gros commerçants qui, à ses yeux, n'étaient que des exploiteurs de la masse paysanne. (272)

[His inexhaustible and innate greed, which he acknowledged impudently but also sincerely despised, without, however, being able to subdue it, did not prevent him from being a sensitive creature who inclined towards helping the poor. True, to make money, he was ready to play the most outrageous tricks, but always to the detriment of colonisers, native chiefs or rich traders, for he considered them exploiters of the peasant masses. (169)]

This passage is a microcosm of the text's strategies to negotiate between Wangrin's weaknesses as an ordinary man and the narrative impulse to create an epic hero. First, Wangrin's voracious appetite for material pleasures and his generally unprincipled struggle to satisfy them are attributed to his *nature*. His nobility, character, and destiny are thus all of one piece. Moreover, even if the young Wangrin, as a school administrator, dreams uncontrollably of a certain lifestyle above his means, it is only in response to provocation by the boisterous and foolish Racoutié that Wangrin actually embarks on his rather shady career.

A second textual strategy is to highlight Wangrin's strengths. Thus once he has decided to compete with Romo, he, as is befitting an honorable man, informs his opponent of his decision. Furthermore, Wangrin can be counted on to keep his word; he espouses traditional values:

Wangrin était filou, certes, mais son âme n'était pas insensible. Son coeur était habité par une intense volonté de gagner de l'argent par tous les moyens afin de satisfaire une convoitise innée, mais il n'était point dépourvu de bonté, de générosité et même de grandeur. Les pauvres et tous ceux auxquels il était venu en aide dans le secret en savaient quelque chose. Son comportement, cynique envers les puissants et les favorisés de la fortune, ne manquait cependant jamais d'une certaine élégance. (197)

[Wangrin was a rogue, true, but his soul did not lack sensitivity. Although his heart was consumed by a desire to make money by any conceivable means at his disposal in order to satisfy his congenital covetousness, there was much goodness, generosity and even grandeur in his make-up. The poor and the many people who had benefited by his unostentatious gifts were well acquainted with that side of his nature. Although his behaviour was cynical towards the mighty and the favourites of fortune, it was at no time despoiled of a certain elegance. (122)]

Wangrin is generous and charitable with widows, orphans, and the poor and is perhaps doubly redeemed by this behavior (in the eyes of readers and characters alike) since charity is deemed good in and of itself and since Wangrin's behavior proves his fidelity: these are virtues recommended to him by his mother. He can be moved likewise by the plight of a victim—even one who figures in Wangrin's own calculations against an enemy. Thus Wangrin rescues de Villermoz's messenger, who was thrown in prison because the papers he carried were stolen (by Wangrin's man, of course). Similarly, Wangrin responds sympathetically to Diofo's pleas to leave Brildji's body interred, but Wangrin's good instincts here as elsewhere are already dictated by or related to his noble origins. This is suggested in the passage above by the emphasis on what does or does not constitute his nature (*âme*), and it is made explicit in the following passage:

> "Non, Wangrin. Tu as sucé un noble lait et c'est du sang pur qui coule dans tes veines de prince. Tu ne déshonoreras pas un homme de même rang que toi, que la mort a privé de tout moyen de défense. Ce serait un lâcheté abominable et tu n'es pas déshonnête au point de violer la bienséance due par un homme noble à la dépouille d'un autre noble. L'identité de vos rangs et conditions sociales te crée des obligations."
>
>   . . . Le discours de Diofo l'avait remué profondément. Deux lourdes larmes roulèrent sur ses joues. (196–97)

> ["No, Wangrin. You were suckled on noble milk; blue blood flows in your princely veins. You cannot dishonour a man of your own rank, now rendered defenceless by death. It would be abominable cowardice; surely you cannot be so dishonorable as to forget the proper way a nobleman behaves when he is confronted with the dead body of one of his peers. The similarity between your rank and social status and Brildji's places you under some sort of obligation."
>
>   . . . Diofo's speech, then, had perturbed him deeply. (121–22)]

Finally, Wangrin's greed is justified entirely by the need to triumph over the French colonials. It is here that the narrative approximates the genuine provocation of the epic: "le héros lutte par légitimité, rarement par ambition" (Koné 40) ["the hero fights for the sake of justice, rarely for ambition"]. The narrator puts forth this rationale as we saw above, and in the recounting of Wangrin's first meeting with de Villermoz, for example, he uses direct discourse to allow Wangrin to "speak" and exonerate himself. The commandant of Diagaramba remarks to Wangrin, "il faut que tu payes les bienveillances que tu dois à la France en la faisant aimer et en répandant sa langue et sa civilisation. Ce sont là les deux plus beaux cadeaux que l'histoire humaine ait faits aux Noirs de l'Afrique. Oui, nous avons mission de faire le bonheur des Noirs, au besoin malgré eux" (38) ["You must pay the debt you owe France by ensuring that she is loved and that her language and civilization are spread far and wide. In the whole history of mankind, these are the two most beautiful gifts ever bestowed on African Blacks. Yes, it is our mission to bring happiness to the Black peoples, if need be against their own wishes" (20)]. With great largesse, he then gives Wangrin three five-franc coins. Given Wangrin's self-interest in maintaining the position of *assimilé*, he plays the appropriate part. In describing the scene to the future narrator of his story, however, Wangrin intimates that he was conscious of French paternalism and that his response to de Villermoz was irreverent, if not contemptuous:

Je m'exclamai: "Oh! Mon commandant!" Le commandant sourit, avec la suffisance princière d'un grand de ce monde venant accorder sa grâce à un besogneux. "Ce n'est rien pour un bon serviteur de la France comme toi, me dit-il. C'est tout juste un petit secours pour t'aider à t'installer dans ce putain de pays où le sacrifice humain est encore pratiqué par certains fétichistes!"

Je ne saurai jamais dire quelle force occulte me poussa à m'écrier en sortant: "Merci, mon commandant! Vive la France!" (40)

[I exclaimed: "Oh, Sir!" The district officer smiled with the princely condescension of the great man who has just bestowed favour on the needy. "It is a mere nothing for someone who serves France as well as you do," he replied. "Just a small contribution to help you settle down in this wretched country where fetishists are known to practice human sacrifices to this very day!"

I will never be able to tell which occult force made me shout, as I was leaving: "Thank you, Sir! Hurray for France!" (22)]

Wangrin mocks the commandant's generosity and observes his own duplicity. Interactions such as these are explanation enough perhaps for Wangrin's subversive career in fraud. He "does battle" with the French as if they have wounded and challenged his ethnic or national pride. The narrator lends support to Wangrin's mission by exposing even further nefarious French intentions and values, as in the following remarks: "A l'époque, le degré de moralité d'un individu se mesurait d'une part à l'importance des services qu'il avait rendus à la pénétration française et, d'autre part, à la situation géographique de son pays d'origine. C'est ainsi que les plus moraux des hommes étaient les Européens blancs" (57) ["At that time, the degree of moral uprightness of an individual was judged, on the one hand, on the basis of how much he had contributed towards French penetration and, on the other, by the geographical position of his country of origin. Accordingly, Europeans were the most moral of men" (32)]. The narrator highlights other anticolonialist protests, such as the small act of rebellion by the Bambara schoolchildren who surreptitiously mock the formula accompanying the sign of the cross. Instead of "Au nom du père, / du fils / et du Saint Esprit / Ainsi soit-il" ["In the name of the Father / and of the Son / and of the Holy Ghost / Amen"], Wangrin and his classmates say in Bambara, "Quoi que ce soit, / moi, / ma participation / n'y sera" (35) ["Whatever may happen, / as for me / there, I won't be" (19)]. Even Tierno Siddi, who recognizes Wangrin's guilt in the "cattle affair" ("Je suis contre toute personne qui abuse de son pouvoir ou de son intelligence, ou de tout autre avantage, pour tromper ses semblables et ravir leurs biens") ["I am against anyone who abuses his power and intelligence, or any other quality he may possess, for the purpose of deceiving and robbing his fellowmen" (62)] helps save Wangrin's skin because the French claim a moral superiority ("Mais je suis également contre les forts qui rejettent leurs fautes sur le dos des faibles" 102) ["But I am equally opposed to powerful men who make less powerful ones pay for their own misdeeds" (62)]. The narrator is thus Wangrin's best accomplice and defender in the campaign against the French.

Wangrin's rivals are intelligent men, although none is as intelligent as Wangrin. When they are noble, as is de Villermoz, their nobility implies education and a sense of honor, but it does not imply, as it does for Wangrin, greatness of spirit or soul. The French administrators are, above all, powerful. As a whole, they are more powerful than Wangrin because they are the agents of a structure bolstered by military might. Yet none of them is individually more powerful than Wangrin, for he knows more than they: he knows their world, its language and protocol, and he knows *his* world, the world in which they must operate. Wangrin's knowledge is his power. He is not exempt from punishment and persecution, of course, but he would be unbeatable in any event, even if he were less intelligent—by some slip of narrative—because destiny is on his side. The administrators, of course, have no singular destiny, except that of being the obstacles along Wangrin's path.

As for his African rivals, they, too, are doomed to fail, but when they are strong, they play their parts valiantly. The most distinguished and respected is Romo, with whom Wangrin engages in a competition of word sparring that augments the grandeur of each, since it is all accomplished through proverbs and metaphor.

Like other epic heroes, Wangrin has his devoted helpers, not least of whom is the narrator, as we have seen. In the story these helpers are numerous and come from all walks of life; they include the god Gongoloma-Sooké, Wangrin's griot Koutena, the elder Abougui Mansou and the marabout Tierno Siddi, assorted functionaries, Wangrin's stepdaughter, old women who dream dreams, and all those others whom Wangrin has saved or helped. Many are with Wangrin always such as his griot Koutena, while others appear and disappear, depending on where Wangrin finds himself. Wangrin wins the admiration and often affection of these individuals because of his personal charisma, his generosity, his respect for tradition and for elders. There are others whom Wangrin must trick into helping him; many of these remain faithful to him because they admire his determination and intelligence. And almost all these individuals derive at least some satisfaction in Wangrin's outfoxing the French. Wangrin's help does not come merely from "individuals," however. Spiritual forces, which manifest themselves in dreams, visions, and premonitions, also guide his actions and come to his rescue.

But if it is Wangrin's destiny to triumph over the French, it is also eventually his destiny to fail. The decline is predicted by the wise man who presides over Wangrin's circumcision and the initiation ceremony: "ton étoile commencera à pâlir le jour où N'tubaninkan-fin, la tourterelle au cou cerclé à demi d'une bande noire, se posera sur une branche morte d'un kapokier en fleurs" (24) ["I can see that your star will begin to set the day N-tubanin-kan-fin, the dove with a black ring round one half of her neck, comes to rest on the dead branch of a kapok tree in full bloom" (12)].

Inevitably, Wangrin will be undone, and the text manifests this degeneracy as Wangrin's growing laxity with regard to cultural traditions and interdictions, which is, in the final analysis, a weakening of his bond to the spiritual order. His first faults are thus poor social behavior: he has begun to hunt for pleasure rather than for food. He has become less generous with the poor and with widows and orphans. But his final infractions are of a different order entirely. He forgets to perform a ritual ceremony in honor of his ancestors, he has forgotten to bring his ritual symbolic stone which will eventually be thrown out by Blanche Terreau, he unintentionally kills the sacred python. This crisis, over which he seems to have no control (the text names it "involuntary suicide"), is the only truly reprehensible one of Wangrin's abuses. His manipulation of others, his greed are negligible; they seem allowable in someone of Wangrin's stature. But the inability to stay in harmony with tradition assures his downfall. Wangrin is aware of his self-destructive behavior, which is sometimes intentional and sometimes not. But he is unable to stop it.

It is not surprising that Wangrin's weakness should be situated in his deviation from prescribed customs and laws. It is ironic, however, that Wangrin's deviation from custom should be presented as his central flaw, for Wangrin is, by nature, already a deviant from "pure tradition." He is already straddling the French and African worlds, and this is actually his strength. It is one and the same person who is, on the one hand, "outré de voir ainsi maltraiter la belle langue française" ["dismayed by hearing the beautiful tongue he had learnt at school so ill used"] and contemptuous of his African brethren who speak "forofifon naspa," *tirailleur* French, in which "les verbes n'avaient ni temps ni mode et les noms, prénoms et adjectifs, ni nombre ni genre" (32) ["verbs had neither moods nor tenses and nouns, adjectives and pronouns, neither number nor gender" (17)] and who, on the other hand, wishes to help African farmers maintain greater control over their produce.

The Organization of Plot and the Problem of Agency

What is implied by the narrative structure of *Wangrin*, that is, the relationship between the events of Wangrin's life as they are narrated?

Theorists of the novel make a number of claims about narrative structure that are instructive in this regard. It is not to the structuralist models of narrative that I will refer, but rather to theories about the cultural bases and biases implicit in the novel. Bakhtin argues that in the (European) novel we come into contact with the "spontaneity of the inconclusive present" (*The Dialogic Imagination* 27), that "reality as we have it in the novel is only one of many possible realities; it is not inevitable . . . it bears within itself other possibilities." Furthermore, "there always remains in [the hero] unrealized potential and unrealized demands" (37). This dimension of the novel triggers a reaction on the part of novel readers, according to Bakhtin: they are always enticed by the desire to know "what's next?" Because this open-endedness and sense of possibility imply the ability to choose, "the individual acquires the ideological and linguistic initiative necessary to change the nature of his own image" (38). Bakhtin and Marxist critics seem to agree: the randomness and "originality" of protagonists' experiences in the novel manifest and foster a sense of individual power.

For many theorists the novel has its archetype in the detective novel, in which the plot is driven by suspense and the ending (frequently consisting of a revelation of something new) forces a rereading of the beginning. Many factors come together to create this new form. Lennard Davis, in a materialist interpretation, situates this climactic structure in a new attitude toward history (215): endings can alter what was previously thought to be a fixed destiny. In "teleogenic" narratives (those focusing on endings), Davis argues, the possibility of rereading is experienced by the reader as the ability to reshape a personal destiny. Thus, if for Bakhtin the novel is an appropriate form for "modern" life because it captures the "inconclusiveness" of reality, for Marxists it promotes a false and dangerous sense of individual power, which both reinforces capitalist ideology and distracts from more meaningful social action.

Unpredictability ("What's next?") and transformation of beginnings—these are two of the features that, according to these and other theorists, characterize narrative structure in the novel, in particular, the European novel from the early modern period to mid-twentieth century. With these theories in mind, we are able to see the particularity of *Wangrin*. In Bâ's novel, the ending does not force a rereading of the beginning, and there is little of the unpredictability to which Bakhtin refers. Having been made aware of Wangrin's singularity through the emphasis on his birth and his exceptional qualities, we know from the very first pages of the text the direction of the hero's future. His destiny, the rise and decline, is foretold. The narrator leaves no doubt about the credibility of the prophecy when he says, "Le récit qui va suivre verra l'exacte vérification de cette prédiction" (24) ["The narrative which is about to begin will show just how exact that prediction turned out to be" (12)].

The narrative structure of *Wangrin*, consistent with the story's stress on destiny, is a narrative where events are consecutive and cumulative. Episodes are relatively autonomous and overt; they do not contain the elements of a covert reading, only available at the end. And so there are two pleasures in Bâ's text: on the one hand, the minor suspense and desire to know how Wangrin will manage *this* time and, on the other hand, the even more encompassing joy of repetition, of fulfilled expectations. Accordingly, Bâ's narrative makes excellent use of what Eric Havelock has called the "echo principle" of oral poetry and narrative (177–78). The narrative is peppered with dreams, warnings, signs, functioning to alert both the actors and the readers as to how to read events. Havelock attributes such forecasting in the Greek epics not to the alleged fatalism of Greek culture but to the conditions of oral performance in which an audience, unless it is warned to listen, may fail to hear important passages that go by only once. In *Wangrin* these signs, which are manifest in the story and which touch therefore both actors and readers, are paralleled in the discourse by the narrator's proverbs to which readers alone are privy. Yet if we agree that narrative not only manifests culture but also shapes it, then the inclusion of dreams, warnings, and signs in narrative, even if they are due to the demands of performance, may in fact feed back into culture and create a disposition in which they become acceptable predictors. Then they not only tell what will happen but they *limit the sense of what can happen,* as does the emphasis on destiny and on a given immutable order.

And this is the significant point, it seems to me. For if the European novel, as described by its theorists, creates a false sense of individual power, the epic tendency of *Wangrin* creates simultaneously a false sense of power (though not of just any individual) and a false sense of stasis, that is, of undefiable order, and therefore of impotency.

Let us examine this paradox more closely. At one level, *Wangrin* is an empowering text. As Amadou Koné writes:

> Vis-à-vis du passé et de l'avenir . . . Wangrin conserve un ton serein et les aspects du héros traditionnel. Il est l'étalon, admiré par le narrateur et aussi par les lecteurs. Il se veut un modèle et . . . assume les valeurs traditionnelles telles que l'honneur, la parole donnée. Il sait que la société traditionnelle est en train de mourir et que de nouveaux soleils naissent. Il est un témoin et un acteur lucide de la métamorphose des temps. En fait, le récit semble être un témoignage sur les temps coloniaux, l'épopée d'hommes qui surent s'adapter à ces temps difficiles. (128)

> [With regard to the past and the future . . . Wangrin retains a serene tone and traits of the traditional hero. He is Man, admired by the narrator as by the readers. He sees himself as an example and . . . assumes traditional values such as honor or the keeping of a promise. He knows that traditional society is dying and that new suns will rise. He is a clearminded witness and actor in this transitional era. The narrative seems in fact to give witness to the colonial period, to be an epic about men who knew how to adapt to such difficult times.]

Like *Le Devoir de violence* (with which it superficially has very little in common), *Wangrin* asserts a forceful African response to the changes wrought by colonialism and thus a certain heroism— although the terms are obviously different in each text. Far from being a passive victim, Wangrin is hardy and resilient in the face of enormous, and often traumatic, change. He and other characters devise innumerable, creative anticolonialist strategies. The children's deformation of the sacred language of the sign of the cross is an exemplary instance, combining as it does three targets of revolt—language, education, and religion.

None of these small strategies, however, has the impact of Wangrin's gargantuan subversive plots, as in his rerouting of the "produits de la cueillette" ["fruits of the harvest"]. Thus while the French rule superficially, they are nonetheless being tricked, and French colonial policy is being subverted by this native son. We might even speak of a mild romanticization of colonialism, as Wangrin's vast playground, where the bullies are clearly in view. Because what is good for Wangrin is good for Wangrin's people, Wangrin's acts stand out as culturally heroic. The novel is governed by an epic impulse, which assimilates the hero to his people. *Prima facie*, it is the welcome assertion of an African triumph of sorts over Europe.

But Wangrin's heroism is so compromised that the triumph is dubious. While his heroic narrative predecessors act out of outrage toward injustice or wounded national or ethnic pride, which does, of course, have the consequence of enriching them and the populace, Wangrin is motivated primarily by the possibility of financial gain. His whittling away at the colonial structure is more a happy consequence of his actions rather than their motive. I make this comment not out of commitment to high moral values but because the reshuffling of motives, which correlates to the possibilities inherent in this colonial setting, mark a significant shift toward the trivialization of the challenge that the hero faces. The epic hero's motive and the measure of his power have shifted from epic to novel, from a hierarchical society, where nobility and heritage are aligned with justice, to the more random context of colonialism, where nobility and destiny justify greed and assure access to the new sign of heroism (wealth and its pleasures, including ultimately an affair with Blanche Terreau).

At best, Wangrin's achievements (like those of many a trickster) suggest that no system, regardless of its power, is invulnerable to cunning and intelligence. This is valid enough, but it is also a deficient and perhaps deceptive lesson when it is made to stand alone, for it is obvious that individual intelligence and cunning are not sufficient to combat a structural problem. Wangrin's defiant acts, which are so satisfying to his friends and the reader, are mere dents and scratches on the carapace of colonialism, which remains firmly in place. One is hard put to demonstrate any disruption whatsoever of the colonial machinery, as a result of his interventions. Above all, Wangrin lives within and profits from the system, thereby reinforcing and perpetuating it. His achievements, if they can be so called, vis-à-vis an overriding colonial structure are trivial. They are the achievements of a trickster and yet have become worthy of the stature of epic. The implication is that while the structural problem may persist, one can live within it, shadow-boxing and being "successful," too, if one is sufficiently smart, for no other outlets for heroic action seem possible. The narrative recognizes the need to adapt, but there is nowhere for heroism to go. The old heroism is gone, and in its new avatar, it can only work toward personal, material gain.

Because both the motive for and object of heroic action have shifted in *Wangrin*, the efficacy of individual action is questioned and the heroism of the hero is undermined. Furthermore, the relationship of Wangrin to those "represented" in his heroism is worth noting. Sundiata stands in "synecdotal" relationship to his people; even as he has a greater role that emphasizes his singularity, his difference, he is nonetheless one of them. His is a collective victory. In *Wangrin,* that relationship is fractured and could be characterized, at best, as "metaphorical." It is a rather arbitrary identification of the hero and his group, for the people do not and cannot come with Wangrin into victory. He cannot, as Scheub states, usher in a new age or propose a new vision.

There is an additional reservation to be made regarding Wangrin's heroism. With its content (Wangrin's success), the narrative extends the promise of individual force yet takes it back with the irreversible order of its form, for Wangrin's strength is not of his own making. He is able to accomplish what he does only because it is his destiny to do so, because he is heir to Silâmaka and to other epic heroes, because time and history, like the sequence of narrative events, move forward inexorably. It is clearly not for everyone to act.

And yet the narrative does not recognize the limits of Wangrin; it creates an old-style hero, justified every step of the way. Indeed, part of what redeems Wangrin—and it is helpful to think once again of Ngũgĩ's thieves in *Devil on the Cross*—is his nobility, his origins, which confer the right and the power to succeed. Similarly, it is the arbitrariness of success (exploitation) in Ngũgĩ's narrative that contributes to the viciousness of the process. Ngũgĩ depicts a "jungle," in which any man who is sufficiently greedy and heartless steps forward.

It would seem too little, in my view, to see in Bâ's familiarity with certain traditional forms a sufficient cause for this marriage of hero and form, for in this (conscious or unconscious) assembly lies a significance. Despite the charisma of Wangrin, the exuberance of his personality, and the satisfaction engendered (in accomplices and readers alike) by his successful adventures, the narrative ultimately seems to me paradoxically to project a state of blockage and to justify inaction. The apparently individual cunning and intelligence of Wangrin are not individual at all: there can be no individual initiative because the ability to act is predetermined. The role of destiny and the foreordained sequence of actions effectively relieve the individual of the burden of acting. Given a nonexceptional place in life, small subversions seem sufficient and indeed the only actions possible.

My conclusion is not that Bâ's remarkable novel is a false epic or that a writer should be advised to return to "true" epic. Rather, the aspiration toward epic (that is, the appropriation of epic narrative structure) in *Wangrin* is a strategy (a retreat into the authority of birth and destiny) to overcome what might be called a crisis in leadership. It is a strategy whose limits are also quite clear.

5

The Democratization of Epic:
Les Bouts de bois de Dieu

Like *L'Etrange Destin de Wangrin*, Ousmane Sembène's *Les Bouts de bois de Dieu* (1960) participates in the tradition of realism in African novels. It focuses on "ordinary" individuals in social interaction, and its considerable and evident artifice notwithstanding, the novel has come to be regarded as documentary fiction. Structurally speaking, it uses an epic framework, but it does this differently from *Wangrin*, modifying the traditional form significantly. It is a revision of epic, which shifts the emphasis from birth, destiny, and oracles. My objective is not therefore to prove its similarity to epic but rather to examine how the novel qualifies epic form, to see how the shape of heroism and social change are related to narrative form.

There has been little written about the epic impulse of *Les Bouts de bois*.[1] Sembène's stance against the mystification of the past and of oral literature is well known. In an interview with Mineke Schipper, Sembène stated in this regard:

> we must not forget contemporary reality, and let us no longer dream sentimentally about dear old Africa in the past. . . . Very soon Africa will no longer orally transmit its old stories to the younger generations. On the one hand this is sad, of course, but on the other hand it is very comprehensible. . . . [T]he ambition of the young generation reaches much farther than the horizon of the village. (567)

So forceful and adamant is Sembène on this point that readers and critics, by and large, have given up *Les Bouts de bois* to the other camp, so to speak. Mohamadou Kane writes, "Certes l'oeuvre de certains écrivains, tels Sembène . . . paraît vierge de ces survivances des formes traditionnelles" ("Sur les formes" 559) ["Of course, the work of certain writers, such as Sembène, . . . seem to carry no vestiges of traditional forms"]. Kane's judgment is based partly on questionable categories of oral tale *taken from a social transformation* not *birth, genealogy etc.*

and novel, as we have seen, but it also takes into account Sembène's acknowledgment of the influence of Western writers and thought on his work. In any discussion of literary origins or intertextuality, *Les Bouts de bois* is inevitably associated with Zola's *Germinal* or Malraux's *La Condition humaine*, and with good cause, since the latter is woven into the story as the inspiration for Tiémoko's initiative to try Diara before the other strikers. A further reason for dismissing any possible connection between *Les Bouts de bois* and epic form is the political nature of the latter. If the Sundiata epic, for example, is a verbal production of a ruling class (Koné, 62; Mbele, 15–18), it is clear that *Les Bouts de bois* has another agenda entirely.

Yet there is also general agreement among readers and critics that *Les Bouts de bois* attempts something more than most African novels. Palmer calls it "a story of . . . epic proportions" (190). Soyinka says, "It is a work which reaches beyond mere narrative in its meticulous delineation of human strengths and weaknesses, heroism and communal solidarity, and it attains epic levels. As with all good epics, humanity is recreated" (117). Soyinka's disparaging comment on "mere narrative" notwithstanding, one may infer that he regards *Les Bouts de bois* as a narrative whose focus is larger than the experience of the solitary individual.

This sense of something epic in Sembène's novel is rich in implications. First of all, genres of narrative are *logical* categories, and in any single narrative itself, categories may and do overlap. Bakhtin, it will be recalled, argues that the novel is by definition that genre which incorporates and parodies other genres. Still more important, to signal an epic impulse (that is, to assert something larger) in Sembène's novel is not necessarily to project it into a nostalgic past. Nor does it necessarily mean, as Kane's argument may imply, that narrative categories themselves are essentially of one culture or another. The epic self of *Les Bouts de bois* does not suggest a particular Africanness, a cultural imperative, but rather the working out of a particular issue. The fact that Sembène's previous novels do not reveal epic structure and aspirations substantiates this hypothesis. His choice of design, regardless of his ability or willingness to name it as I am doing, is the consequence not of the hero's birth or the dictates of literary tradition or even of chance but of a particular sense of society and social transformation.

Narrative Prototypes and Historical Events

In their discussion of *Beowulf* Robert Scholes and Robert Kellogg make the following remarks which must be taken with reservations but are relevant in a consideration of form in *Les Bouts de bois*:

> the values preserved in the myths of an oral tradition may be summoned up as a guide for comprehending the present event and how the present event is thereby incorporated into the tradition. . . . [T]he historical event

[intrudes] upon the traditional stock of myths and *topoi,* as requiring some sort of readjustment in the tradition to accommodate it. . . . A prototype of Beowulf doubtless existed in the Anglo-Saxon epic tradition before the events of sixth-century Denmark and Gotland were associated with him. And the Old French epic tradition had prototypes of Roland to whom the events of history were attracted in the process of evolving the *Chanson de Roland.* (36–40)

With two caveats, this analysis is useful. First, there seems to be little reason to limit the scope of the phenomenon Scholes and Kellogg describe to the oral tradition—this quarantining of the oral tradition betrays a misunderstanding—or even to literature, for that matter. In recent years, politicians often seem to take their cues from "heroes" in the mass media. Moreover, scientists, social scientists, and humanists, as is well known, also tend to see what they have been accustomed or trained to see. Our myths and history play a large role in what we are able to perceive and to narrate, no matter the discipline. Lévi-Strauss's metaphor of the "traveler in the train" makes precisely this point (Chapter 1).

Second, there is an obvious condition in this process that we may tend to overlook: multiple prototypes or structures are available, and storytellers or writers select, consciously or unconsciously, those that suit their needs. Thus the prototypes of Beowulf and Roland were not universally useful in narrative; they were appropriate models for narrating heroic deeds and not simply for shaping any and all plots. In other words, heroism was not the only model available; there were others that could be seen and chosen. There is some determination, but no overdetermination.

Nonetheless, Scholes and Kellogg posit correctly, it seems to me, that narrative structures of legend and myth which predate historical events provide structures for understanding and enshrining those events; they accommodate new "raw material." In this exchange events take on, wrap themselves, in the seemingly atemporal authority of myth and legend, which are transformed by the new conditions that obtain, and the structures of myth and legend are perpetuated in new stories. The tradition lives on as it bends to new substance, and the new events are perceived in the context of a society's history and past, in continuity and harmony with its deepest, most resonant chords.

This, in my view, is the case of Sembène's *Les Bouts de bois.* This narrative appropriates and alters the structures of epic for its not-so-distant subject, the 1947–48 strike of the Dakar-Bamako rail workers, and I shall read it against the example of D. T. Niane's *Soundjata* and Laye's *Maître de la parole.* It is the *structure* of these two texts which illuminates *Les Bouts de bois,* not an implicit nostalgia for past days of glory and authority. In its very dialogue with the Soundjata epic, Sembène's novel distinguishes itself and makes that point clear. Let me repeat that the reference to epic is an effective design for particular ends (ends which may be inferred from the text and not necessarily those "intended" by the author) and not a necessary and purely "aesthetic" (that is, functionless) heritage from the traditional storyteller, as some persist in claiming.

Ihechukwu Madubuike, for example, closes his eyes to the particularity of Sembène's text in order to make it fit into preconceived, hand-me-down formulas about what constitutes African narrative. One example of this tendency is his unconvincing claim for the "linearity" of *Les Bouts de bois*, a claim that keeps the narrative within his model of the Senegalese novel, which is inherently indebted, Madubuike claims, to the traditional storyteller:

> The Senegalese writer seems to cut off, voluntarily, details and subplots in order to better focus attention on the main subject of the novel. Not even Sembène Ousmane's *God's Bits of Wood*, with its amazing welter of anecdotes and apparently disconnected incidents, fails to reflect and respect this progressive linear structure. (159)

To claim that Sembène's novel is linear is either to ignore the evidence or to render the term meaningless. That the novel is well constructed around a single issue is unquestionable. But to subsume its numerous plots, its cinematic shifts in location, its many moments and various personalities under the term *linear* is to give in to a hasty, facile formula that distracts us from examining the power and uses of form. Mohamadou Kane, on the other hand, recognizes that by his definition of the cluster of traits of the traditional tale (unity of action, linear progression, and the single protagonist), *Les Bouts de bois* cannot be characterized as being derived from traditional form. Indeed, by Kane's terms, it cannot; yet, like the Sundiata epic, Sembène's novel depicts the battle of a society against an external aggressor, it focuses on the hero and his helpers, and it heralds the dawn of a new age and a new vision. Let us examine these points of similarity and the novel's modification of them.

Who Is Bakayoko?

Les Bouts de bois does not privilege origins and heritage: Bakayoko's grandeur is a grandeur of soul. His authority is justified by neither birth nor nobility but rather by personal qualities of intelligence and vision. The bases of his authority thus cannot be situated by the text either in a village or a kingdom or in his ties to deity or in genealogy, as they are for a Sundiata or for Wangrin; thus there can be no appeal to prophecy, no predictions of Bakayoko's power.

It is paradoxically the *absence* of Bakayoko in the first two thirds of the story that accords him his extraordinary power over both the other strikers and the reader. Since Bakayoko cannot be depicted as he who is "destined" to be great, he is made great instead by the voice of other characters from Thiès to Bamako to Dakar—a fitting measure in a novel of social transformation, as is this one, since it is the esteem of his people which elevates Bakayoko and not a specious birthright. Bakayoko is made present to all in the reiteration of his words, which like new "proverbs" punctuate the narrative and legitimize the other characters' decisions and actions. Keita states, "Il y a quelque temps Ibrahima Bakayoko me disait: 'Non seulement nous ferons le grand brassage dans ce pays, mais encore nous le ferons avec ceux de l'autre bord du grand fleuve'" (154) ["Ibrahim Bakayoko said to me, not long ago: 'When we have succeeded in stirring up the people of this country, and making them one, we will go on and do the same thing between ourselves and the people on the other side of the ocean'" (*God's Bits of Wood* 157)]. Samba says, "Bakayoko a dit: 'Ce ne sont pas ceux qui sont pris par force, enchaînés et vendus comme esclaves qui sont les vrais esclaves, ce sont ceux qui acceptent moralement et physiquement de l'être'" (45) ["Bakayoko has told us: 'It isn't those who are taken by force, put in chains and sold as slaves who are the real slaves; it is those who will accept it, morally and physically'" (58)].

Bakayoko is the point of reference, the buoy in the ocean of ideas that now dominate the strikers' lives and thoughts. Tiémoko, for example, reflects after the trial of Diara: "C'est un échec pour moi . . . tout cela vient de mon manque de savoir, mais la prochaine fois, ce sera plus sérieux. Dès ce soir, j'écrirai à Bakayoko" (155) ["He has beaten me now, because I don't know enough about these things, but it will be different next time. I must write to Bakayoko tonight" (159)]. Thus he is present in the rumors of his vision and moral bravery that circulate endlessly among his admirers. Daouda, who is jealous of him, sums it up best, perhaps: "Quel était donc ce Bakayoko, on aurait dit que son ombre était sur chaque chose, dans chaque maison; dans les phrases des autres, on retrouvait ses phrases, dans leurs idées ses idées à lui, et mon [sic] nom même se répétait partout comme un écho?" (110) ["Who was this man whose shadow reached into every house, touching every object? His words and his ideas were everywhere, and even his name filled the air like an echo." (115)]. Absent physically, he is all the more present and powerful because he dominates the moral vision of the strikers.

A further consequence of Bakayoko's physical absence during most of the story is a sense of suspense and expectation (on the part of characters and the reader) by which his stature and talents can be gauged; when he finally appears, an air of enigma surrounds him. There is a lack of emphasis on the private detail of his life, and there is an insistence instead on Bakayoko's singularity of purpose and vision, a treatment that is perplexing. And it is this enigmatic personality which contributes to Bakayoko's stature as an epic hero and which we must consider.

The tensions in Bakayoko's private and public selves have brought forth a range of interpretations. Madubuike, for example, comes to the erroneous conclusion that Bakayoko "is there simply to express the thinking of the group. . . . The individual disappears in the wake of a popular movement for survival" (40). Comments such as these fail to account for the *entire* novel. Indeed, a number of factors may contribute to our inability to perceive the texture of *Les Bouts de bois*. We may perhaps confuse individuality with the literary tradition of psychological realism; we may subscribe unquestioningly to prevailing wisdom, which in this case denies the role of individuality and self in Africa and African literature, or we may sense that Sembène's Marxist orientation precludes such roles. Recognizing and refusing such prejudices may allow us to see that, on the contrary, individuals make up the popular movement in Sembène's story. And, of course, to say that Bakayoko (or, for that matter, any other character) is an individual, and even more a hero, is not to deny the force of collectivity. Clearly, there could be no strike, no change without the people, nor can Bakayoko's particularity and role in the narrative be ignored or wished away. Sembène's novel is not an allegory; his characters are not a faceless mass.

Bakayoko's aloofness is, of course, likely in epic heroes, who are typically somewhat unfathomable, but unlikely in the protagonist of psychological realism that characterizes many mimetic novels. Eustace Palmer's judgment of Bakayoko, for example, seems to be premised on just such a model. Recognizing his strengths and appeal, Palmer also attributes to Bakayoko a certain "callousness and lack of consideration for the feelings of others." Palmer concludes that Bakayoko is evidence that "the rather special situation [political action] demands men who will not allow feelings or sentiments to interfere with their singleness of purpose; but there is no doubting the stress laid on Bakayoko's harsher qualities" (193). If for Madubuike there is no individual, for Palmer, Bakayoko is strikingly individualistic. Palmer's comments betray a gender bias (clearly heroic women like Ramatoulaye act out of their feelings, but men à la Saint Exupéry do not). Palmer's comments also betray a certain disembodied idealism (human beings, especially males, are above feelings; we develop, we can think and act *apart* from what we feel; thus Bakayoko's dedication to this cause or his reaction to the old woman in the crowd, for example, has nothing to do with feelings about injustice, suffering, exploitation, or racism). Palmer's comments fail to integrate all the evidence. It is only when Bakayoko is viewed as a descendant of the epic hero that Madubuike's and Palmer's perceptions can be reconciled, the view that he is, on the one hand, in a special relationship to his people and that he is, on the other hand, distinctive, full of determination and vision. Soyinka describes these two dimensions of Bakayoko in this way:

> Bakayoko is a Promethean creation. . . . Amoral in the mundane sense of the word, Bakayoko appears to be sculpted out of pure intellect and omniscience. . . . [B]ecause Bakayoko is portrayed as understanding and controlling the future . . . he supersedes all existing moral authority. . . . [T]he portraiture . . . is somewhat romanticised—necessarily so. He is a man of mystery . . . and dominating to all. . . . [H]e represents a gifted world. . . . He tends to the poetic, and his perception of the world takes from his own innate grandeur. . . . Thus, the world and his people are constantly transformed with his own reflective glow. (117)

Bakayoko's singularity is, indeed, atypical in fiction of this kind, and Northrop Frye's distinctions help to show why. The protagonist of most realistic fiction, according to Frye, is "superior neither to other men nor to his environment [but] is one of us: we respond to a sense of his common humanity, and demand . . . the same canons of probability that we find in our own experience." Bakayoko, on the other hand, is the protagonist who is "superior in degree to other men but not to his natural environment . . . a leader. He has authority, passions, and powers of expression far greater than ours, but what he does is subject both to social criticism and to the order of nature." This, Frye contends, is the hero of most epic and tragedy (33–34). Because the hero heralds the dawn of a new age, and because that transformation requires an agent of vision, ability, and great appeal to those around him, he must be magnetic, charismatic, to forge the many wills and destinies into one. (This does not preclude, of course, the hero's having his share of flaws.) Bakayoko is thus like the hero of epic and takes us by surprise in a novel such as this one.

Soyinka's term *sculpted* is perhaps not gratuitous, for Sembène's very presentation of Bakayoko contributes to this effect. If Bakayoko is mysterious to us in the first two thirds of the story, it is because we know him through rumor: he is not "represented" to the same extent as others but evoked, symbolized in the speech of others. Once he has appeared, however, he remains enigmatic, being less developed—mimetically speaking—than other characters (not *more*, as Madubuike claims in his discussion). In addition to the very qualities of exceptional intelligence, vision, and will that make him less malleable than other men and that set him apart, Bakayoko is presented "economically," that is, through his salient features only, and not with the alluring intimacy through which other characters are espied.

The portrayal of Bakayoko is, I suggest, a literary equivalent of this principle of sculpture. Writing of sculptures of Benin and Ife kings, Jean Laude describes the refusal of "individual accidentals" (*l'arbitraire individuel*) and a will to signify the essential:

> l'homme tend à être conçu et perçu comme personne distincte, même s'il ne s'agit en aucun cas de psychologie au sens occidental du terme. Ce ne sont pas les traits particuliers du souverain qui sont représentés, mais sa puissance, sa majesté et une sorte de beauté qui expriment dans leur perfection les caractères physiques d'un groupe ethnique. (135)

> [here man tends to be conceived and perceived as a distinct person, although this is never a matter of psychology, in the Western sense of the term. What is represented is not the particular traits of a king, but his power, his majesty and a type of beauty which, in their perfection, express the physical characteristics of an ethnic group.]

If the refusal of "representation" and the preference for signification are common values throughout the continent, as a number of scholars have indicated, Bakayoko's portraiture may be an adaptation of this aesthetic. Bakayoko is not for this reason—nor is a Benin or Ife king—a mere mouthpiece or transparent image of his people, as Madubuike has suggested. Bakayoko is rather an individual whose most fundamental traits (those important to the narrative) are presented with measure and discretion. He is part of a community and symbolic of it. He is not simply a hollow medium through which his people may be perceived.

Bakayoko's portraiture may be further explained by reference to what Robert Farris Thompson designates "the aesthetic of the cool": "control, stability, and composure." Thompson notes that "the 'mask' of coolness is worn not only in time of stress but also of pleasure. . . . The cooler a person becomes, the more ancestral he becomes. . . . Men and women have the responsibility to meet the special challenge of their lives with the reserve and beauty of mind characteristic of the finest chiefs or kings" (41–42). This moral and aesthetic aspiration is perhaps the best explanation of Palmer's judgment that Bakayoko is callous.

If Bakayoko is as grand as a king or epic hero, there is an important distinction to be made between his function and that of other cultural heroes. While the epic of Sundiata is a monument to a glorious past, the heroism of Bakayoko is a call to an historical future. Thus in the epic of Sundiata, the particularity of the hero is singularly important. His names, his lineage, his totems, the predictions of his birth—all are known and verifiable. Obviously, as a mimetic fiction, *Les Bouts de bois* also situates itself in space and time and history, but paradoxically Bakayoko's heroism is freed from time and space because it embodies the force and virtue of a people. Despite his position in this highly mimetic fiction, Bakayoko is less substantive than is Sundiata. It is no accident, it seems to me, that Bakayoko's mother dies and that he becomes the son of the old woman in the crowd, Fatou Wade:

> —Je te cherchais, fils, dit-elle à Bakayoko, pour te demander quelque chose: As-tu encore ta mère?
> —Non, grand-mère. Elle a été assassinée par les gendarmes quand je n'étais pas à la maison.
> 　　Bakayoko, tout en parlant, regardait la vieille femme. Elle lui rappelait Niakoro, et il se souvint des paroles de Bakary. Un regret lui serra le coeur.
> —Dorénavant, je serai ta mère, dit la vieille en lui prenant la main qu'elle lui caressa un moment. Mon mari est mort à la première guerre, à la seconde mon aîné. Et maintenant ils m'ont pris mon fils. . . . Si tu restes à N'Dakarou, viens habiter chez moi, il y aura toujours une natte pour toi.
> 　　Et tout heureuse d'avoir retrouvé un enfant, la grand-mère Fatou Wade s'en fut en gonflant ses joues et en plissant les lèvres comme le faisait Niakoro. (330–31)

> ["I have been looking for you, my son," she said to Bakayoko, "to ask you something. Do you still have your mother?"
> 　　"No, Grandmother. She was murdered by the police while I was away from home." Bakayoko looked at the old woman steadily as he

spoke. She reminded him of Niakoro. He remembered the words Bakary
had said to him and a little twinge of regret caught at his heart.

"From today on, then, I will be your mother," the old woman said,
taking his hand and holding it for a moment. "My husband died in the
first war and my oldest son in the second. And now they have taken
my other son. . . . If you stay in Dakar, my son, come live with me.
There will always be a place for you."

She walked off and left them, sucking her cheeks as Niakoro had
done, filled with joy at having found a son to replace her own. (317–18)]

It is once again neither birth nor blood lineage but the baptism by
fire in collective action that reforges and extends familial bonds. Fatou
Wade's symbolic adoption of Bakayoko suggests that he belongs to the people, whose desire and will he embodies. Bakayoko's moral vision is the
promise of their future. It is the precise role of "the people" in this heroic
novel which we shall examine next.

Agency: From Helpers to Heroes

Scheub notes, it will be recalled, that in many tales and epics, the hero
achieves his objective with the assistance of "helpers." These may be humans, animals, or objects, as the research of Calame-Griaule, Paulme, and
Görög-Karady demonstrates. In the Sundiata epic, for example, the future
emperor is helped principally by his brother Manding Bory, his griot Balla
Fasseké, and his sister Nana Triban; there are, in addition, spiritual forces,
magic objects, and a cast of kind hosts, valiant allies, and soothsayers.
In Wangrin the hero's helpers include his griot, the marabout, deities, and
numerous individuals. The chief characteristic of the human helpers is
obviously their devotion to the hero. They facilitate his triumphs and contribute to *his* glory, which ultimately—so the tradition would have it—
accrues to the whole people.

In *Les Bouts de bois,* there is a significant modification of the dynamic
between hero and helpers, for the latter are no longer mere extensions
of the hero. Bakayoko himself is not personally aggrandized by the actions
of the strikers. They are not simply joining him in *his* quest; they themselves quest and are transformed into heroes in the process. They cease
to be helpers, then, for the enterprise that they undertake is collective,
and they are no longer in a supporting role. The vision of the future is
no longer merely that of the hero, to which other characters attach themselves. It is not simply shared but is instead reworked as each and every
one grows in understanding and awareness. The text is explicit on this
point, as in the following passage in which the narrator describes
Tiémoko's sense of accomplishment at having persuaded his comrades of
the need to bring Diara to trial:

> Tout en marchant, il mettait son plan au point tandis qu'une puissante
> exaltation s'emparait de lui. Pour la première fois de sa vie, une idée

de lui allait mettre en jeu le destin de centaines de milliers d'êtres humains. Ce n'était pas l'orgueil qui était en lui, simplement il venait de
découvrir sa valeur d'homme. Tout ragaillardi, il entonna à pleine voix
Soundiata. (147)

[As he walked, he considered all of the points of the plan he had in
mind, and a sense of exultation swept through him. For the first time
in his life, an idea of his was going to play a part in the lives of thousands
of others. It was not pride or vanity he was experiencing, but the aston-
ishing discovery of his worth as a human being. . . . He began singing
aloud an ancient Bambara hymn to the founder of the empire of Mali,
the *Soundiata*. (150)]

Bakayoko's initial absence permits (and necessitates) such initiative
and reflection on the part of the strikers. The text thus envisions a role
for leadership, but does not conceive of heroism as the exclusive quality
of designated leaders. Indeed, it cannot be, for if the struggle in Sundiata
and other epics is frequently a physical battle, a show of prowess, then
in the novel it has become moral strength, wisdom, endurance, solidarity—a test which, as it has often been pointed out with regard to Sembène's
fiction, knows no gender. Given these extended parameters, women also
cease to be mere helpers or extensions of masculine identity and purpose,
as they necessarily are in traditional epics and in *Wangrin*.

Apart from Bakayoko's vision, the other great force for truth and therefore for heroism is "the machine," as the train is known. It lays bare the
lie of discrimination. Of race, class, and wealth it has no experience, and
it cannot be tutored, as people are, in such ideologies and social constructions ("la machine . . . elle, n'a ni langage, ni race" 127) ["the machine
knows neither a language nor a race" (132)]. Thus the text insists on distinguishing between technology as a catalyst for new vision and change, a
source of beauty and of human power, on the one hand, and, on the
other, the racism, class and economic interests that pervade its use. Those
passages isolating the tool from the web of societal bias, from its use in
exploiting other people's resources, are among the most brilliant and the
most beautiful:

Une fois par semaine seulement la "Fumée de la savane" courait à travers
la brousse, conduite par des Européens. Alors les grévistes tendaient
leurs oreilles, tels des lièvres surpris par un bruit insolite. Pendant un
instant, le passage de la locomotive apaisait le drame qui se jouait dans
leur coeur, car leur communion avec la machine était profonde et forte,
plus forte que les barrières qui les séparaient de leurs employeurs, plus
forte que cet obstacle jusqu'alors infranchissable: la couleur de leur peau.
Puis, la fumée disparue, le silence ou le vent s'installait de nouveau.
(128)

[Only once each week did the "smoke of the savanna" rise above the
brush, from the trains run by the Europeans. On those days the strikers
would stop whatever they were doing and turn their heads to listen,

like hunted animals startled by an unwonted sound. For a moment, the passage of the locomotive would calm the torment in their hearts, because their fellowship with the machine was deep and strong; stronger than the barriers which separated them from their employers, stronger even than the obstacle which until now had been insurmountable—the color of their skin.

Then the smoke would disappear, and there would be only silence again, or the sighing of the wind. (132–33)]

The train diffuses the cloud of contradictions and illogic that dominates the strikers' lives. Regardless of social constructions of class and race, the strikers are drawn to the train, and its simple "unschooled" machinery confirms their conviction that status and color do not matter ontologically. That the train and the strike usher in a new age hardly needs insistence. It is evident in people's thoughts and deeds: Ramatoulaye finds the strength to slay Vendredi "dans les cuisines aux foyers éteints" (124) ["beside a cold fireplace in an empty kitchen" (129)]; past and present come together in this historical event, the narrator states, "pour féconder un nouveau type d'homme" (127) ["to breed a new kind of man" (132)]; at the trial of Diara, the participants are struck by "la nouveauté d'avoir à prendre eux-mêmes une décision de ce genre" (132) ["the very newness of being forced to make a decision of this kind for themselves" (136)]. It is thus not only the uprightness and magnetism of *Bakayoko* but also the power of a *collective* vision and enterprise that constitute the epic dimension of this novel. Sembène enlarges the definition of heroic action and the very notion of hero. People become the agents of their own destiny.

From Perfect Past to Imperfect Future

If the relationship between heroes and helpers is altered in *Les Bouts de bois* (from that of epic), so is the relationship between the telling/reading of the story and the attitude toward the past. Sembène's novel is not a nostalgic, complacent tribute to the past; to the contrary, the novel seems to me to extend an invitation to build a future. For this reason, *Les Bouts de bois* seems to propose a view of epic and novel similar to that of Bakhtin, who, it will be recalled, characterized the epic as belonging to an "absolute past" that is already fixed, stable, and valorized with no sense of open-endedness. *Les Bouts de bois*, on the other hand, uses every means available to stress inconclusion, dynamism, and possibility—an as yet imperfect (that is, unfinished) future.

Claims for the open-endedness of *Les Bouts de bois*, the implication of an uncompleted future, may seem doubtful in light of Sembène's dedication: "Les hommes et les femmes qui, du 10 octobre 1947 au 19 mars 1948, engagèrent cette lutte pour une vie meilleure ne doivent rien à personne: ni à aucune 'mission civilisatrice', ni à un notable, ni à un parlementaire.

Leur exemple ne fut pas vain: depuis, l'Afrique progresse" (8) ["The men and women who, from the tenth of October, 1947, to the nineteenth of March, 1948, took part in this struggle for a better way of life owe nothing to anyone: neither to any 'civilizing mission' nor to any parliament or parliamentarian. Their example was not in vain. Since then, Africa has made progress" (10)]. As Mineke Schipper points out, the dedication can leave no question about who the victors will be and the direction the narrative will go (568–69). But if this note suggests to the reader that it is the destiny of the people to succeed in their strike, this is the knowledge of hindsight. The narrative itself undermines the notion of destiny, as it should, for if the strike and its revolution were ideas whose time had come, it became obvious to us only once they were ended. There are no reliable predictors of destiny (birth, nobility, oracles) in this narrative. Victory is not taken for granted, the consequence of a predetermined order, for at the moment in which the events occurred, their outcome was not known. From the perspective of the present, past historical events may seem to have been destined to occur, but such a view beforehand may be a costly luxury.

Les Bouts de bois de Dieu does not present itself as a narrative of inexorable destiny, as does the Sundiata epic or *Wangrin,* in which the hero's and the narrative's destination is already fixed, the path already indicated— only the details being left to the imagination of the reader before the text fills them in. Sembène's novel does not propose a necessary evolution, in which the past is viewed only from the vantage point of the present. The past does not move toward its "natural" end—to use another metaphor—like lightning following a lightning rod. Rather, Sembène undoes the view of history as progressing mechanically. He does this both in the context of specific events and in the story as a whole. One example of the first type is the death of Maimouna's twin under the bicycle. It is a complex interaction, the concurrence of events and beings, the accumulation of small incidents, none of which alone would have sufficed to kill the child: the chance that the bicycle was where it was; the baby's curiosity and random movement toward it; the man who grabs and then lets go of the handlebars; Bachirou's flight from the militia; finally, the militiaman's hunting down Bachirou.

In the larger story, the narrative stresses history *in the making.* The strike and the transformation it brings about are dynamic events created organically by the presence of the train, French colonial bureaucracy, racism, financial interests, and the needs and experiences of the strikers' individual lives and those of their families. This complexity is manifest in Sembène's mobile, multivoiced narration, which shifts from town to town, from memories to current actions, which gives the perspective of each and every actor. Particularity and interdependence (both in the sense of mutual reliance and random interplay) are the elements of which history is made. Obviously, the train itself is the best expression of this dynamic, binding individual lives and acts together across the miles.

The Battle: Exhortation, Confrontation, Defection

To the antagonists in this struggle we have paid little attention so far, and the novel's elaboration of the challenge that the heroes of this narrative face merits attention, even if the fate of the colonial agents as individuals is, as Soyinka writes, of little interest to the author (120). The French management of the railway line embodies the larger problem, colonialism. Just as the text shows the making of history, here it rejects the conflated term, *the clash of cultures,* in which the African-French "contact" was frequently discussed, and isolates instead the many dimensions of colonial ideology. Given the literary (and historical) context in which Sembène was writing, the novel's fictional reappraisal of that encounter and its redefinition of terms are bold and innovative.

Racism is obviously the mainstay of the colonial mind. Indeed the railway administrators ultimately have a more difficult time combating the strikers *because* they are racist; the fact that they do not believe that any of the African strikers could be honest and principled [*"intègre"*] means that they waste their energy in a futile effort to buy them off. The belief that the African strikers are children being led by a few outside agitators blinds the French to the truth they will arrive at eventually and with great pain, that, as Isnard puts it, "il y a du solide dans ce qu'ils disent" (61) ["there's a good deal in what they are saying" (73)]. Sexism combines with racism on a number of occasions, as when the French administrators, awaiting the arrival of the strikers' delegates, do not hear what the women are singing because they cannot, of necessity, believe there is anything to hear. A new and thus untutored French administrator asks,

> —Est-ce que vous comprenez ce que chantent les femmes? Ça a peut-être un rapport avec la grève.
> —Penses-tu! répondit Isnard. Des cris, comme d'habitude. La grève? Qu'est-ce que tu veux qu'elles y comprennent! Elles font du bruit, elles aiment ça! (276)

> ["Do you understand what the women are singing? It may have something to do with the strike."
> "Don't be a fool," Isnard snapped. "It's just shouting and yelling, as usual. What do you think they know about the strike? They're just making noise because they like to make noise." (272)]

Obviously this same attitude is responsible for the managers' lack of competence in any African language, which thus reinforces the barrier between self and "inferior" other.

Colonial ideology is crystallized most sharply in the negotiation between strikers and management and in the latter's refusal to consider the demand for family subsidies because the strikers are polygynous. Polygyny is, of course, justification for the managers' racism and sense of superiority. The narrator voices Dejean's reflections:

céder sur la question des allocations familiales, c'était beaucoup plus que d'agréer un compromis avec des ouvriers en grève, c'était reconnaître pour valable une manifestation raciale, entériner les coutumes d'êtres inférieurs, céder non à des travailleurs mais à des Nègres et cela Dejean ne le pouvait pas. (280)

[To give in on the question of family allowances was much more than a matter of agreeing to a compromise with striking workers; it would amount to recognition of a racial aberrance, a ratification of the customs of inferior beings. It would be giving in, not to workers but to Negroes, and that Dejean could not do. (276)]

Losing control, Dejean resorts to claims for the racial and national superiority of the French, grounds on which the workers refuse to debate (as Sembène refuses them in the novel). The issue is class interests—which the managers cannot admit, to which they are nearly blind, so racist are they.

Another sort of ideological obfuscation exists among the workers themselves in the initial stages of the strike. It is exposed in the following discussion between Arona and Deune, two union men in Dakar:

—Il y a des Européens qui sont venus de là-bas pour briser la grève, et voilà que d'autres nous envoient de l'argent pour continuer. Tu ne trouves pas ça drôle, toi?

—Il y a encore plus drôle: C'est les gars du Dahomey qui nous ont envoyé des sous. Ça, je ne m'y attendais pas! . . . Avant les Dahoméens, je les chinais, et tu sais pourquoi? . . . Parce que je les considérais comme mes inférieurs. Tu te souviens de la causerie de Bakayoko sur "les méfaits de la citoyenneté"? Et bien maintenant, j'ai compris et j'ai honte. Oui, Bakayoko a raison, cette grève nous apprend beaucoup de choses. (74)

["You have Europeans who have come all the way from up there, just to break the strike, and then there are other Europeans who send us money to go on with it. Don't you think it's odd?"

"There are other things that are even odder—those guys from Dahomey who sent us money. I certainly never expected that! . . . I used to make fun of people from Dahomey before—and do you know why? . . . Because I thought I was better than they are, that's why. Do you remember the talk Bakayoko gave, on 'the pitfalls of citizenship'? Well, now I understand what he was talking about, and I'm ashamed of myself. Bakayoko is right—this strike has taught us a lot of things." (81–82)]

In this conversation Sembène once again draws attention to the divisive nature of racial prejudice and the concept of nationality. The financial aid of the European workers in France and of the Dahomeans shows Deune that essentialist views work to their disadvantage. The strike is thus both means and end. Not only will it improve the material conditions of the strikers' lives, but it is also a process in which the strikers learn to recognize and overcome the secondary enemy, which is their own blindness and limitations. The novel thus redefines the meaning of the heroic challenge.

The strikers' long battle is marked by other episodes and embellish-
ments that are typical of epic struggles. Just as Soumaoro loses the benefit
of his gris-gris through the flight of Balla Fasséké and Nana Triban, the
colonial agents' loss of moral authority, their solidarity in a coherent ideology, is signaled by the defection of LeBlanc. Just as Balla Fasséké, once
back with Sundiata, intones a chant before battle, the women on the long
road to Dakar also raise their voices in song. The latter instance has been
seen as pure vestige of the oral tradition, but it is more meaningful to
see it as an integral feature of the epic self of Sembène's text. Song in
both instances, then, plays a role of preparing for battle, lifting hopes,
voicing the future. It announces and accompanies both death and birth,
a break with the past and an embrace of a new beginning.

Sembène's Realism

It is a widespread idea in African literary circles as in others that realism
is an "imitation of reality": thus when we label a text *realist* we are postulat-
ing its desire to reproduce the "real" world in writing. Mineke Schipper,
for example, in an article that brings out many aspects of Sembène's writing, begins a discussion of realism in the African context with the issue
of authorial attitudes toward reality and its representability. "My starting
point," she writes, "is that only [one] conception—the author's belief that
reality exists in itself as an object of knowledge and that it is possible
to represent it 'as it is' in literature—is to be called realistic and its product
realistic literature" (560). Apart from the difficult, if not impossible, task
of ascertaining an author's beliefs, the problem that this definition signals
is the general acceptance of the idea that it is possible to "represent it
'as it is,'" that realism is an objective account.

Les Bouts de bois is obviously a novel in the realist tradition. My use
of the term, however, refers to Sembène's textual practice; realism is a
mode of representation that purports (and that the narratee infers, although the reader should not) to be an "objective" and almost photographic
record. As such, it tends to emphasize concrete and frequently visual images, gesture, dialogue, social interaction, physical description of place
and characters; it may refer to historical moments, real places, and people.

Shifting the discussion to textual practice allows us to see the ambiguity of *Les Bouts de bois*, which is not (and cannot be) a mirror image of
reality, for Sembène intervenes and, what is more, undermines the world
he projects by disassembling and scrutinizing its usually invisible dimensions. He does indeed fabricate a material world, made of sensual images
and social interaction, but he questions the reality or, to be more precise,
the *necessity* of the world he represents. There is no pure and simple rein-
scribing of the "real" world. Above all else, he exposes the danger of sub-
mitting to appearances; he challenges the apparent order of things. *Les
Bouts de bois* breaks the pretense that the world is what it is "naturally"
and shows rather that it is constructed and therefore mutable. The novel

rejects the belief in the necessariness of the world it represents and shakes loose its premise of reality. To speak of realism, then, as an equivalence between text and world is to misconstrue, for Sembène's profound impulse is not to inscribe a given reality, believed to preexist outside the text, but to deconstruct a "given" world inside his text. If Sembène gives the impression of a world "as it is," it is only to show that the world does not have to be that way.

The impulse of this realist text is thus diametrically opposed to that of texts like the Sundiata epic, which—despite the romantic mode of their fiction—espouse wholeheartedly the order of the world they describe and propose that world as both Given and True. Epic thus identifies with and seeks to justify the order it perceives. Sembène's quarrel with "accepted" truth and apparent order is, in effect, the parodying gesture of the novel to which Bakhtin refers.

If birth and nobility can no longer serve as standard measures of goodness and heroism, there also can be no textual faith in the "real world." Thus Mabigué's appeal to divine authority to explain why the current reality (of French domination, African elite privilege, poverty) should exist and why it cannot be challenged fails to convince the reader as it fails to convince Ramatoulaye, who has just begged her brother to help her procure rice for her starving family. Mabigué argues:

> "Crois-tu réellement que les toubabs céderont? Moi, non. Je suis sûr qu'ils auront le dernier mot. Tout ici leur appartient: l'eau que nous buvons, les boutiques et les marchandises. Cette grève, c'est comme si une bande de singes désertaient un champ fertile; qui est-ce qui en bénéficie? Le propriétaire du champ! Et puis nous n'avons pas à lutter contre la volonté divine. . . . Je sais que la vie est dure, mais cela ne doit pas nous pousser à désespérer de Dieu. . . . Il a assigné à chacun son rang, sa place et son rôle; il est impie d'intervenir. Les toubabs sont là : c'est la volonté de Dieu. Nous n'avons pas à nous mesurer à eux car la force est un don de Dieu et Allah leur en a fait cadeau. Vois, ils ont même fermé les robinets." (83)

> ["Do you really think that the *toubabs* will give in? I know better—I know that they will have the last word. Everything here belongs to them— the shops, and the merchandise in the shops, even the water we drink. This strike is like a band of monkeys deserting a fertile plain—who gains from that? The owner of the plain! It is not our part in life to resist the will of heaven. I know that life is often hard, but that should not cause us to turn our backs on God. He has assigned a rank, a place, and a certain role to every man, and it is blasphemous to think of changing His design. The *toubabs* are here because that is the will of God. Strength is a gift of God, and Allah has given it to them. We cannot fight against it—why, look, they have even turned off the water." (89–90)]

Mabigué is a spokesman for the real order and would be, not coincidentally, the perfect auditor for the epic. He adheres to the "real" because it is already in place, and the fact that it is already in place is all the justification required. He can claim therefore that God Himself has ordained it. Mabigué is one with the world as it is. And indeed there may be those who espouse such views honestly, disinterestedly, but Mabigué is not one of them, for his is an "interested" vision. Mabigué profits from this order and so does not and will not see that it is constructed. He does not see the arbitrariness of what is inscribed materially, because it serves him. He thus expresses that reality and intervenes to perpetuate it, but it is this very arbitrariness that Ramatoulaye and the strikers recognize and that Sembène exposes in his text. *Les Bouts de bois* is the answer to Mabigué's assertion of divine will and right, of tradition, of given hierarchy.

Of Narrative Form

Sembène's rejection of authority based on divine will or tradition and his assertion of a world that is, on the contrary, constructible is apparent not only in verbal exchanges between Ramatoulaye and Mabigué or between the strikers' delegates and French managers, but also in the form of the narrative, which involves numbers of people and shifts in time and space. The inexorable destiny of the hero in the Sundiata epic and in *Wangrin* and the smooth, unalterable progression of narrative sequences (even where the path is strewn with obstacles) have been replaced by the interdependence of multiple actors and events. *Les Bouts de bois* challenges the very premise of epic, the inviolability of established hierarchy. It is a compelling narrative that revises the epic, thematically and formally, because it imagines significant change and a plurality of agents.

Sembène's text has moments of satire ("N'Dèye ne savait pas exactement qui serait ce Prince Charmant, ni quelle serait la couleur de sa peau, mais elle savait qu'il viendrait un jour et qu'il lui apporterait l'amour" 100) ["N'Dèye was not at all sure who this Prince Charming would be, nor what color his skin would have, but she knew that he would come some day, and that he would bring her love" (106)]. But on the whole the text moves away from satire unlike other classic realist novels, Oyono's *Une Vie de boy* and *Le Vieux Nègre et la médaille*, Béti's *Pauvre Christ de Bomba*, all of which exploit the discrepancy between what the protagonists and narratees understand of the story. Rather than ridicule the unsavory world it creates, *Les Bouts de bois* reveals its arbitrariness and thereby implies its mutability.

It is surely no coincidence that both Sembène and Ngũgĩ have written novels of epic tendencies, texts in which historical moments are seen not as destined and determined exogenously but as dynamic processes involving individual choices and lives. Both *Les Bouts de bois* and *A Grain of Wheat* are situated at moments of historical transition; both relate the interdependence of history and individuals—with a difference in nuance. Ngũgĩ's text is interrogative: a call to assessment; Sembène's is declarative: an exhortation.

Initiation Story

6

Authority Reconstructed: *Le Regard du roi*

There are competing voices in Camara Laye's *Le Regard du roi* (1954), one that posits Africa as Europe's "other" and another that parodies that view; one that proposes subjective approaches to knowledge and another that proposes "tradition"; one that insists on the importance of *doing* and another, of *being*; and, finally—symbolic of all these—one that is partial to the individual-centered novel and another that favors the traditional story. These tensions—Jameson's term *marbling* is excellent for such textual discontinuities—become perceptible when we consider the narrative structure of *Le Regard*. If *Wangrin* and *Les Bouts de bois* adapt an epic structure with relative ease, there is more tension between the aims of the traditional initiation story and another set of assumptions that informs *Le Regard* and that it strives to correct. One can conclude from this tension that the impetus for creating such a novel is singularly compelling. In this instance Bakhtin's claim that the novel incorporates other genres to make *them* the object of representation, to show their limits and subvert them, seems valid. We shall see that *Le Regard,* modeled on the initiation story, does indeed challenge a set of intertextual references, French literary myths of Africa. The novel is neither slavishly imitative nor derivative of oral traditions: rather it invokes a traditional genre that must be seen not as the point of origin of the novel but as an element in the elaboration of a message, a solution to the questions that Laye's narrative raises.

Studies of *Le Regard* generally ignore its narrative structure entirely or fail to ponder its implications; they most frequently dwell on its symbolism and, in particular, on the many possible interpretations of the climactic scene in which the worn but wise Clarence is embraced by the king. By and large they tend to argue for a spiritual resolution and a universal lesson.[1] That we focus on the symbolism of Laye's work is perhaps inevitable, since the narrative's images are as vaporous and elusive to readers as are the experiences of the journey south to Clarence. Soyinka, on the other hand, expresses an impatience with the insistence on salvation through the sacred order: "Despite the mystical effusion at the end, the aesthetics of the novel are secular, based on the harmonies of social relationships and human functions. *The Radiance of the King* remains our earliest imaginative effort towards a modern literary aesthetic that is unquestionably African, and secular" (126). I share this sense that the novel has often been misread. At the very least, the religious emphasis of most interpretations has blinded us to other facets of the novel, or, still more likely, our inability to see other dimensions of the text has allowed us to be guided, like Clarence, solely by the light of the king at the end of the text.[2]

Le Regard is a recalcitrant text for literary taxonomy: our fascination with symbolism may manifest an uncertainty about exactly how the novel fits into generic categories. The novel is unquestionably faithful to the art of the novel in the usual acceptation of the term—the emphasis on the individual consciousness that grows in self-knowledge through a complex set of experiences. *Le Regard* is at the same time characterized by a boundless, timeless landscape, a series of magical events and characters, and a strong didactic intention, all of which give it an air of both surrealism and allegory, typical of traditional stories. Of the many insights which consideration of narrative structure offers, the most important is perhaps the hierarchical nature of that structure. Regardless of the text's spiritual lessons to "the white man" or to all of us, the novel is, above all, a response to a felt dilemma. *Le Regard* represents a desire to reassert a menaced or lost order. Once again, the writer is not the puppet of a literary tradition: the form of the narrative is more than the sign of his origins.

Before considering the narrative structure of *Le Regard* and those traditional stories which illuminate it, we will make a brief excursion of our own into the French Africanist discourse whose premises the structure of the novel helps parody. We will examine three writers in particular, Baudelaire, Loti, and Gide, and the critic Roland Lebel; each brings a particular emphasis to the discourse on Africa, the view of the continent as menace or goodness.

Alterity and "L'Odeur du Sud"

The choice of title of the fourth chapter of Part I of *Le Regard,* in which Clarence undertakes his journey, situates Clarence's adventure in a matrix of images, journeys, and texts from Baudelaire, writing in the 1840s and 1850s, through Cendrars, writing one hundred years later. Laye's text enters and alters that tradition.

Without retracing Christopher Miller's careful itinerary in *Blank Darkness,* let us recall that the sense of smell is the most pregnant of senses for Baudelaire and the one that figures in any number of his poems as the impetus for his poetic journeys "south." As we shall see later, Clarence himself expresses skepticism about the north/south, winter/summer dichotomies of evocations like this one from "Parfum exotique":

> Quand, les deux yeux fermés, en un soir chaud d'automne,
> Je respire l'odeur de ton sein chaleureux,
> Je vois se dérouler des rivages heureux
> Qu'éblouissent les feux d'un soleil monotone; (52)

> [When, on an autumn evening, with closed eyes,
> I breathe the warm dark fragrance of your breast
> Before me blissful shores unfold, caressed
> By dazzling fires from blue unchanging skies.
> ("Exotic Perfume" 31)]

The world of reverie whose origin the poet situates in the sense of smell in "Parfum exotique" is occasioned in "La Chevelure" both by smell and by rhythmical movement and the sensation of depth, which Baudelaire associates with water:

> La langoureuse Asie et la brûlante Afrique,
> Tout un monde lointain, absent, presque défunt,
> Vit dans tes profondeurs, forêt aromatique!
> Comme d'autres esprits *voguent* sur la musique,
> Le mien, ô mon amour! *nage* sur ton parfum.
>
> . . . .
>
> Je *plongerai* ma tête amoureuse d'ivresse
> Dans ce noir *océan* où l'autre est enfermé;
> Et mon esprit subtil que le *roulis* caresse
> Saura vous retrouver, ô féconde paresse,
> Infinis *bercements* du loisir embaumé! (53, emphasis added)

> [Asia the languorous, the burning solitude
> Of Africa—a whole world, distant, all but dead—
> Survives in thy profundities, O odorous wood!
> My soul, as other souls put forth on the deep flood
> Of music, sails away upon thy scent instead.
>
> . . . .
>
> In this black ocean where the primal ocean roars,
> Drunken, in love with drunkenness, I plunge and drown;
> Over my dubious spirit the rolling tide outpours
> Its peace—oh, fruitful indolence, upon thy shores,
> Cradled in languor, let me drift and lay me down!
> ("The Fleece" 21)]

This mythologized South, metaphorically constructed and evoked by Baudelaire as aromatic and as a cadenced, fluid substance, potentially lulling or passionate, into which the poet and reader—obviously men—plunge or descend, undergoes a series of avatars in other writers. If for Baudelaire the "languorous" South is escape, for Pierre Loti in *Le Roman*

hi (1881), its sensuality engulfs and weakens the European "prey"
midst:

y avait trois ans que Jean Peyral avait mis le pied sur cette terre d'Afrique, —et depuis qu'il était là, une grande transformation s'était faite
en lui. Il avait passé par plusieurs phases morales; —les milieux, le cli-
mat, la nature avaient exercé peu à peu sur sa tête jeune toutes leurs
influences énervantes; —lentement, il s'était senti glisser sur des pentes
inconnues; —et, aujourd'hui, il était l'amant de Fatou-gaye, jeune fille
noire de race khassonkée, qui avait jeté sur lui je ne sais quelle séduction
sensuelle et impure, je ne sais quel charme d'amulette. (21)

[It had been three years since Jean Peyral set foot in Africa—and since
he had been there, an important change had occurred in him. He had
passed through several moral stages; little by little the surroundings, the
climate, and nature had exercised on his young mind all their draining
influence; slowly he had felt himself slip onto unknown slopes, and today
he was the lover of Fatou-gaye, a young black girl of the Khassonké race,
who had cast on him I know not what carnal and impure seduction,
I know not what amulet charm.]

Here "Africa" is more than an autumn evening's armchair reverie.
Loti had spent considerable time in Sénégal, and his knowledge of fauna
and flora, of African names and customs, sustains the pretense of the
fiction as "true" and provides sufficient detail of an unfamiliar ambiance
so as to create the sought-after impression of *dépaysement* [defamiliariza-
tion]. But Africa does not because of Loti's enhanced local color, escape
the mythologizing discourse so eloquently constructed by Baudelaire. Africa is still "blank darkness." In the passage above, Loti situates Africa
metonymically in nature and in the female—both elements that aggres-
sively overwhelm the (European white male's) senses and reason. It becomes obvious, then, that Clarence's nocturnal passion, his vision of the
femmes-poissons [fish-women], and his incapacity parody such mythology.

In the passage above, the passivity implicit in Baudelaire's status as
observer and tourist is inscribed and extended thematically in the choice
of verbs and in verb tense: Peyral has acted only once (he set foot in Africa)
and has been unacting ever since ("since he had been there," "he had
passed through several moral stages," "he was the lover of Fatou-gaye").
Rather, as the reflexive verbs communicate most effectively, he has been
acted upon, against his will ("an important change had occurred in him,"
"he had felt himself slip"). It is worth noting, however, that the passage
seems to betray the tenuousness of its assertions of African potency and
of Peyral's blamelessness in his degeneracy. Its repetition of "I know not
what"—intended to suggest the excessive power of African charm or,
should we say, bewitchery—discloses quite honestly, to the contrary, Loti's
silence before the absurdity of his proposition, his inability to articulate
an adequate rationale.

Peyral's feebleness, which can be called justifiably his "effeminacy," earned Loti poor marks in Roland Lebel's *L'Afrique occidentale dans la littéra-ture française* (1925). Lebel characterizes Loti's novel as merely exotic, a tourist novel, whose plot was the typical "aventure sentimentale" ["senti-mental adventure"] and was a "prétexte à décors" ["pretext for new set-tings"] (190), the type of novel which simply catered to the tastes and escap-ist desires of French readers. More important, from Lebel's point of view, was Loti's failure to participate in forging a new type of literature, the *roman colonial*, in which the protagonist would be "l'européen dans la beauté de son action colonisatrice, . . . le grand colonisateur, le créateur d'empires, le conducteur d'hommes, le bâtisseur de routes, le civilisateur, l'homme en action" (234–36) ["the European in the beauty of his colonizing act . . . the great colonizer, the creator of empires, the leader of men, the road builder, the civilizer, the man of action"].

Lebel's prescriptions for the hero of the colonial novel are the indices of a particular historical context and ideology. Like many of his modernist contemporaries including Marinetti, Pound, and Hemingway, Lebel was anxious about the perceived "softness" of Europe, its "feminization" (see Nixon). Africa, indeed all the European colonies, seemed to hold out the promise of regeneration. In Lebel's view, it was not merely for reasons of trade and commerce that colonization was necessary, but for psychologi-cal reasons as well. Colonization provided the opportunity to "sauver notre race" ["save our race"] because the colonies were "un réservoir des forces morales, d'énergie, de volonté rajeunies et accrues . . . une école de virilité . . . une formatrice d'hommes" (234) ["a source of moral strength, of energy, of strengthened and rejuvenated wills . . . a school of virility . . . a molder of men"]. Africa provided an opportunity to forge and test one's mettle, one's masculinity, and Loti's effeminate novel was not imbued with this vision.

André Gide's *L'Immoraliste* (1902) is a narrative generally overlooked in this context. It participates more precisely in Orientalist (rather than Africanist) discourse. It is informed simultaneously by the Baudelairian desire for an "elsewhere" (an escape into a sensual realm) and by Nietzsche's philosophy of the will. In the latter regard, *L'Immoraliste* an-nounces the modernist crisis of "masculinity," which will be articulated some twenty years later in Lebel's study, cited above, on the image of West Africa in French literature.

Michel is, of course, another wanderer to the South, where he discov-ers and basks in his own sensuality. In the Baudelairian tradition, this discovery is for Michel a release from the constraints of his schooling and upbringing; it fills him, as Nietzsche would have it, with a sense of his own energy and the will to live, regardless of the consequences. But Gide's protagonist ultimately is not the hero Lebel will require, for two reasons: Michel's homosexuality works against the Lebelian model of masculinity, and Michel, even as he stereotypes North Africa and the North African children, is quite conscious of their *opacity*. Michel recognizes the "other-ness" of North Africa, even if he fails to see it as anything more than what he believes he is not and what he strives to be. Gide's narrative is distinctive on this score, but it could hardly be called progressive.

With Gide, then, the pendulum swings away slightly from Loti's absolute fear of difference and toward Baudelaire's delight in what he imagined it to be—with a new emphasis, however: it is not merely the individual who seeks to escape; it is rather a deadened civilization that requires rejuvenation, rebirth in its association with "Africa." This will be Lebel's objective, but Gide's Michel believes he is learning *from* Africa, from the "other" (whom Michel continues to define, of course, in opposition to his rational self and as immoral), while Lebel sees Africa as "setting" (*décor*), the passive (although challenging), unparticularized site in which Europeans will perform their own triumphant moral transformation.

There is a continuous vacillation in Africanist literature of the colonial period well through the mid-twentieth century on the nature of the north-south rapport. With Conrad's *Heart of Darkness* (1902) and Céline's *Voyage au bout de la nuit* (1932), the purported sensuality of Africa and its closeness to "nature" rather than "culture" are, above all, menacing to European "civilization," while Cendrars, Tzara, and the Surrealists generally cling to a belief in the "poetry and spirituality" of African life from which Europe might learn. In 1963, Tzara articulated their hope: "L'humanisation nous reviendra peut-être de là-bas" (Blachère 177) ["It is perhaps from Africa that we will relearn how to be truly human"].

These many protagonists, ideologies, hopes, and fears create the tradition in European texts to which Laye's Clarence and "l'odeur du Sud" are heir. It is to these European voices that *Le Regard* responds. Clarence himself recognizes early in his journey that meaning or value is determined by the vantage point of him who thinks, that the exotic South (of Baudelaire) is the imagining of a northern mind. Shortly after the outset of his journey with the beggar and twins, Clarence thinks to himself:

> "Ah! c'est fameux le Sud quand on habite les pays du Nord! On se berce, on se chauffe, on s'échauffe: on est comme devant un grand feu de bûches, au coeur de l'hiver. Et ce qu'on voit? Un hamac accroché à deux cocotiers, en bordure du lagon! Et puis il y a ce souffle vanillé et presque imperceptible qui fait frémir un peu les cils et les ailes du nez, et qu'on appelle l'alizé. Et ensuite des plantes plus vertes et des fleurs plus bariolées, des fleurs comme des oiseaux et des plantes comme des jets d'eau; et une mer plus bleue, plus transparente et plus bleue . . . Que ne voit-on pas? Mais on le voit parce qu'il bruine, ou parce qu'il y a du givre sur les vitres, parce qu'on n'y va pas voir!" (95–96)

> ["Yes, the South!" Clarence mutters to himself. "Oh the South, it's marvellous, the South, when you live in the North! You sway gently, you are warm, at times you even get over-heated: it's like being in front of a great log fire in the dead of winter. And what do you see? A hammock hanging between a pair of coconut palms at the edge of a lagoon! And then there's that vanilla fragrance, almost imperceptible, which makes the eyelids quiver and the nostrils faintly flare, and which is called the

trade winds. And the foliage greener than anywhere else, and the flowers more brilliant—flowers like birds, and plants like fountains; and a sea that was of a profounder blue—more transparent, more intensely blue . . . What could you *not* see? But you see it only because it is drizzling, or because there is frost on the window-panes, because you think you will never see such things!" (*The Radiance of the King* 104)]

Color, fragrance, warmth—elements that appear in the Baudelairian poems recur here as Clarence thinks of the contrast in northern realities and desires which together spin the discourse of the exotic South. Yet Clarence is unable, for the time being, to experience the South as anything more than the disappointment of those illusions:

"—Et on ne devrait jamais aller voir, poursuit-il à voix haute. Les plantes ne sont pas plus vertes, elles seraient même plutôt grises, plutôt cendreuses. Et le ciel? . . . Mais on voit à peine le ciel! Et les fleurs? . . . Qu'importe! C'est l'eau bleue qui passe tout. Où est l'azur, où est la limpidité de cette eau? . . . C'est l'eau croupie des mares et c'est l'eau trouble des rivières. Si on en boit, c'est comme une boue qui . . ." (96)

["And you should never see such things, or go to see them," he goes on, talking to himself. "The foliage is no greener; it's even rather grey, rather ashen. And the sky? . . . But you can hardly see the sky! And the flowers? . . . What does it matter? It's the blueness of the water that is the most wonderful thing. But where is the azure limpidity of the water? There is the stagnant water of ponds and the muddy water of the rivers. If you drink it, it's like a mouthful of mud that . . ." (104)]

The South fails, of course, to measure up to its exotic mythology. Clarence has gone south, and although he recognizes in his hallucinatory lucidity the origins and contradictions of that mythology, he remains trapped by it nonetheless, disappointed that the South does not live up to expectations. He will remain an outsider until he overcomes the barrier of that mythology and learns to be receptive to what the South *is*.

Thus the text reveals two impediments to knowing the other that is Africa: on the one hand, the view that it is the exotic elsewhere of carefree, joyous existence to which one flees; on the other, it is the expatriate mentality of him who is present and yet an outsider, the annoyance and resentment that it is not the otherness of one's dreams but an opaque reality of its own. It is precisely this lack of true experience that the beggar signals when he asks in response to Clarence's complaint about the muddy water one drinks in the South, "—Avez-vous, jusqu'ici, bu beaucoup d'eau?" (96) ["Have you drunk much water?" (104)], to which the answer is, of course, no, Clarence has not drunk the water of which he complains.

"L'odeur du Sud" ["the odor of the South"], spun by literary and political practice, is precisely the butt of the novel's critique, but Laye does not simply make his critique discursively. The profound impulse of the novel is to parody and mock stereotypes and received ideas. Clarence's "petits services" ["small services"] are the most obvious example—it is the European who, having no culturally useful talent or training, becomes for once the "stud"—"Man become man," elemental and biological. There are likewise the continual word games that baffle Clarence and all his ideas, and there are winks between author and reader as when Clarence, standing in the crowd, finds that "il émanait de ces hommes étroitement agglomérés sous le ciel d'Afrique une odeur de laine et d'huile, une odeur de troupeau, qui plongeait l'être dans une espèce de sommeil" (11) ["An odour of warm wool and oil, a herd-like odour that seemed to dull the senses into a kind of trance, emanated from these men packed tightly together under the African sky" (21)]. Characteristically, the Africans "give off an odor" that puts one to sleep—"the one," the sentient being in question, is, of course, the European outsider. The text highlights another such stereotype when Clarence hears the cries of the master of ceremonies and thinks, "Certainement le sang ne tarderait pas à couler. Peut-être arrêtait-on au premier sang? Mais non, rien ne les arrêterait; c'étaient *de vrais sauvages*" (168–69, emphasis added) ["It would certainly not be long before blood was drawn. Perhaps they stopped then? No, nothing would stop them—they were nothing but *savages*." (172)].

Le Regard is very nearly a clown show, a carnivalesque fiction, in Bakhtin's terms. The parody of ideas, manifest in the verbal jousting between Clarence and his guides and hosts, is complemented and extended in the novel's organization as a traditional initiation story. The implication, it seems to me, is that the mythology of the South is so compelling that it elicits not simply a verbal argument on its own terms within the story but also a radical restructuring of narrative.

The Initiation Story

The form of initiation story to which I refer is not comparable to the realist or mimetic novel (*Bildungsroman* in European traditions), which narrates the youthful life and development of its major character. Although both genres relate the growth of an individual, the emphases are entirely different. Laye's autobiography, *L'Enfant noir,* an example of the second, describes the boy's separation from his home and the growth and experiences that tend to differentiate him from family and that thrust him out of a familiar world. *L'Enfant noir* is more nearly open-ended, outward-bound, characteristics which Bakhtin attributes to the novel. There is a search for values in such narratives not unlike that which Michael McKeon identifies in the early English novel, the debate over the merits of birth versus wealth, personal ambition and initiative, and received "truths" versus personal experience and decision making. The implication is that the individual has a good deal of control over the direction of his or her life.

Two traditional West African initiation stories to which we can refer in studying *Le Regard* are Birago Diop's "L'Héritage," a traditional tale of the Sahel, included in *Les Contes d'Amadou Koumba,* and a more complex form of this narrative, the Pular *Kaïdara,* recounted by Amadou Hampâté Bâ.[3] These initiation stories, unlike the *Bildungsroman,* seek to preserve an already extant order, to preach the virtues of continuity and conformity to an established set of truths. Of the official or established artists who perform narratives such as *Kaïdara,* Amadou Koné writes: "Leurs dits visent à . . . enseigner et à maintenir intacte l'architecture d'une société qui croit avoir résolu ses problèmes majeurs et donc ne se remet pas en question. Le griot est en quelque sorte un poète officiel. Il veut éduquer dans l'esprit consacré de la tradition" (23) ["Their words aim at . . . instructing and holding in place the architecture of a society which believes that it has resolved its major problems and therefore does not question itself. The griot is a sort of official poet. He wants to instruct in the spirit of a hallowed tradition"]. This is initiation *into* an order, rather than the story of supposedly novel individual experiences and choices. Here there is no suggestion of shaping our own destiny, except to the extent that we follow the path "charted" for us since birth. The difference between the *Bildungsroman* and the initiation story of the oral tradition is precisely the difference between subjective and traditional approaches to knowledge, between stressing the virtues or the vanity of human agency.

In both "L'Héritage" and *Kaïdara* modest heroes embark on journeys, during which they encounter a series of unintelligible signs and at the end of which they arrive at "Truth." With regard to narrative structure, they fit the pattern described by Denise Paulme as "un manque initial comblé" ["an initial lack fulfilled"]. Like these traditional narratives, then, *Le Regard* takes as its subject the journey whose goal is to transform a state of blindness and ignorance to one of sight and wisdom. There can be little doubt of the author's intention that the moral of Clarence's journey should be easily perceived by his readers. Through the contrast of Clarence's new behavior with the old, and the social endorsement of the new, expressed in advice and friendship offered him by Samba Baloum, the blacksmith, and the king, *Le Regard* takes care to make Clarence's transformation obvious, just as the traditional narratives do. Thus if there is much debate about the symbolism of *Le Regard,* all are agreed nonetheless on its themes of learning, Clarence's deculturation and acculturation, and the metamorphosis he undergoes from pride to humility.

Le Regard resembles the traditional narratives also in that it rejects the illusion of actuality and chronology, which we associate with realism in favor of the limitless setting of the tale and myth. It, too, contains the sequence of "surrealistic" or fantastic occurrences that are symptoms of the protagonist's malaise and riddles that beg answers. In *Le Regard* these paradoxical phenomena begin to occur before Clarence actually undertakes the journey south: the twins Noaga and Nagoa exchange identities at will. Similarly, the menacing judge soon reappears as a gracious host and father of the dancing girl who—by chance, of course—becomes Clarence's protector. The courthouse itself is revisited as her father's abode. Clarence's assorted experiences, like those of the brothers in "L'Héritage" and the companions in *Kaïdara,* constitute a pattern of repetition. Each experience is shaped by a principle of metamorphosis and mystery. One thing is never what it seems to be and always something else. The continual word games of Noaga and Nagoa and of the beggar are further examples of the infinite possibility and variability in Clarence's environment. Clarence is unable to make out whether the frescos on the wall of the fortress are scenes of war or of religion: "une suite de sacrifices, un long déroulement de captifs, conduits vers des autels où des prêtres, des rois peut-être les égorgeaient" (31) ["a series of sacrifices, a long procession of captives being led to altars where priests—perhaps kings—were cutting their victims' throats" (41)]. He then asks the twins the story of the frescos. One twin claims the king is punishing his unfaithful vassals; the other claims that guilty blood would profane the altars and so only faithful vassals could be worthy of death. "'Quel conte me faites-vous là?' dit Clarence. Il ne concevait pas que le roi pût immoler ses vassaux fidèles ou que le sacrifice fût une récompense; pourtant, en y réfléchissant . . ." (31–32) ["'What sort of nonsense is all this?' said Clarence. He did not understand how the king could sacrifice his most devoted vassals, or how such a sacrifice could be a reward. Yet when you came to think of it . . ." (42)].

The issues of sight, wisdom, and metamorphosis are presented right from the start. This argument underscores what it is that Clarence, like the travelers of the traditional stories, is unable to do: *decipher* meanings. The indeterminate quality of reality and the uncertainty of standard premises and fixed truths are suggested by Clarence's inability to see and to hear. His initial confusion is caused by his failure to understand the sacrificial scene: does it signify the violence of war or the purity of religion (categories which are, in fact, often indistinguishable)? Once he establishes that the sacrifice involves the king and his vassals, a second enigma is posed: is sacrifice a punishment or a reward?

As the journey actually begins, the prejourney ambiance of mild mystery and metamorphosis yields to one of more intense enigma, and a certain initial realism in description and events gives way to a far more suggestive prose. The brothers of "L'Héritage" travel to a faraway land; the companions of *Kaïdara* travel to a subterranean world, and Clarence makes his way through the forest whose kinship to the world of the traditional narratives is implied from the outset, when Clarence thinks to himself, "Je devrais faire des marques . . . marquer mon passage, semer des cailloux blancs, ou briser des branches, ou cocher les arbres . . ." (88) ["'I ought to leave signs,' he thought, 'to mark where we have been. I could lay a trail of white pebbles, or break certain branches, or notch trees . . .'" (97)]. Clarence enters a veritable marsh of illusions, in which he, too, will be unable to sort out the countless sensations and absurd impressions he experiences.

Ways to Knowledge

It is through Clarence's loss of subjectivity and individual power, those qualities most closely associated with the novel in its many avatars, that *Le Regard* discredits personal reason and truth and valorizes traditional knowledge and wisdom. Let us see precisely how this shift in epistemological approach is effected.

Le Regard begins as the typical novel of individual growth and achievement. We infer that Clarence finds himself in Africa because he has proudly sought adventure, experience of the world. Proud, willful, presumptuous, Clarence begins his more immediate journey as a quest for employment in the king's service and thus for the money that will merely allow him to play out his adventure. Clarence, unlike the protagonists of the traditional stories, does not know that he is on his way to learning anything. In the other stories the heroes humbly seek knowledge, they are disposed to learning, since they recognize an order outside themselves, greater than themselves, of which they are or must become a part; their goal is "wisdom," which suggests connectedness, a harmonious relationship with both the natural world and the human community, while in the novel, Clarence aims for "adventure" and sensation, proper to the subject and to his private thoughts and satisfactions.

Yet the text immediately begins to undermine the bases of subjectivity and of learning through individual perceptions. First of all, the world in which Clarence finds himself is not easily knowable, and, second, language fails to communicate knowledge effectively. We read of the king, for example:

> Cette façon inattendue de descendre de cheval donnait *l'impression d'une extrême pesanteur*, mais *apparemment n'était-ce qu'une impression*, et *assurément une impression fausse*, car *tout* dans la personne du prince *donnait à l'inverse l'impression d'une merveilleuse légèreté*; *la première impression pourtant persistait* parallèlement à la seconde. Sitôt que le roi eut mis pied à terre, deux pages danseurs se portèrent à sa droite et deux autres à sa gauche, et ils lui relevèrent les bras; alors Clarence découvrit que ces bras étaient cerclés de tant d'anneaux d'or que le roi n'aurait pu les lever sans aide; *l'impression de pesanteur* venait de cette invraisemblable profusion d'anneaux. En même temps que les pages avaient levé les bras du roi, la robe royale s'était entrouverte sur *un mince torse d'adolescent*. (22, emphasis added)

> [This unconventional method of dismounting gave the impression of extreme heaviness, but apparently it was only an impression, and a false one, for everything about the prince's person gave on the contrary an impression of miraculous lightness; yet the first impression lingered on with the second. As soon as the king reached the ground, two of the pages or dancers placed themselves at his right hand, and two at his left, and slowly lifted his arms. It was only then that Clarence discovered that these arms were encircled with so many golden bracelets that the

king would never have been able to lift his arms without help: and it was this extraordinary profusion of gold bracelets that gave the impression of heaviness. At the same time as the pages were lifting the king's arms, the royal robe was falling open to reveal the slender black torso of an adolescent boy. (32–33)]

Contradictions are rife in the world in which Clarence finds himself. The king is both heavy and light and, as we learn later, both young and old, fragile and robust. The world itself thus refuses to be known by easy labels and mutually exclusive categories. The text conveys this impression of unresolvable contradiction not only in what it states but in the very manner in which it states Clarence's experience. First of all, Laye's narration frequently relies on indirect free style and innumerable instances of the present and imperfect tense, both of which place the narratee in the realm of Clarence's rather nebulous thoughts. Moreover, as in the passage above, a typical procedure is to further discredit the logic of a statement with a series of questions or with a series of reservations (usually in the form of adverbs) and then, finally, in a complete reversal, to reassert the first, now discredited, hypothesis. The unreliability of Clarence's impressions is thus expressed in the hesitancy of the language, its careful modifications and nuances, which little by little whittle away at and subtly contradict its first meaning, leaving the narratee in complete doubt as to the nature of what has occurred. The narration is thus marked by a very effective use of language that, in its confusion, communicates Clarence's disarray. And it is not only Clarence's integrity as a thinking, controlling subject that is eroded by such language but also that of the reader. The text sabotages its own intelligibility at a certain level such that the reader's ability to judge is nearly as impaired as is Clarence's.

In addition to his murky sensual impressions of all kinds, Clarence's lack of linguistic ability is a sign of his failure to assess the world accurately, and it thus becomes an object of the narrator's discrediting language. The words by which Clarence is accustomed to judge are continuously under assault, as in the following passage. The beggar says of the boys Noaga and Nagoa: "C'est parce qu'ils sont du Sud, qu'ils sont si fripons" (94) ["It's because they come from the South that they are such rascals" (102)]. And Clarence wonders: "Fripons? . . . Oui, sans doute sont-ils fripons; ils le sont même certainement. Mais sont-ils seuls à l'être. . . . Clarence pense que le mendiant qui, depuis des semaines, lui fait parcourir le même sentier est plus fripon encore . . ." (94) ["Rascals? . . . Yes, it's quite likely they *are* rascals; in fact, they certainly are. But are they the only ones? . . . Clarence feels that the beggar who has been leading him down the same old garden path for days and days, for weeks even, is still more of a rascal . . ." (102)].

Clarence's linguistic skills are useless; he is unable to read the inscriptions above the courtroom entrance and to comprehend the simplest statements or to ascertain their truth. The inability to manipulate language is thus a further challenge to the primacy of the thinking subject. Clarence has great difficulty learning from what people say. Rather, as we shall see, truth can be known only as it is learned from activity, from example, what others *do*. *Le Regard* thus discredits words, which even in dialogue are less effective than the lessons of the flogging, the blacksmith's ax, and the king's glance—the ultimate source of knowledge. This is meaning which Harry Berger describes as "inscribed in bodies," thereby preserving its authority in remaining unwritten (151).[4] The critique of subjectivity thus carries with it a profound mistrust of language that is not moored. Truth, the text seems to argue, is beyond mere words; it cannot be so superficially grasped and represented. Indeed, in Mande culture, true knowledge is held to be deserving of silence rather than desacralizing speech (Niane, *Soundjata* 78–79).

Le Regard thus challenges—it obviously cannot destroy—the authority of the subject (both Clarence and the reader) and of the language through which Clarence and the others communicate and through which it communicates with the reader. Not only does Clarence's subjectivity cease to be effective but the reader is also made aware of the limits of subjectivity.

To the extent that the novel questions the value of rational and subjective approaches to knowledge, it proposes in their place learning through apprenticeship. Significantly, Clarence's fulfillment—knowledge and clarity—do not come through memory or a self-conscious restructuring of identity, as is the case in many novels. Clarence's journey is spatial rather than temporal—just as the journeys of the traditional narratives represent knowledge through the experience of displacement to a mysterious but paradoxically more truthful world. Clarence leaves a world of apparent but false order for the seemingly slippery one in which individual perception and subjectivity, empirical theories and rules, are no longer meaningful. Thus Clarence himself does not engineer the changes he undergoes; he is formed by his many mentors as are the traditional travelers by the sages whom they have gone to meet. Despite the attention paid to individual consciousness, the story does not end with the individual triumphant but with the lesson learned.

The critique of subjectivity implied by the style of narration throughout the novel is reinforced also by the very type of narrator. This story of an individual experience, rich in ambiguity and irony, almost begs a first-person narrator. Yet it is told not in the first person by Clarence himself but by a "traditional" narrator who is both omniscient and wise and who nonetheless is frequently just the medium of Clarence's confused thoughts. For this subjective experience, the novelist situates authority outside the subject, which allows him to minimize reader empathy for Clarence's alienation and to parody Clarence's cultural and moral clumsiness. The narrator serves as a corrective lens to the protagonist's self-absorption and distorted vision of others.

The text comments on its own dynamic between outside authority and subject in the conversation between Diallo the blacksmith and Clarence, who interrupted the "display" during which the master of ceremonies was disciplined for revealing the nature of Clarence's "small services" in the chief's employ:

> —Vous n'auriez pas dû interrompre la fête, dit Diallo.
> —Ne comprenez-vous pas que le derrière du maître des cérémonies n'est pas un fragment de fer?
> —Eh bien, tout le monde comprend cela. Mais ce maître des cérémonies n'avait pas volé sa fessée. On lui façonnait l'entendement, en traitant son derrière comme je traite le fer sur l'enclume.
> —Et s'il n'avait fait que déclarer la vérité? dit Clarence.
> —Toute vérité, voyez-vous, n'est pas bonne à dire.
> —Mais elle est toujours bonne à entendre.
> —Ni bonne à dire ni bonne à entendre, dit Diallo.
> Il avait retiré le fer du foyer et le martelait à petits coups précis.
> —Vous n'êtes pas parvenu à votre âge, reprit-il, sans savoir que toutes les vérités ne sont pas bonnes à entendre? (185)

> ["You shouldn't have stopped the display," said Diallo.
> "But can't you see that the master of ceremonies' backside is not a piece of red-hot iron?"
> "Well, everyone can see that. But the master of ceremonies well deserved the spanking he got. He was having some sense knocked into him, and they were dealing with his backside as I deal with iron on the anvil."
> "And what if he had only been speaking the truth?" Clarence demanded.
> "It's not always nice to tell the truth."
> "But the truth is always worth hearing."
> "It's neither worth speaking nor hearing," said Diallo.
> He had pulled the iron out of the fire and now was hammering it with sharp little blows.
> "Surely you haven't reached your present age," he went on, "without knowing that certain things are better left unsaid?" (188–89)]

This passage draws the parallel between the metal which Diallo is fashioning "with sharp little blows," the behind of the master of ceremonies, which has undergone a series of lashes, and Clarence's "understanding," which Diallo also forms, little by little. Repeated visits to the blacksmith permit Clarence to be "shaped" (*impressed* like the iron, like the flesh) by Diallo's example. In place of the discovering, discursive subject, the text proposes then, particularly in the form of the blacksmith and the final embrace of the king, an apprenticeship in traditional wisdom, learning from lived experience in community rather than from personal reflection. We may refer to a passage of *Kaïdara* in which a wood spirit and Hamtoudo, one of the nonnoble and thus less discerning companions, exchange two views of learning. Hamtoudo says:

Les yeux voient des phénomènes
que la raison ne comprend pas.
Tout ce qu'on voit est Kaïdara
Tout ce qu'on entend va chez Kaïdara.
Notre maître est Kaïdara.
Pourquoi le coeur ne voit-il pas
et n'enseigne-t-il pas le sens des symboles
qui nous intriguent dans les terres
du royaume de Kaïdara? (55)

[The eyes see wonders
that the mind fails to understand.
All we see is Kaïdara.
All we hear is Kaïdara.
Our lord is Kaïdara.
Why does the heart fail to see
and to teach the meaning of the symbols
that entice us throughout the lands
of the kingdom of Kaïdara?]

Hamtoudou speaks metaphorically of his sense of the nature of knowledge when he refers to "the heart." Knowledge should be acquired as if
by intuition, spontaneously, effortlessly. Since the heart resides in the body,
no effort need be made to codify knowledge and communicate it beyond
the self. Knowledge is thus akin to a passive state of being, an intuitive,
harmonious oneness with nature and world, acquired at no cost because
it is inherent in each human.

The wood spirit replies and offers yet another view:

L'apprenti-forgeron actionne les soufflets
pendant de longues années
avant que son maître lui apprenne
le sens secret des choses
lui donnant puissance
de transformer les métaux
pour en faire des outils fort utiles. (55–57)

[The apprentice blacksmith works the bellows
for many a long year
before his master instructs him
in the secret ways of things
giving him power
to transform metals
into the most useful of tools.]

The wood spirit's view contrasts sharply with Hamtoudou's. Knowledge does not reside within us; nor, we infer, is it an answer to a question
that can be provided and thus acquired instantaneously. It is a *process of
learning* rather than a thing to be possessed. Like an apprenticeship, it

requires time, patience, and humility. It is a far cry from the "initiation" of the book or lecture or college education—all dependent on "the word." True learning, this traditional Pular text argues, is acquired gradually in an appropriate social context, and it is realized, completed in some sense in a creative act of communal value. The blacksmithing metaphor suggests, as does the entire narrative moreover, a limitless process that can and indeed must continue.

In *Le Regard* we find an echo of this juxtaposition in Clarence's initial cavalierness, his expectation of quick results, his inflated sense of his own worth, on the one hand, and, on the other, the process of his education, which is furthered considerably by his friendship with the blacksmith. He visits the forge often, where he both witnesses the manual magic of Diallo and hears (but rarely accepts) the wise, sometimes sententious, advice of the blacksmith. In each instance, as in a repeated episode of a traditional narrative, some event is reinterpreted and its "unlikely" significance or import explained to Clarence. In the conversation regarding the behind of the master of ceremonies, the would-be rational rule of thumb, "Truth is a universal good," is shown to be inadequate, for the context, the act of communication with its speaker and listener, is as much a factor in what is "good" as is the message or text itself.[5] Diallo's final question in that conversation suggests once more the themes of all three narratives: that age, experience, and community living are the bases of knowledge, and thus, by corollary, that knowledge or wisdom is not "given" or easily acquired by the young and uninitiated, that there is a season for coming of age. The wordplay, the repetition and antitheses in this conversation are once again like riddles that punctuate the narrative and ornament this crucial message so that it is preserved in a memorable way.

It could not be accidental that it is the blacksmith who guides Clarence in the process of learning, for the father in *L'Enfant noir* is also a blacksmith whose wisdom and whose knowledge of gold working grow out of each other and fascinate the young child. As in *Le Regard*, the issues of growth, initiation, and learning are paramount. Laye writes of the circumcision rites and the test of "Konden Diara":

> Plus tard, j'ai su qui était Konden Diara et j'ai su aussi que les risques étaient inexistants, mais je ne l'ai appris qu'à l'heure où il m'était permis de le savoir. Tant que nous n'avons pas été circoncis, tant que nous ne sommes pas venus à cette seconde vie qui est notre vraie vie, on ne nous révèle rien, et nous n'arrivons à rien surprendre.
>
> Ce n'est qu'après avoir participé plusieurs fois à la cérémonie des lions, que nous commençons à vaguement entrevoir quelque chose, mais nous respectons le secret: nous ne faisons part de ce que nous avons deviné qu'à ceux de nos compagnons qui ont une même expérience; et l'essentiel nous échappe jusqu'au jour de notre initiation à la vie d'homme. (*L'Enfant noir* 105)

[Later I got to know who Kondén Diara was, and I learned these things when the time had come for me to learn them. As long as we are not circumcised, as long as we have not attained that second life that is our true existence, we are told nothing, and we can find out nothing.

We begin to have a vague understanding of the ceremony of the lions after we have taken part in it many times. But even then, we are careful to share our knowledge only with those companions who have had the same experience. And the real secret lies hidden until the day we are initiated into our life as men. (*The Dark Child* 106)]

As in the rite of Konden Diara, *Le Regard,* "L'Héritage," and *Kaïdara* challenge the authority of the subject, the ability and the right to "read" signs and to learn on one's own. Knowledge, truth, and wisdom are held in secret and disguised; they can be shared only by those having had the appropriate experience and consequent humility. With regard to their common themes—journey, growth, knowledge—the narratives express a single sensibility, which Alpha I. Sow describes this way:

> en Afrique noire, il est dans la logique des choses que le grand savoir s'affuble d'apparences dérisoires et marginales pour écarter les profanes, les disciples "fermés" que le maître ne réussira pas à "ouvrir" à la "lumière" des connaissances ou dont il ne pourra pas "percer l'oreille", les curieux, les envieux et les superficiels qui en tout état de cause, ne méritent pas d'acquérir les secrets de la nature et d'être initiés aux mystères. (34)

> [in black Africa, our logic holds that true knowledge disguises itself in demeaning and marginal forms in order to discourage the profane, "close-minded" disciples whom the master will not succeed in "opening" to the "light" of understanding or whose ears he will be unable to penetrate, the curious, the envious, and the superficial who by their very nature do not merit acquiring the secrets of nature and being initiated into these mysteries.]

Wisdom is thus frequently masked until the initiate is ready to "see." "Le savoir doit être un secret," says Mamadou Kouyaté in the Soundjata epic (*Soundjata* 78) ["learning should be a secret" (*Sundiata* 41)]. So it is that Clarence's peregrinations and the blacksmith's tutelage initiate Clarence to Truth and Wisdom and that the reader of Laye's narrative experiences a subversion of rational, subjective approaches to learning, characteristic of many novels, and a reassertion of the value of tradition and apprenticeship, characteristic of traditional initiation stories.

Human Agency: The Case for Humility

The most significant issue in Clarence's reeducation, one which relates to both the narrative structure and the epistemological approach of the traditional story, is the question of how best to determine human worth and "goodness": by what one does or by what one is? This distinction may, of course, be more logical than real. What Clarence is (his new disposition) is not a purely internal and therefore intangible quality, but is made manifest to the reader in Clarence's changed attitude toward himself and toward Samba Baloum and Diallo when he seeks out their advice. The text nonetheless juxtaposes doing and being. An important debate on the subject takes place between the master of ceremonies and Clarence. The villainous master of ceremonies is the spokesperson for the rather existential notion of goodness (we are what we do), against whom Clarence, who has done little of any merit, must defend himself.

Samba Baloum, the keeper of the harem, and Diallo have been arguing all along against the existential view, represented by the master of ceremonies. They see that perfection or great achievement is an ideal and, as such, is out of reach. One must simply *strive* for it, because full humanity resides in the struggle, not in the perfection of one's gift or product or in the accomplishments to which one can point. These, no matter how many or how beautiful, will never be enough, as Diallo demonstrates in his continual reforging of the ax that he wishes to offer to the king.

The constant tending toward perfection echoes the sense of knowledge and Truth as an ongoing learning process. Thus Diallo proposes a principle for daily behavior and living: humbly desiring to do the "right" thing and doing one's best, while recognizing that one's human best is a far cry from absolute (divine) perfection, for regardless of our perfection, we can never *merit* salvation. He says, "Peut-être ne puis-je faire autre chose, peut-être, en dépit de tant de défauts, peut-être parce que je suis comme cet arbre et que je manque de moyens, le roi malgré tout considérera-t-il ma bonne volonté. Mais la hache en soi?" (188) ["Perhaps I can do nothing else . . . perhaps, in spite of having so many faults, perhaps because I am like that tree and lack the means to do anything but this; in spite of everything, the king will give me credit for my good will . . . but as far as the axe itself . . ." (191–192)]. The king has no need of Diallo's ax and will accept it because it represents the faith and striving of a less than perfect being.

When Clarence, nude and offering only his good intentions, finally is embraced by the king, it is the rigidly existential philosophy of the master of ceremonies that is discredited. As Clarence approaches the king, he thinks to himself:

> "Personne pourtant n'est plus vil que moi, plus dénué que moi, pensait-il. Et vous, Seigneur, vous acceptez de poser le regard sur moi!" Ou était-ce son dénuement même? . . . "Ton dénuement même! semblait dire le regard. Ce vide effrayant qui est en toi et qui s'ouvre à moi; ta faim qui répond à ma faim; ton abjection même qui n'existait pas sans ma permission, et la honte que tu en as . . ." (252)

> ["Yes, no one is as base as I, as naked as I," he thought. "And you, lord, you are willing to rest your eyes upon me!" Or was it because of his very nakedness? . . . "Because of your very nakedness!" the look

seemed to say. "That terrifying void that is within you and which opens to receive me; your hunger which calls to my hunger; your very baseness which did not exist until I gave it leave; and the great shame you feel . . ." (252)]

What saves Clarence is his very attitude of receptivity. The king offers an all-encompassing love that is nearly blind to deeds. It is a seductive embrace (as is the story), for it absolves completely:

—Ne savais-tu pas que je t'attendais? dit le roi.
Et Clarence posa doucement les lèvres sur le léger, sur l'immense battement. Alors le roi referma lentement les bras, et son grand manteau enveloppa Clarence pour toujours. (252)

["Did you not know that I was waiting for you?" asked the king.
And Clarence placed his lips upon the faint and yet tremendous beating of that heart. Then the king slowly closed his arms around him, and his great mantle swept about him, and enveloped him for ever. (252–53)]

What Clarence has done matters less than his disposition to do. It is therefore easy to read into this embrace a Christian theology: we do not and indeed cannot save ourselves; rather we are saved by grace, still more perhaps, *chosen* for grace. The novel thus advocates *being* rather than *doing*.[6] More precisely, *Le Regard* is the triumph of a philosophy that might be read, at worst, as an apology for inaction or, in a positive sense, as a stoic response to the vanity of human schemes. The novel's ambiguous philosophy corresponds, in fact, to Denise Paulme's claim that traditional West African tales do not extol exceptional behavior.[7] Werewere Liking warns against the typically disempowering interpretation given to initiation stories and rituals, especially to those characterized by blind obedience. Her criticism is significant with respect to the use of the genre in *Le Regard*. She writes that her students perceive "tradition" as "un système figé et rigide, prônant la non responsabilité et 'l'irresponsabilisation' de l'homme, favorisant l'esprit d'assisté . . . et interdisant le dépassement de soi et du modèle, aucune réflexion personnelle et aucune question n'é-tant tolérées" (7) ["a fixed and rigid system, extolling nonresponsibility and human 'incapacity,' promoting a mentality of dependency . . . and prohibiting one from stretching beyond oneself and the norm—all personal reflection and questioning being strictly forbidden"]. It is precisely for these reasons, I believe, that this particular narrative structure is crucial to Laye's novel.

In contrast to those novels which Davis describes as teleogenic, in which a revelation or surprise ending necessitates a rereading of what has gone before, *Le Regard* uses its ending, then, to affirm the veracity of what has preceded, the order that was implied. Thus the anguish that Clarence experiences in the search for the meaning of his life and in the waiting is reminiscent of that of Vladimir, Estragon, and others of Beckett's tramps;

but this anxiety is counterbalanced by the structure of the story, our knowledge as trained listeners and readers that the initiation story will gratify the quest, that the king will come and the riddles will be resolved.

What seemed only barely visible throughout the story is thus made clear in its ending. To the extent that the epic is controlled to its finish by its beginning (the hero's origins predict his future), the initiation story is controlled from its beginning by its ending (the path of Clarence's journey homeward will be seen to have been inscribed and meaningful all along, though he did not know it). In this sense, *Le Regard* is close to *Wangrin*: although superficially about two entirely different types of protagonist, both novels insist on an a priori order that cannot be circumvented.

Le Regard expresses structurally what *L'Enfant noir,* Laye's first narrative, expresses lyrically: the nostalgia for a predictable and harmonious world, experienced by the adolescent boy about to leave home. The novel is dedicated to a French official, Monsieur Bernard Cornut-Gentille, High Commisssioner of the Republic of French West Africa, "en témoignage de respectueuse amitié" ["in testimony of respectful friendship"]. It is not by chance, it seems to me, that this novel takes the pattern of the traditional initiation narratives, for it both wrests authority from those European writers and their protagonists, for whom the experience of the "sensuality" and "primitive" life of Africa inevitably leads to the depravity and dissolution of European civilization, and, at the same time, it absolves them. It is a nostalgic gesture—not simply because the novel constructs a seemingly atemporal utopia—but because it posits an incontrovertible order, perhaps the only order that could counter an inflated and reckless European individualism.

7

An Ambiguous Quest: *La Carte d'identité*

A hybrid text, Jean-Marie Adiaffi's *La Carte d'identité* (1980) is both a prose narrative, punctuated with poetry, and a philosophical essay. Alternating between the mythic, noble quest and "initiation" of a disinherited prince and its comic, sometimes bawdy sketches of popular life, it thus combines and contrasts several tones and forms of narrative, focusing on different classes and yet expressing a common impulse to challenge a demeaning colonialist authority and mentality and to reclaim subjectivity. *La Carte d'identité* focuses on a crisis in self-vision, and the narrative diagnoses the cause of the current paralysis as political and cultural disenfranchisement. Adiaffi situates his narrative metonymically in the colonial period. There may be contextual (practical) reasons for such a choice by contemporary writers. The colonial period is a safe substitute target (as is the fictional Katamalanasia in Sony Labou Tansi's *La Vie et demie*) for a text that would be critical of current political practices.

   Thus Mélédouman's trivial (and nonetheless consequential) "identity card" situates him in an alienating system outside himself and his community and thereby renders him an object. The very existence of the identity card and its subsequent loss symbolize a crisis in self-definition, for the "colonialist" writing (interpretation) of African history and of the African subject strips Mélédouman of his identity and an entire people of their vision and strength. If the initiation form is used in *Le Regard du roi* to assert an external authority, requiring the initiate to abandon his pretensions to a vain subjectivity, that authority in *La Carte d'identité* is called upon paradoxically to sanction the initiate's struggle to achieve self-definition.

   Mélédouman's journey is thus a spatio-spiritual exercise in which he will "read the map" (*la carte*) of his identity and values and will thereby strive to answer the haunting question that Toundi asks at the end of his rude initiation: "Mon frère . . . que sommes-nous? Que sont tous les nègres qu'*on dit* français?" (*Une vie de boy* 13, emphasis added) ["Brother, what are we? What are all those blacks known as French?"]. The focus on the (African) initiate's attempts to assume the position of subject is not new, of course, but the distinction of *La Carte d'identité* is perhaps its emphasis on self-knowledge as a first step in envisioning the future.

Adiaffi's novel is an innovative narrative whose many tensions signal the power and strictures of its form. On the one hand, *La Carte d'identité*—not any less than *Le Regard du roi*—is an attempt to retreat into a certain authority. Clearly, narrative form is chosen (not given), for the identical "problem" (the absence of an identity card) is the element around which Ousmane Sembène spins another type of text altogether, *Le Mandat* (1966), a mimetic and secular critique of the abuses of neo-colonialism and of the Brother Jeroes that neo-colonialism spawns. So Adiaffi's novel is, as is Laye's, a philosophical and "spiritual" defense of African civilization, and it takes on the issue of which view of that civilization—a Eurocentric or an Afrocentric view—shall prevail. It, too, derives its moral force from its structure as initiation story.

The use of the initiation form is not, then, the simple manifestation of an emphatic aesthetic heritage but reveals an anxious formulation of issues, an inability to forgo a certain nostalgia whose time is clearly past. *La Carte d'identité* signals an enduring fascination with the origin of a problem, with a distracting and futile discourse on cultural superiority and inferiority, and ultimately with essence.

On the other hand, the narrative admits the need to go beyond issues of authenticity and identity. This is suggested formally, as we shall see, in its departure from the norms of the initiation stories we have seen. First of all, *La Carte d'identité* valorizes individual consciousness that attempts, as in the detective story, to reread the signs that society has misread. Mélédouman thinks as he begins his journey, for example, "Remonter patiemment le cours du temps *à la recherche du temps perdu*. Jouer au *Sherlock Holmes* de l'histoire, de la mémoire, du destin" (67, emphasis added) ["To go patiently back up the stream in search of things past. To play the Sherlock Holmes of history, memory, and fate"]. Mélédouman will not undergo an apprenticeship into an order clearly visible and comprehensible to the reader; he will not be "embraced" as is Clarence and integrated into a society. His learning is effected, rather, as is Proust's or Sherlock Holmes's, by his own actions, by the force of his courage and intelligence. Second, the narrative punctuates the quest with sketches of popular culture. Indeed, its best moments are those in which Adiaffi counterbalances the excessive seriousness of Mélédouman's plight with the (comic) uprisings of those who, rather than philosophize, are "cultivating their gardens."

An Absurd and Accidental Authority

When Mélédouman, the aged Agni prince, is arrested early one morning by the French commandant, Kakatika Lapine, and his African subordinate,

Gnamien Pli, the narrator begins what will be the continual juxtaposition (in the text and in Mélédouman's thoughts) between material and moral orders, between the commandant's definition of Mélédouman and the latter's self-definition. Mélédouman has no control over the first order of things, and the narrative characterizes his disadvantage at the outset of the story by a rather obvious loss of name:

> —C'est bien toi, Mélédouman (*soit: "je n'ai pas de nom", ou exactement: "on a falsifié mon nom"*)?
> —Oui, c'est bien moi, le prince Mélédouman.
> —Prince! prince! Qu'est-ce qu'il ne faut pas entendre. . . . Eh bien, suis-moi au cercle, prince, prince de la principauté de mon cul!
> Prince ou pas, Mélédouman savait par expérience ce qu' "aller au cercle" veut dire dans cette "encerclée" colonie. (3)

> ["Are you Mélédouman?" (*meaning "I have no name" or more precisely, "they have falsified my name."*)
> "Yes, I am prince Mélédouman."
> "Prince! Prince! The rubbish one hears! . . . Well then, prince, come with me to the district, prince of the principality of my ass!"
> Prince or not, Mélédouman knew from experience what "going to the district" meant in that captive colony.]

The commandant Kakatika addresses Mélédouman disparagingly in the familiar form (*tu*) and is unwilling to admit any but his own interpretation of Mélédouman's existence. Mélédouman, on the other hand, is quite conscious of his status within another system, since he has accepted, presumably, the nonname given to him by circumstances. In the circumscribed space of the colony, his sense of his own status does not matter ("Prince or not"); he cannot ignore the directives and the material force of "the other."[1]

A similarly important sequence in the early part of the narrative is Kakatika's interview of Mélédouman, which establishes and reinforces the pivotal opposition between paper truths and essence, appearance and reality, material force and moral authority. Kakatika asserts the validity of the first term of these oppositions. In a transparent reading of circumstances and events, he interprets might as right and says to Mélédouman:

> Quant au présent, sois réaliste, à défaut d'humilité et de sagesse. Regarde les chaînes à tes pieds, les menottes à tes poignets et les gardes autour de toi; cela doit te suffire pour comprendre que le présent, lui m'appartient totalement, absolument, sans partage. (31)

> [As for the present, if you can't be modest and wise, be realistic at least. Look at the chains on your feet, the handcuffs round your wrists and the guards surrounding you. That should be enough to make you see that the present is utterly and unequivocally mine.]

The commandant sees definitive meaning in appearances that are obviously changeable; he also fails to realize that interpretations are conditioned by vantage point or ideology. Thus for Kakatika, the French "civilizing mission" gives him an absolute right and duty to "frapper sans défaillance chaque fois que ce sommeilleux serpent venimeux enfoui au fin fond du Noir lève un tant soit peu la tête, se manifestant par quelque signe que lui, Kakatika, est, bien entendu, le seul à déceler et à interpréter sans autre forme de procès" (21) ["to strike unhesitatingly each time the poisonous snake sleeping deep within the Black man reared his head ever so slightly, revealing himself by some sign that Kakatika was, of course, the only one to notice and judge summarily"]. Meaning is determined by one intelligence, that of the authority in place. But Mélédouman realizes only too well that material and moral victory are no longer one, that meaning is debatable.

Frustrated by the commandant's refusal to state the charges against him, Mélédouman argues:

> Eh bien! Je vais satisfaire votre curiosité puisque vous insistez, si cela peut faire effectivement avancer la noble cause de la justice et de la vérité. Je suis, en tant que prince héritier du trône, le fondement de tout pouvoir dans ce royaume. Toute forme de pouvoir donc, qui ne traverse pas mon sang de près ou de loin, toute forme de pouvoir, tout acte juridique ou légal qui ne bénéficie pas de cet aval, de l'aval de la famille royale de Bettié, détentrice de la vraie légitimité, tout acte qui n'a pas le bénéfice de ma caution spirituelle, morale ou politique, ou celle de ma famille ne peut être qu'usurpation, expropriation illégale, illicite, illégitime et spoliation. (30)

> [All right then! I shall satisfy your curiosity since you are so insistent and if my answer can serve the noble cause of truth and justice. I am, as prince and heir to the throne, the seat of all power in this kingdom. Any form of power that is unconnected to my blood, any form of power, any legal or judicial act that is unauthorized by me or the royal family of Bettié, who hold real legitimacy—any such act performed without benefit of my spiritual, moral, or political approval or that of my family can be nothing more than usurpation, illegal expropriation, unlawful and illegitimate spoliation.]

In other circumstances, as we infer, Mélédouman would have been the subject of epic, in which material and moral triumph are one. Ironically, his authority is historically legitimate, but he is powerless. Mélédouman offers a pertinent analysis of that incongruency when he says to Kakatika, "Votre pouvoir est un pouvoir technique, policier et militaire. Quoi que vous puissiez penser, j'ai le droit, la justice, la liberté, la dignité de mon côté. J'ai le pouvoir moral et spirituel" (38) ["Your power is technological, the might of the police and the military. Regardless of what you may think, right, justice, freedom, and dignity are on my side. My power is moral and spiritual"]. It is this disparity between outside and inside, between the accidental and essential which creates the absurdity and anguish of Mélédouman's situation and experience.

Mélédouman reconciles himself to this injustice by rationalizing: the immaterial moral and spiritual force of man is ultimately, if not immediately, stronger than material power. Unlike the glib Clarence, then, Mélédouman does not come to his initiation with excessive pride and self-assurance that need to be undone before the initiation can begin or as a part of the initiation. Paradoxically, Mélédouman articulates compelling arguments, but his problem is to hold onto a sense of self and self-worth when faced with the technical victory of his colonizer. *La Carte d'identité* aims to undo the enslaved self and to create the confident and free one. Accordingly, Mélédouman is not the butt of parody as is Clarence, who represents that against which *Le Regard du roi* is written. The reader of *Le Regard*, it will be recalled, experiences Clarence's disorientation—the narrative undermines Clarence's subjectivity by challenging all its textual counterparts or manifestations—but the reader knows nonetheless that the signs which the initiate cannot decipher *are* interpretable, that meaning is there and lies in the quest, in humility—all of which are made manifest in the embrace of the king. The sympathetic reader of *La Carte d'identité*, on the other hand, has much more at stake, is not superior in this sense to Mélédouman, and shares his anxiety about the resilience of African morale.

"Jouer au Sherlock Holmes de l'histoire, de la mémoire, du destin"

With the loss of his identity card and the obligation to search for it, Mélédouman experiences profound disarray and alienation, despite the fact that he is a sturdier man than most—proud of his integrity and heritage, stronger (rather than weaker) because of his French schooling.[2] He no longer is certain of his age, of where he lives, of his parents' identity. Moreover, his torture in prison has led to blindness, and he asks his granddaughter Ebah Ya to bring him a mirror. We read in this too patently symbolic infirmity and its corrective the status of every initiate: he has not yet acquired knowledge and does not yet know how to read signs. Mélédouman thus says, "O morts. . . . N'est-ce pas vous qui dans ce vent m'adressez cet étrange message que je n'arrive plus à déchiffrer, à décrypter?" (131) ["Oh, my dead. . . . Is it not you speaking to me through the wind's voice this strange message I can no longer decipher or decode?"]. But Mélédouman's blindness is also indicative of a certain innate skepticism regarding appearances and obvious answers and his willingness to grapple with more challenging interpretations. As Mélédouman explains to Ebah Ya, "Quand on met du piment dans tes yeux, sois reconnaissante à cette main criminelle. Elle est en train d'ouvrir tes yeux pour te révéler le monde" (75) ["When someone puts pepper into your eyes, be grateful to that criminal hand: it is opening your eyes to show you the world"]. Thus, as we saw above, Mélédouman does not interpret material, technical victory as moral authority as does the commandant who "reads" naively, confusing the accidental and the essential.

The initiatory journey is consecrated (and highlighted textually) by Mélédouman's poetic invocation to his ancestor, Anoh Asséman:

> Me voici mon frère Anoh Asséman
> Debout au gouvernail rude et aride
> De mon peuple au destin
> De hérisson et de taupe
>
> . . . .
> Levons-nous prompts
>   Avec le coq
> Pour guider ce peuple mien
> Ce peuple encore aveugle
> Sur le chemin incertain et sinueux
> Qu'il va falloir emprunter
> Pour traverser le fleuve
> De triste mémoire.
> Si nous voulons échapper encore une fois
> A l'humiliante vie de l'esclave
>   Pour un destin Pokou
>   De liberté
>   De gloire
>   De joie
>   De bonheur (61–63)

> [Here I am brother Anoh Asséman
> Standing at the harsh and barren helm
> Of my people's destiny
> A destiny of hedgehogs and moles
>
> . . . .
> Let us arise promptly
>   With the cock
> To guide this, my people
> Still blind
> On the uncertain and winding path
> We will have to take
> In order to cross the river
> Of sorrowful memory.
> If we want to escape once more
> The humiliating life of a slave
>   And follow the destiny of Pokou
>   Of freedom
>   Of glory
>   Of joy
>   Of happiness]

By juxtaposing the people's blindness and enslavement with the allusion to the Agni Queen Pokou, who sacrificed her infant son so that her people might be saved,[3] the image of the captain governing his ship and the prophetic dawn, this invocation situates Mélédouman's initiation in historical tradition and myth. It leaves no doubt about the apocalyptic nature of Mélédouman's initiation.

Mélédouman's journey is symbolic, first of all, in its objective: to find his identity is to reinterpret "history, memory, and destiny." Second, Mélédouman represents an entire people who must also enact a journey. Thus Adiaffi strives to present Mélédouman, not as a superior, but as one who is of the people. The relationship between Mélédouman and those whom he represents, or the interdependence of leaders (or, presumably, intellectuals) and popular classes, is suggested in several ways.

First of all, Mélédouman carries his mirror, which signals his lack of self-sufficiency, his need for *external* confirmation of his existence and identity. He is guided furthermore by Ebah Ya, a necessary participant in his life, whom he calls "mes yeux, ma déesse" (128) ["my eyes, my goddess"]. This couple embodies the complementarity and interdependence of old age and youth, male and female, wisdom and innocence: "J'ai mis ta mère au monde et toi tu me mets au monde aujourd'hui; je suis ton fils, tu m'as arraché au monde des morts. . . . [T]u es ma nanan aussi, comme je suis ta nanan" (128) ["I brought your mother into the world and you bring me into the world today. I am your son, you have snatched me from the world of the dead. . . . [Y]ou are my nanan too, as I am your nanan"]. Yet the homage to feminine virginity and virtue, implied in Ebah Ya's participation in the journey, suggests a defensive and stale conception of possibilities for women: the only virtuous female is either the exceptional and legendary Queen Pokou or the prepubescent handmaiden, that favorite of Christian iconography.

The imbalance in the representation of the feminine becomes still more obvious when we consider the narrative's inclusion of scenes of popular culture. Those scenes forge the bond between the demeaned Mélédouman and the brutalized people whom he represents. In particular, *La Carte d'identité* exploits the image of rape to suggest the social decay that a loss of identity and vision has occasioned in the Agni populace. Let us examine the power and limits of that metonymy so as to better grasp the sense of Mélédouman's journey.

An Ambiguous Epidemic

After his interview with Mélédouman, the commandant Kakatika judges four cases of rape, three of which, like many events of the story, involve competing interpretations. Here, as elsewhere, signs and their meaning(s) are a fundamental issue.

Taken all together, the rapes that occur in Bettié are the image of a malfunctioning society. It is an easy intention to grasp, since Kakatika himself bemoans the impossibility of friendship with Mélédouman ("une amitié avortée" ["an aborted friendship"]) and complains, "Quelle époque! Epoque d'avortement et de viol" (46) ["What an era! An era of abortion and rape"]. Later, Mélédouman also refers to "mon identité . . . violée" (68) ["my desecrated identity"] and "le viol [du] peuple" (136) ["the rape of the people"]. The most incontestable link, however, is established by one of the rapists, the insane Kouamé, who conjugates the verb *violer* in all its tenses and persons and then adds: "Le violeur violé. On est toujours violé par quelqu'un, par quelque chose. Et on viole toujours quelqu'un, quelque chose. La terre est habitée par des violeurs qui s'entreviolent" (54–55) ["The raped rapist. One is always raped by someone or something. And one always rapes someone or something. The earth is inhabited by rapists who rape one another"]. The narrator then comments,

> Et si la folie avait raison! Et si la folie du monde s'exprimait ainsi inno-cemment à travers la folie d'un violeur! Un odieux violeur devenu fou à cause d'un crime horrible et d'un viol insupportable. Kouamé était affreux et pitoyable à voir. Avec ses yeux hagards qui regardent on ne sait où. Le monde absurde de la violence, peut-être, le monde bestial de l'agression, sans doute. (55)
>
> [And if madness were truthful! If the world's madness were expressed thus—through the artless madness of a rapist! A detestable rapist gone mad because of a horrible crime and an unbearable rape. Kouamé was wretched and pitiful to see. With his haggard eyes looking who knows where. Perhaps the absurd world of violence; no doubt, the bestial world of aggression.]

Reciprocal violence and madness are characteristic, the passage im-plies, of Bettié. Even the commandant himself falls ill—from what combi-nation of supernatural and natural forces we are not told—when he con-siders the unrealized potential and waste all around him in the colony. The rape metonymy is ineffective, however. In addition to the fact that the narrative does not motivate the supposed decay and that the several rapes stand virtually alone as a symbol of societal degradation, Adiaffi unfortunately subverts the metonymy in two ways. In two of the four cases of rape, the degree of female complicity is so important as to challenge the very notion of violation and lack of respect. The wife's silence, by the narrator's ambiguous account, vis-à-vis her own reaction in Rape II implies that she desired the sexual relations with the rapist and was not averse to making a fool of her husband: "elle ne s'en aperçut que lorsque la puissante chose érectile était profondément entrée en elle, et déjà la chatouillait. Elle tut à ce niveau sa propre réaction, après le criminel, le coupable chatouillement" (53) ["she only realized what was happening when the powerful and erect thing was deep inside her and already tickling her. She had nothing to say about her own reaction once the reprehensible tickling had commenced"]. In Rape IV, the case of "the mad virgin," the girl is raped by a young man as she sleeps. Opposing her father who argues she has been raped, she claims that she enjoyed the act and is as guilty as the young man: he should not therefore be blamed. She is deemed crazy because young women normally do not ever admit sexual desire—and surely not when so much is at stake.

In Rape I, despite the young girl's plea that the rapist be punished, Kakatika does not punish him but tries instead to establish the girl's ultimate consent to or pleasure in the sexual act and, failing to establish either, orders a doctor's examination for evidence of penetration and ejaculation.[4] Thus the woman who has "enjoyed it" is believed (Rape IV); another refuses to comment, that is, she did enjoy it (Rape II); and the one who says she did not enjoy it is not believed (Rape I). Two women are pleased to have been forced, and Kakatika's refusal to pronounce judgment on behalf of the third is not only contemptuous but also credits the view that women are always pleased in such circumstances, despite themselves.

One might attribute this failure of justice to Kakatika's masculine blindness and racism, but it seems rather to emanate from the narrative itself: Rape III is the only rape in which guilt is undeniable because the rapist also kills his victim. The heinous crime thus ceases to be called rape and is called murder instead, and the perpetrator ceases to be thought of as one man among men and is viewed instead as mad—a different category of being altogether. With such narrative and semantic magic, Adiaffi belittles the crime of rape and pleads insanity for the man who is truly guilty.

The second narrative subversion of the rape metonymy is the tone of these episodes. *La Carte d'identité* contains innumerable instances of popular back talk and challenges to authority, which supplement the story's emphasis on the mythic initiation of Mélédouman. These intrusions into the classic story anchor the protagonist in his community and also reveal the indomitable spirit of popular revolt: the women's erotic purification dance which disrupts an official routine (the arrest of Mélédouman), and the people's caricaturist nicknames for Father Joseph ("Fetish-Father"), Kakatika ("Evil Spirit of the Forest"), and the garde-floco ("Big God"), who, like all such colonial intermediaries, has illusions of grandeur and likes to assert his superiority vis-à-vis his fellow Africans. Such popular comic "readings" of official language and behavior virtually become an alternative language in Sony Labou Tansi's *La Vie et demie*. In Bakhtin's view, they represent a hardy, healthy response to the numerous manifestations of an alienating authority (see Chapter 8).

As always in *La Carte d'identité*, popular reaction and behavior occasion a humorous and playful scene, as in the following dialogue, which precedes the raiding of the Catholic church:

—Diaaa . . . les Blancs aussi ont des génies!
—Bien sûr, qu'est-ce que tu crois?
—Mais les Blancs, ce sont des hommes comme nous. Et le Fétiche, c'est Dieu qui l'a créé; donc les Blancs aussi ont des fétiches, triompha Koutou Kouakou le raisonneur.
—Il paraît même qu'ils adorent leurs morts comme nous.

—Et les statuettes qui sont à l'église, qu'est-ce que tu crois? Ce sont des fétiches habités par leurs Génies.
—C'est vrai ça?
—Oui, c'est vrai, je jure sur Gnamien. Je jure sur la tête de mon grand-père.
—Un Blanc en transe?
—Allons voir ça.

Les bébés, les enfants délaissés piaillaient à tout rompre, en appelant leur mère rendue sourde et indigne par l'extravagance de la nouvelle. Le chef du village, pratique, réunit, en un tournemain, le conseil du village, les notables. On en conclut à la nécessité d'offrir aux génies des Blancs—un génie est un génie—un mouton, des poulets, des oeufs et du gin. (88)

[—Diaaa . . . White men also have their spirits!
—But of course, what do you expect?
—The Whites are people like us. Fetishes are created by God. So the Whites also have fetishes, reasoned Koutou Kouakou triumphantly.
—It seems they also worship their dead, just like us!
—And the statues inside the church, do you know what they are? They're fetishes inhabited by their spirits.
—Really?
—Yes, it's true! I swear by Gnamien. I swear on my grandfather's head.
—A White man possessed?
—Let's go see!

Babies and children left on their own were whining with all their might, calling their mothers grown deaf and distracted at this sensational news. The village chief, practical-minded as he was, assembled the elders. They concluded that it was appropriate to offer to the White men's spirits—a spirit is a spirit, after all—a sheep, some chickens, eggs, and gin.]

The villagers, like Father Joseph, try to make sense of foreign rites and relics. Their interpretations, based on their own cultural experiences, clash with and mock the haughty view that the self-important Father Joseph expounds. The comedy of this comparative analysis thus exposes Catholicism, as Bakhtin would say, and serves to challenge its authority.

Adiaffi, obeying this comic impulse, then, makes fun of rapists and victims. All three "harmless" rapes are the object of comedy in a narrative where only the buffoons and puppets of colonialism—Kakatika, the garde-floco, and Father Joseph—are ridiculed. Thus the narrator's retelling of Rape II, as we saw above, has the tone of certain ribald songs, and there are countless humorous allusions and double-entendres, "un chasseur revenu bredouille" ["a hunter returning home empty-handed"], "la rapidité chasseresse du geste habile" ["the hunter's rapid and deft movements"], and "on ne badine pas avec . . ." ["you don't play with . . ."] (52–53). Similarly, the pidgin French that the narrative accords to the young girl and her mammoth attacker in Rape I diminishes the seriousness of the incident. The narrator concludes that episode as follows:

Et les garde-flocos de partir de leurs commentaires paillards. Elle n'a pas l'air timide, la petite. Eh, dis, petite, tu as éprouvé du plaisir? Avoue. J'ai un instrument plus précis que ton médecin africain, et attention, ça va vite. Le commandant Kakatika Lapine, qui ne comprend pas les langues locales, ne saura jamais qu'il y a des experts en gynécologie au cercle, et que ce n'était pas la peine de descendre jusqu'au quartier indigène pour dénicher le médecin africain. (52)

[And the floco guards started up with their bawdy comments. The little one seems none too shy. Hey, little one. Tell us, did it feel good? Come on, tell us. I've got a better instrument than your African doctor. And watch out, it works fast. Commandant Kakatika Lapine, who understands no local languages, will never suspect that there are gynecological experts right there in the area, and that there was no need to go down to the native district to seek out an African doctor.]

The switching of registers between the hearty popular idiom of the guards and the groomed, grammatically precise language of the narrator as he expresses Kakatika's obliviousness is part of the pleasure of this passage. The double-entendre and this additional instance of Kakatika's inability to interpret create the comic effect. Furthermore, the coarseness of the garde-flocos and the naive obtuseness of the commandant help ridicule these representatives of a power that is inimical to Mélédouman. But the narrator, too, takes part in this insensitive treatment of rape. If Mélédouman's symbolic quest for respect is treated with reverence, then nonchalance and humor with regard to any violation of humanity are inappropriate and discordant. Thus, when the four rapes have been read, their effectiveness as a sign of corruption has been diminished because the text equivocates and trivializes them. The text privileges their value as comic interlude, as examples of the incompetency or vulgarity of Kakatika and his guards, or as occasions for insights into popular culture.[5] One might even be tempted to argue that the bodily grotesque and popular laughter function here, as Bakhtin has written with regard to Rabelais, to suggest fecundity, the bodily instinct to procreate, which is hardier than colonial might and which will therefore assure the future of society (*Rabelais and His World* 313–14). But it seems to me that *La Carte d'identité* cannot have it both ways. Thus Mélédouman's journey remains a voyage of consequence, but the link between his loss of identity and the society's loss of harmony is tenuous.

The Voyage of Rediscovery

Kakatika gives Mélédouman one week in which to find his identity card. Counting by the "calendrier sacré" of the Akan, he searches on each day in a new place. He will never find the identity card, of course—it has been inadvertently held by the authorities—but the search leads Mélédouman to rediscover and "to dialogue" with facets of his civilization (identity). Mélédouman's initiation is thus simultaneously a rereading of the signs of Africa's past and a wandering in an active, present community. As he and Ebah Ya come upon Abadjinan's artists' shed, Father Joseph's church, Monsieur Adé's school, the historical city Krodasso, now in ruins, the sanctuary of the sacred throne house, Mélédouman ponders art, religion, language, history, medicine. Mélédouman's conversations and reflections respond in effect to the commandant's accusations against African civilization: "Vous n'aviez rien! Vous n'étiez rien! Vous ne connaissiez rien!" (33) ["You had nothing! You were nothing! You knew nothing!"] and to Mélédouman's (and an African) crisis in identity. Let us consider just a few of these encounters.

On Sacred Sunday, Mélédouman begins his search for the identity card with a visit to Abadjinan's shed. Here he is consoled by his rediscovery of the aesthetic principles of Akan sculpture, which the artists ("human genuises") have produced as vessels for the gods ("divine genuises"):

> Tout ici est symbole et s'enracine dans la grande et belle *mythologie akan*. Quelquefois *les lois naturelles sont délicieusement renversées*, comme avec cet audacieux petit rat en argile qui avale un gros serpent boa.
>   *Des scènes comiques* s'incarnent ainsi fertilement dans toutes les matières: argile, bois, cuivre, bronze, or. Profondément imprégnés par cette merveilleuse *culture populaire*, ces créateurs anonymes, aux gestes altiers, concourent, chacun à sa manière, à *résoudre les puzzles*, les mots croisés du grand visage fragmenté de l'Afrique. (78, emphasis added)

> [Everything here is a symbol and is rooted in the beautiful and noble *Akan mythology*. Sometimes *natural laws are pleasingly reversed*, as with this bold little clay rat swallowing a fat boa constrictor.
>   *Comic scenes* thus take form in all sorts of materials: clay, wood, copper, bronze, gold. Deeply steeped in the extraordinary *culture of the people*, these anonymous creators with their proud strokes contribute, each in his own way, to *resolving the large and fragmented puzzle* of Africa's face.]

The principles of traditional art outlined in this passage are precisely those that inform *La Carte d'identité*.[6] The novel builds on Akan mythology and traditions, as in the allusion to Queen Pokou and the Throne Ceremony, which takes place on Sacred Friday. It turns the world upside down, especially on Sacred Wednesday when Mélédouman learns from his "widow" that he "has died" and later when Mélédouman, the small rat, will have the better of Kakatika, the boa. Studded with comic scenes and popular sketches, *La Carte d'identité* strives to decode the signs of Africa's past and future. It is this combination of traditions, imagination, daring, and popular resources that Mélédouman perceives where the commandant Kakatika sees nothing or sees, at best, "des coutumes . . . inintelligibles" (33) ["unintelligible customs"] and where Father Joseph sees art objects and lucrative contraband.

Another significant episode occurs on Sacred Tuesday when Mélédouman encounters a young boy who has been punished by his teacher for speaking Agni. The issue of language, orality, and writing is a veritable leitmotif of *La Carte d'identité*.[7] Mélédouman argues with Adé, the young instructor, about the role of French and of African languages for young people and presumably for an African future. There are echoes of Ngũgĩ, Mudimbe, and Hountondji as Mélédouman and Adé debate the criteria of "beauty," "richness in thought and literature," "the usefulness of a lingua franca," and "aptness for scientific theory and applications."[8] Mélédouman often insists on the term *African language*, whereas Adé slips into using the prejudicial and more common term *dialect*. The discussion of language use, like Mélédouman's earlier conversation with Father Joseph on the comparative value of African and Western religious practices, is curiously inconclusive. The text seeks the authority of the initiation story but, unlike the story in its pure form, does not posit an indisputable set of truths. The question of essence and authenticity, with which the narrative struggles initially, thus seems obsolete: more complex questions have displaced it.

The Fantastic Space of Erasure

If Mélédouman's experiences are, on the whole, rationally explicable, if his ability to reason is his ally in all these encounters and discussions, then the text spins its most elliptic sequence to suggest Mélédouman's most trying problem, faith in himself. As Sacred Tuesday ends, Mélédouman walks through nauseating feces and mud. He implores the rain to wash him and curses his fate of exile and wandering. Mélédouman realizes, as does Clarence, that he is traveling in a fantastic world. He has ignored any number of small signs that told him so. Abadjinan's shed and the school were displaced from their habitual locations; and the whole sequence of events surrounding his arrest—the fact that Mélédouman receives not one of the three summons that Kakatika has sent him, the dead motor of Kakatika's newly repaired jeep, the sudden downpour, the women's spontaneous sexual dance of purification, the inexplicable start-up and steering of the jeep, Kakatika's falling ill after his interview with Mélédouman—all these events could not have been incidental. Considering such mystery, the narrator comments, tongue-in-cheek, "Ah! l'Afrique! l'incompréhensible, l'irrationnelle Afrique!" (13). Mélédouman now realizes that his house is no longer there, that his neighbor's house has, according to Ebah Ya, a roof and no walls, and that the house of another neighbor has walls and no roof. Mélédouman hears violent laughter; he comes across a grey-haired young girl carrying a sleeping old man on her back. The young girl recognizes him and indicates that his house is "just there." Then his widow appears, telling him that Mélédouman has died and been buried and calling him, the man before her, a phantom.

These signs and riddles are strange and confounding, as in the tale

"L'Héritage" or in *Kaïdara*; Mélédouman is unable to discern patterns and causality, to link events one to another, that is, to develop a coherent vision. These many occurrences are not the doing of Kakatika, of course. On the contrary, the text suggests—problematically, in my view, because the novel cannot have its cake and eat it, too—that Mélédouman's journey has been called for, if not orchestrated, by surreal forces, by his dead ancestors, so that he might relearn his history, renew his roots. Moreover, we ultimately learn that the search has no material justification and can have no material outcome because Mélédouman's identity is never in doubt. As he himself says, the commandant must know who Mélédouman is in order to arrest him—and the lost identity card is but a pretext.

In both its form and content, *La Carte d'identité* asserts a higher authority; it insists, at the same time, on the initiate's *self*-discovery. Facing the darkest hour of his journey, Mélédouman decides to consult the cemetery for the definitive answer to the question of his existence. He has begun to doubt everything and to wonder how one even comes to know the existence of others, what constitutes life and death, what permits one *to name*, the very problem signaled at the text's opening.

Here Ebah Ya and the mirror serve to affirm him, but Mélédouman seems to settle for a "discovery" of what he has known all along—that he does indeed exist. The journey of initiation does not have implications beyond the fact of Mélédouman's essence and the truths which he ably articulates at the beginning of his incarceration. Overall, his quest has led to an affirmation of the value and durability of traditional art, to an inconclusive discussion of language and history, and to a feeble assertion of the relativity of religious customs.

Mixed Messages

The most significant outcome of the journey of initiation is not, then, what Mélédouman learns but, rather, what Kakatika learns. By story's end, thanks to the teleogenic revelation that Mélédouman has spent many years in France and in French schools, Kakatika has a "change of heart" (rereads the story, as in detective fiction) and sees Mélédouman, of course, as the exceptional African who proves the rule. Given the story's emphasis on the individual consciousness that reorders history, it should be unimportant what the French officer has understood: there should be no satisfaction in triumph over the colonizing other. The victory should be self-assurance, restored faith, and conviction. But the narrative equivocates on this point. Mélédouman would ignore or minimize the importance of Kakatika's revised opinion, but the narrative's sole achievement is, in fact, that Kakatika has "seen the light." Materially, nothing has changed, and this is precisely the reason why Kakatika's transformation takes on such importance. The narrative settles for a cheap victory. Mélédouman's right to self-definition can only be claimed when it is recognized by him who has deprived Mélédouman of that right. It is as though Kakatika undergoes the initiation.

Furthermore, the choice of an exceptional man as initiate is troubling, as is the fact that Mélédouman's background is hidden to the reader until it is revealed to Kakatika. Mélédouman is clearly not an *alienated assimilé* who seeks a "retour aux sources"; but he represents all along nobility of blood, of character, and of intellect. The revelation of the facts of Mélédouman's French experience to Kakatika at story's end provokes Kakatika's change of heart. It is the narrative's trump card, and so Mélédouman's nonchalance about his experience is meant to compensate by suggesting that those facts are irrelevant, that self-esteem and nobility do not derive from opportunities to assimilate, that the exceptional man is not—or, at the very least, does not feel himself to be—superior to the ordinary man. Yet the tardy revelation of that information leads the reader, too, to speculate that only an exceptional man could reason and speak so eloquently. It is a self-defeating implication.

The significance of narrative form becomes perceptible once again, for the adaptation of the traditional initiation story is, as I have argued, neither necessary nor generic. Adiaffi's text is a discursive and fictional response to accusations such as Kakatika's exclamation, "You had nothing! You were nothing! You knew nothing!" In its initiatory form, the story gains authority, as does *Le Regard du roi*, for the view it proposes, for the moral authority of African civilization(s). As we have seen, it is also an attempt to valorize self-transformation and social dynamism. In the latter regard, *La Carte d'identité* further adapts, indeed popularizes, the traditional form with sketches of the motley and audacious community in which the initiate is rooted and which he represents.

Thus Mélédouman's story borders on the naive and nostalgic, the reverie of a dispossessed, disillusioned class longing for an illustrious past transposed to the present, but the text is governed as well by a strong urge to transcend such sentimentality, to discover the possibilities for a collective future. Indeed, the past (or an ahistorical zone) is not, as Bakhtin has written, absolutely valorized and distanced in *La Carte d'identité* as it is in *Le Regard du roi*, precisely because the contemporary and popular world constantly impinges upon and supplants the heroic vision. In those instances, *La Carte d'identité* seems to admit that "modernity" is not an aggregate of outside elements to be assimilated but is the syncretic space in which we all operate. Hallowed tradition and irreverent innovation, community and self, indigenous media and technology as well as borrowed ones are resources that a healthy culture cannot afford to overlook, as Mélédouman implies: "Quand on va étudier l'intelligence des autres, ce n'est pas pour abandonner la sienne . . . mais la multiplier indéfiniment, fort de cet apport de l'autre" (136) ["When one goes to acquire others' knowledge, it's not in order to forgo one's own . . . but to increase it many times over, strengthened from another's contribution"].

Given its mixed agenda, *La Carte d'identité* suffers from a textual malaise. For the matter of where authority lies or the retreat into essential truths and definitions seems anachronistic. The narrative itself surpasses the issue of identity (attaining self-knowledge). The locus of the problem, European power and African disempowerment, seems to lie elsewhere.

Fable

8

"The Emperor's New Clothes":
The Lens of Fable in *La Vie et demie*

"Un souverain nu, pensait Chaïdana, c'est le
sommet de la laideur."

["A naked ruler," thought Chaïdana, "is the
height of ugliness."]

The novels we have seen so far adapt features of the epic and initiation
story. In so doing, they assert an order of one sort or another and present
a particular view of the possibilities for agency. *Wangrin*, in the context
of an intransigent colonial situation, imagines and represents victory, au-
thorized (and limited) by birth and destiny. *Les Bouts de bois de Dieu*, on
the other hand, revises the epic as we see it in *Wangrin* and represents
a new authority of collective faith, will, and sweat. *Le Regard du roi* parodies
Eurocentric mythologies of Africa, but spins nonetheless its own mythology of plenitude, grace, and absolution seemingly outside history and beyond action. *La Carte d'identité* paradoxically and uneasily seeks to recon-
struct an authentic subjectivity through a form that situates authority
outside the subject. In this chapter we turn to a text, *La Vie et demie* (1979),
whose profound impulse is to empower, as is that of *Les Bouts de bois de
Dieu*—yet not this time through a narrative tradition of glorification and
realism but, rather, as we shall see, through a tradition of ridicule and
fable.

Sony Labou Tansi tells us in the *avertissement* to *La Vie et demie* how
he sees what he has written, and his comments signal a number of important issues concerning narrative form in the novel:

Et à l'intention des amateurs de la couleur locale qui m'accuseraient
d'être cruellement tropical et d'ajouter de l'eau au moulin déjà inondé
des racistes, je tiens à préciser que *la Vie et Demie* fait ces taches que
la vie seulement fait. Ce livre se passe entièrement en moi. Au fond,
la Terre n'est plus ronde. Elle ne le sera jamais plus. *La Vie et Demie*
devient cette *fable* qui voit demain avec des yeux d'aujourd'hui. Qu'aucun

aujourd'hui politique ou humain ne vienne s'y mêler. Cela prêterait à confusion. Le jour où me sera donnée l'occasion de parler d'un quelconque aujourd'hui, je ne passerai pas par mille chemins, en tout cas pas par un chemin aussi tortueux que la fable. (10)

[And for the benefit of lovers of local color who would accuse me of being cruelly tropical and of adding fuel to racist fires already in flames, I must point out that *La Vie et demie* makes blemishes that life alone has made. This book takes place entirely in me. In truth, the Earth is no longer round. Nor will it ever be again. *La Vie et demie* has become that *fable* that sees tomorrow through the eyes of today. Let no political or human "here and now" get mixed up in it. That would lead to confusion. The day that I have occasion to speak of a perchance "here and now," I won't take a thousand detours, in any case, no detour as twisted as the fable.]

These comments accurately describe, in my view, the formal stance of the novel. Let us begin by noting that *La Vie et demie*'s fabledness is not a matter of the anthropomorphization of animals, associated with a wide variety of African tales, *Aesop's Fables,* and the fables of La Fontaine.[1] Fabledness obviously does not depend on the species of a narrative's characters but is rather, in Scholes and Kellogg's terms, related to "an intellectual and moral impulse" (14). More specifically, the fable is for Labou Tansi a form of indirect expression ("a twisted detour"), which circumstances dictate. The story is utterly imaginary ("takes place entirely in me"), but it is truthful if not true ("makes blemishes that life alone has made"). Since the life and world that it seeks to evoke have gone amuck ("the Earth is no longer round"), the text does not therefore tell a standard and pretty story in a novel and exotic setting. Thus *La Vie et demie* is "fabulous," first of all, in its pose as (moral) metaphor and evocation of a certain reality rather than realist representation, and, second, in the unpredictable schemes and metamorphoses that it imagines.

I have stated above that *La Vie et demie*, like *Les Bouts de bois de Dieu*, seeks to empower. Even though it is secularist and even though it contains moments of satire and humor, *Les Bouts de bois* is, on the whole, a reverent narrative. *La Vie et demie*, on the other hand, is the profane, carnivalesque counterpart which is also fervently committed to similar ideals and as respectful of life. Thus, although its tyrants are tropical Ubu-Rois whose antics are the object of caricature and satire, Sony Labou Tansi's fable is characterized nonetheless by faith in the hardiness of "the people" and of popular culture—expressed both thematically and formally in its central, recurring motif: the stabbed, sabered, shot, ground and eaten Martial refuses to die. This motif is found, of course, in traditional tales[2] and is reminiscent of the "mythological" or "magical" realism of the Caribbean and Latin America.[3] As Sony Labou Tansi's *avertissement* states, the novel refuses to be bound by the rational and by the documentary impulse of many first-generation African novels. Indeed, *La Vie et demie*'s fundamental urge is to acknowledge the existence but deny the authority of *la vie* as it is "given"—wherefore the novel's surreality, its assumption of a form that allows free rein to the imagination.

The context in which Sembène's and Labou Tansi's texts were written is significant, it seems to me, with regard to the form through which each narrative manifests the impulse to empower. We noted in Chapter 5 that Sembène conceptualizes (and we experience) historical process—the multitude of hands and hearts, the success, failure, and suspense—in and through his writing. But his is nonetheless a confident text, for he writes at a moment in which that particular battle is won. He chronicles after the fact. Moreover, the enemy is, for the most part, *the other*. Thus *Les Bouts de bois* bears witness to an historical triumph and proposes that particular victory as an omen of others that must come, that the narrative itself will help bring about.

La Vie et demie is a "more desperate" text than *Les Bouts de bois*; its demons are more powerful. It is written in less optimistic circumstances—in the trenches, as it were, for the battle is being waged here and now. And the easy labels of race and nationality that once seemed dependable indices of allegiance—they were always questionable, however—now clearly have lost their validity. The familiar manifestations and institutions of racism and colonialism disguise themselves and take new forms under neo-colonialism. The state in this era is itself a new type of political entity, robotlike and unreasonable, hostage more than ever to its leaders and to international pressures. Given its compounded problems, the world that Labou Tansi would actualize calls for powerful, unconventional narrative strategies, for the neo-colonial situation in which African writers find themselves is uniquely challenging, as Ngũgĩ states bitterly in *Decolonising the Mind*:

> How does a writer, a novelist, shock his readers by telling them that these [heads of state who collaborate with imperialist powers] are neo-slaves when they themselves, the neo-slaves, are openly announcing the fact on the rooftops? How do you shock your readers by pointing out that these are mass murderers, looters, robbers, thieves, when they, the perpetrators of these anti-people crimes, are not even attempting to hide the fact? When in some cases they are actually and proudly celebrating their massacre of children, and the theft and robbery of the nation? How do you satirise their utterances and claims when their own words beat all fictional exaggerations? (80)

Writers take a variety of approaches to this problem, of course, and in Chapter 9, we shall see the strategies that Ngũgĩ himself chooses in *Devil on the Cross*. I shall refer briefly, however, to Ayi Kwei Armah's *The Beautyful Ones Are Not Yet Born* (1969), which, in my view, illuminates Labou Tansi's particular strategy in *La Vie et demie*. Both texts are "autocritical" in the sense that they point to internal responsibility—in the first case, exclusively, and in the second, to a large extent—for the grotesque and deplorable state of affairs in which African nations find themselves. Armah, who writes in the tradition of realism, modifies that tradition from the very beginning, however, when he names his protagonist "the man"; we are on the verge of a more allegorical (rather than purportedly documentary) form, even then. The text is then governed by a paralyzing naturalism, achieved to large extent through Armah's reduction of the human person to organs and functions—teeth, lips, excrement, and bodily secretions—devoid of spirit, imagination, and will. In the world of *The Beautyful Ones*, characterized by greed and lust for power, the man is inadequate, futile, alien, and—it is important to note—the text is engulfed in its own despair until its very last moments.

In *La Vie et demie* realism is abandoned more deliberately. To the extent that documentary prose takes as its premise the view that the mere description of an awry and unjust world is sufficient, realism seems unequal to the task that Sony Labou Tansi takes on. In the tradition of realism (as in Oyono's *Une vie de boy*, for example) the individual, in time and through his or her experiences, evolves and may learn to understand—often ironically—what is "true" (accurate), that which the narratee has already decoded. But *La Vie et demie* stresses the arbitrariness and absurdity of a world to which realism would perhaps afford too much credence and authority.[4] *La Vie et demie* does not propose the familiar satisfaction of reading the naiveté of an individual protagonist to whom the narratee feels superior. Because Katamalanasia is absurd, because official pronouncements of the state are not meant to tell the truth but to lie, to conceal, to fail to communicate, the text subverts the view of reality and language as ordered and acceptable—a view which a naive reading of realism would allow. Thus *La Vie et demie* does not merely *expose* the ugliness of an apparently immutable world to self-satisfied readers. As I read *La Vie et demie*, it seeks to threaten and destabilize that world.

For Labou Tansi, then, the choice is not only fable but also laughter, a liberating strategy, which Bakhtin describes as though he had read *La Vie et demie* himself:

> Laughter has the remarkable power of making an object come up close, of drawing it into a zone of crude contact where one can finger it familiarly on all sides, turn it upside down, inside out, peer at it from above and below, break open its external shell, look into its center, doubt it, take it apart, dismember it, lay it bare and expose it, examine it freely and experiment with it. *Laughter demolishes fear and piety before an object, before a world,* making of it an object of familiar contact and thus clearing the ground for an absolutely free investigation of it. Laughter is a vital factor in laying down that prerequisite for fearlessness without which it would be impossible to approach the world realistically. As it draws an object to itself and makes it familiar, *laughter delivers the object into the fearless hands of investigative experiment—both scientific and artistic—and into the hands of free experimental fantasy.* (*Dialogic Imagination* 23, emphasis added)

With its fabled portrait of Katamalanasia, then, *La Vie et demie* makes a massive assault on the reality it evokes but does not name, for it demolishes our fear and piety before the (unfounded) authority of that world. Were it done in mimetic fashion, the text would be *less*, not more, empowering because it would give in, as does *The Beautyful Ones*, to naturalism and fatalism, a sense of being "stuck," of having no alternatives. Laughter seems a more forceful response because it refuses to take the terms proffered by the system portrayed, it makes us step out of the ring of authority of that world. Furthermore, it derives from a popular response to unpopular authority.

That Bakhtin's comments, which we may infer are based in part on his reading of Rabelais's *Gargantua*, so accurately describe *La Vie et demie* confirms the sisterhood between these two texts whose resources—granted their particularity—are an iconoclastic laughter, which Bakhtin sees as characteristic of "low" genres and folk traditions,[5] and a regenerative conception of lower bodily strata (*Rabelais and His World* 1–58), although *La Vie et demie*'s use of blood, copulation, and death are often violent, as we shall see.

The Bad, the Ugly, and the Good

If *La Vie et demie* had been published twenty years earlier, it surely would have been viewed as proof once again of the irresistible pull of (the oral) tradition. This interpretation still can be put forth, of course. But if we accept this explanation and attribute all to the sway of origins, the past, and tradition, we shall fail to see that Labou Tansi *constructs* a story, that the fantasy and character types which we find in the novel are textually and ideologically functional. As we have already noted, the fantasy of the novel allows it to evoke rather than name and to refuse the rules of the "real" world. With regard to character types, we shall see that they, too, are not gratuitous but correspond to the dehumanization of human beings under abusive power. These are the two dimensions of narrative form we now shall consider.

In the opening sequence of the novel, the "Providential Guide," as he ironically is called, goes about eating his lunch and eliminating the opposition leader, Martial, "avec le même couteau ensanglanté" (12) ["with the same bloody knife"]. We are not long in doubt that this is a world in which characters are far from the tradition of psychological realism; they are, in fact, types, usually identifiable by a few traits. The Guide has before him Martial and the latter's wife and children. After several attempts to kill Martial by stabbing and shooting him—all to no avail—the Guide is at his wit's end:

> Le Guide Providentiel se fâcha pour de bon, avec son sabre aux reflets d'or il se mit à tailler à coups aveugles le haut du corps de la loque-père, il démantéla le thorax, puis les épaules, le cou, la tête; bientôt il ne restait

plus qu'une folle touffe de cheveux flottant dans le vide amer, les mor-
ceaux taillés formaient au sol une sorte de termitière, le Guide Providentiel les dispersa à grands coups de pied désordonnés avant d'arracher
la touffe de cheveux de son invisible suspension; il tira de toutes ses
forces, d'une main d'abord, puis des deux, la touffe céda et, emporté
par son propre élan, le Guide Providentiel se renversa sur le dos, se
cogna la nuque contre les carreaux, il en serait mort sur le coup, mais
ce n'était pas un homme fragile. (16)

[The Providential Guide got truly mad. Thrusting blindly with his gleaming gold saber, he set about carving up the torso of the wreck-father;
he dismantled the thorax, then the shoulders, the neck, the head; soon
nothing was left but a wild tuft of hair floating in the bitter void; the
chopped-off pieces on the ground formed a sort of termite hill. The Providential Guide kicked them every which way and set them flying before
he snatched the tuft of hair from its invisible suspension; he pulled with
all his might, first with one hand, and then with both; the tuft gave
way and, carried away by his own momentum, the Providential Guide
fell over on his back and knocked the nape of his neck against the tile
floor. He would have died on the spot, except that he was not a fragile
man.]

This scene, like many in the novel, is conceived theatrically. Sony
Labou Tansi is, of course, a playwright and director. Here is the slapstick,
farcical behavior of buffoons, from Laurel and Hardy to Bugs Bunny, but
who are, in this instance, Machiavellian. The passage contains a plethora
of "action" verbs, almost all of which are written in the *passé simple*. The
Guide thus exhibits much behavior, all of it furious and heinous. The exclusion of all psychological sounding in the narration suggests not only an
absence of reflection on the part of the Guide on this occasion but the
very incapacity for thought. The Guide is what we call a "type" character,
then, not because it is part of an aesthetic heritage, but because the one-
dimensional caricature corresponds in this instance to a lack of the depth
we hold to be the basis of humanity. It is not clear whether power turns
one into this sort of one-dimensional inadequate human being or whether
one-dimensional inadequate human beings tend to gravitate toward
power. Regardless of the direction of causality, one-dimensionality corresponds to the practice of power in Katamalanasia.

The "gleaming gold saber" in the foregoing passage is a detail worth
pondering also. All at once this image suggests the preoccupation with
wealth that motivates the Guide, and it is an ironic evocation of the tradition of heroic narrative (epic) in which gleaming swords are always on
the side of the good guys. Here we have come a long distance from the
protagonist of epic to the Providential Guide who, as with his would-be
heroic predecessors, also vaunts his illustrious line of 362 ancestors. The
Guide is, as this passage demonstrates, violent emotion and bungling,
brutish force (he kicks, he swipes), devoid of all capacity for thought or

compassion. The passage suggests as well that such mindless violence is a menace even to oneself: the Guide's bestiality toward the other—a common procedure in slapstick—makes *him* fall over. This clumsiness then becomes the occasion for a superb bit of understatement and irony in the final phrase, "he was not a fragile man." To state that the Guide is neither physically vulnerable nor sensitive is ludicrous because it is all too kind: it is obvious that he is nothing more than a brute.

The initial sketch of personality—temper, physical force, and stupidity—is reinforced and further developed in later scenes. In his frenzy to machine-gun the brutalized torso of Martial, who reappears one evening, the Guide slaughters by accident his presidential (providential) guards:

> Quand le lieutenant s'était retiré après avoir fait débarrasser la pièce des cadavres des gardes et laver les carreaux, le Guide Providentiel réveilla Chaïdana en lui tirant les oreilles comme on les tire à un enfant réfractaire. . . .
>
> —Ton père était là, dit le Guide Providentiel, la voix estompée par la rage. S'il revient, je te mettrai en morceaux.
>
> Il but une bouteille de champagne, fuma sa pipe, puis s'étendit sur le lit, les yeux cloués au plafond. Le lendemain matin, le cartomancien Kassar Pueblo vint le voir tout furieux.
>
> —Martial est venu se plaindre. C'est une honte: tu as essayé.
>
> —J'ai eu envie, expliqua le Guide Providentiel. J'en ai marre de frotter tout seul. Je me blesse la queue. (24)

> [When the lieutenant retreated after having had the room emptied of the guards' bodies and the tiles washed, the Providential Guide woke Chaïdana by pulling her ears the way one pulls the ears of a disobedient child. . . .
>
> —Your father was here, said the Providential Guide, his voice filled with rage. If he comes back, I'll hack you into pieces.
>
> He drank a bottle of champagne, smoked his pipe, then stretched out on his bed, his eyes glued to the ceiling. The following morning, the card-reader Kassar Pueblo came to see him in a fury.
>
> —Martial came to complain. It's a disgrace. You tried.
>
> —I felt like it, explained the Providential Guide. I've had enough of rubbing all by myself. My thing's getting sore.]

The same character traits surface—rage, violence, and lack of thought, conveyed once again by the preponderance of action verbs in the *passé simple*. There are additional nuances this time. The Guide is a creature of strong appetites and carnal desires that, in his frenzy to satisfy them, lead him to threaten all human life around him. Subject to his flesh, which may overpower him at any moment ("I felt like it"), he is pure ego, infantilized by his desires and completely out of control. Finally, the vulgarity of the Guide's reply to Kassar Pueblo ("I've had enough of rubbing all by myself. My thing's getting sore.") confirms his identity as the "non-fragile" being we recognized from the start. Furthermore, the dumb masturbation that results in bruised flesh, the frustrated attempt to "possess" Chaïdana, and, ultimately, the inability to satisfy his needs make him a pathetic specimen of humanity; by association, the authority of the government headed by such a buffoon is, as Bakhtin says, "drawn into a zone of crude contact" and laid bare.

Labou Tansi's distinction between a dose of "local color" and the reality of "la vie *tropicale*" ["tropical life"] is thus an important one. Ngal defines *tropicalité*, a term that occurs often in Sony Labou Tansi's writings, as "sexe ou idiotie commise sous les tropiques" (140) ["sex or inanity committed in the tropics"]. *La Vie et demie* both uses the term and depicts numerous "tropicalities," as in this instance. The polyvalence of the term, its connotation of both the sex act and stupidity, is a further index of the fabled nature of the novel. In its comic portrayal of the nature and functions of the body, the novel is a parody of "Authority" and, as we shall see later, a sign of the hardiness of life.

Thus the dictators of Katamalanasia are prey to their appetites, subject to tantrums, ruthless in order to have their way. Puppets of their passions, they are unable to perceive and empathize with *otherness*. This blindness to all else but their inexorable instincts and drives, the lack of "fragility" and compassion, give them their robotlike quality. Humanness, *La Vie et demie* suggests, is predicated, not on the ability to contemplate and satisfy self, but on the ability to sense and respond to another.

Katamalanasia, of which the dictators are the representatives, is as violent, voracious, and uncompassionate as they. Guided by its leaders' instincts, appetites, and narcissism, the state is a veritable house of horrors for their citizens and compatriots: inkspots and bloodspots, the telltale traces of crime that do not wash out, the dead who will not die and who hound the living, arbitrary and gratuitous rules, carnage and cruelty, violation of persons and moral integrity, official language meant only to lie.

Opposed to the tyrannical state is the dead but ever present Martial, who serves as the prophet of those who attack it. But Martial is also a "type," a reduced human being, mechanical in his political antagonism and more vengeful than thoughtful. He, too, is consumed by a passion, paternal jealousy, for he rapes Chaïdana, thereby committing incest, to punish her for her sexual murders of government officials.[6] If Martial's jealousy and anger are not pitted per se against his political activism, they nonetheless impugn his virtue. Men will be "Men," after all, the text seems to say, even if they are politically revolutionary. Again we see that power infantilizes; only marginal men in the early stages of this chronicle, Layisho for example, are untainted by the corrupting influence of and ambition for power. Chaïdana, both female and heroic, is the exception who proves the rule: she is a complex, feeling, and thoughtful human being, to whom we shall return.

Narrative License

A sense of the disorder (and thus the nonbasis of authority) in Katamalanasia is created not only through synecdoche in the absurd automatons
who head the government, but through the depiction of life itself in Katamalanasia, which is delirious. There are several occasions, for example,
in which the time of the story and of its telling are not always reconciled.
The innumerable flashbacks and flashforwards, especially in the initial
phases of the story, create a sense of disorientation and nightmare. Bits
and pieces of history briefly rush into consciousness for Chaïdana and
for the former presidential physician, Doctor Tchitchalia, who, having
helped Chaïdana escape, is now being tortured by the Guide. This interweaving of past and present, of unbelievable and more believable scenes
creates a disarming sense of confusion about where the real can be delineated from the nonreal—the cognitive effect on which this narrative hinges.
Instances of narrative incongruency (and delirium) are repeated ad in-
finitum.

Still more important, the surreality that is manifest in Martial's refusal
to die and his continual visits to the Guide and later to Chaïdana takes
other forms as well throughout the narrative. Hyperbole in numbers is
one such form.[7] We have already seen that the Guide has 362 illustrious
ancestors. Jean-Coeur-de-Pierre will father two thousand little Jeans.
Chaïdana's sisterhood with Gargantua's mother becomes apparent when
her pregnancy lasts eighteen months and twenty-two days. In the year
"Coeur-de-Père," Katamalanasia celebrates 228 holidays, including "la fête
des noms, la fête des guides, . . . la fête du dernier mariage du guide,
la fête du fils du guide, la fête des immortels, la fête des caméléons du
guide, la fête de la méditation, la fête du spermatozoïde, la fête du boeuf
. . . la journée des cheveux de Chaïdana, la journée des lèvres, la journée
des ventres" (129) ["the feast of names, the feast of guides . . . the feast
of the guide's latest marriage, the feast of the guide's son, the feast of the
immortals, the feast of the guide's chameleons, the feast of meditation,
the feast of spermatozoa, the feast of beef . . . the day of Chaïdana's hair,
the day of lips, the day of abdomens"]. Kapahacheu, the adoptive brother
of Chaïdana, the daughter, catches in his traps "sept cent quarante-deux
sangliers, deux cent vingt-huit civettes, huit cent trois chacals, quatre-
vingt-treize chats, quatre crocodiles, deux léopards, d'innombrables rats
de toutes tailles, ainsi que quatre boas et treize vipères" (93) ["seven hundred forty-two wild boars, two hundred twenty-eight civet-cats, eight hundred three jackals, ninety-three cats, four crocodiles, two leopards, innumerable rats of all sizes, as well as four boas and thirteen vipers"]. These
aphasic lists and hyperbolic numbers, which continually disrupt a smooth
reading, are another form of the comic and create a Brechtian refusal of
the "reality" depicted.

Immensity, moreover, both situates the story in a fabulous and crazy world and is a memorable index of personalities and events. Thus we come to know the Guide's pretensions to nobility, the extent of Jean-Coeur-de-Pierre's sexual appetites, and Kapahacheu's skill as a hunter. Chaïdana becomes pregnant, of course, after having been raped by 363 soldiers. The preponderance of holidays (228 out of 365) is not merely a commentary on governmental self-aggrandizement and the work that does not take place in Katamalanasia; the comic and disconcerting heterogeneity of the holidays[8] is also a reminder of the randomness and arbitrariness with which the regime governs life and its conflation of the country's interests with the leader's personal life, as in "the feast of the guide's latest marriage" and "the feast of the guide's chameleons." The "simple" humor of hyperbole and the implausible overblown proportions of life (and often misery) are then compounded by the narrator's insistence on statistics, precise measures of exorbitance—a procedure that Rabelais uses in *Gargantua*. In Katamalanasia, characterized as it is by deceit and excess, the narrator's unfailing commitment to truth in numbers is ironic and absurd.

It becomes clear, then, that the struggle between real and surreal, between authority and laughter, is manifested also in the language of *La Vie et demie*. Let us consider briefly how that language operates.

The authority of the pathetic dictatorial regime is nonetheless real: the regime privileges certain signs (the color blue, for example, and slogans such as "les aspirations nationales et la cause du peuple" ["national aspirations and the people's cause"]) and censors others (as in the war against black and the outlawing of the term *enfer* [hell]). Governmental decrees for or against these signs entail the burning of books, death penalties, experimentation with blue mice, and so on. Paradoxically, these acts, which assert the regime's strength, also expose its terrible defensiveness, as for example in the strenuous regulation of colors, which are so patently nonthreatening. We infer that an abusive power fears any sign which is not under its control, for signs, by their nature, allow for individual interpretation, the bane of officially sponsored ideas. It is hardly surprising, then, that the definitive article of the new constitution is written in a language no one comprehends, for language in totalitarian Katamalanasia is always false, always distorted, since the government or the dictator imposes meaning, regardless of the conventions governing words and signs.

But imagination and laughter triumph, because the truth seeps out in popular language, despite government efforts. People in the streets refuse government gibberish and reinterpret it in comic and sometimes vulgar terms. The novel thus exposes the contradictions of language under tyranny; it desacralizes power and hierarchy still further through other procedures. As though the "reality" of his world demanded more than the simple lexicon of everyday existence, Labou Tansi coins ironic phrases ("providentiel," "excellentiel") and terms of terror ("les à-fusiller," "les à-surveiller" ["those-to-be-shot," "those-to-be-watched"]). He employs nearly silent terms for those acts and beings which cannot be named ("la *use fable/ allow SLT to after death + create revenants*

puissance étrangère qui fournissait les guides" ["the foreign power that furnished the guides"]) and reductive metonymies à la Armah that show how human life has been debased ("la loque-père," "leur eau," "ta viande" ["the wreck-father," "their water," "your meat"]). Likewise, the novel depicts the regime in the crass jargon of commerce, television, and sports. The linguistic license of popular culture and that of the novel's discourse thus serve the cause of parody and laughter that challenge Katamalanasia's authority.

We are treated once again to subversive surrealism in the proliferation and replication of dictators and their children, signaled in their similar names. Thus, though the name may vary, Henri-au-Coeur-Tendre, Jean-Coeur-de-Père, or Jean-Coeur-de-Pierre, a dictator is always a dictator in Katamalanasia—characterized by the same voracious and uncontrollable passions, vicious and dumb. The little Jeans of Jean-Coeur-de-Pierre are produced at a rate of fifty a year (following the Guide's copulating annually with fifty virgins), and each Jean eventually chooses a name beginning with the letter of the alphabet for that year: in the first year, the aphasic and thus comic list of names includes Jean Crocodile, Jean Clarinette, Jean Carburateur, Jean Coupe-Coupe, Jean Classique, Jean Canne-à-Sucre . . . Of course, the alphabet is eventually exhausted and a system of numbers is instituted—there is excess everywhere. In the final hours of this fantastic chronicle of Katamalanasia, many of these sons will ally themselves with their grandmother Chaïdana, daughter of Chaïdana and granddaughter of Martial, and will wage war against their father and stepbrothers. No system is impervious, and each carries the possibility of its own destruction.

Alongside the outrageous excess, then, there is improbability: the blue mice and blue grass, genetically engineered during "l'ère du bleu" ["the blue period"], and the fact that Chaïdana manages to poison dozens of cabinet ministers, takes 243 identities, marries often and even marries the Guide a second time—to be sure, he does not recognize her. The most striking surreal occurrence, Martial's refusal to die and his continual visitations to the Guide and Chaïdana, is rich in connotations. This narrative device is a brilliant adaptation and usage of the traditional belief that, as Birago Diop writes in "Souffles," "les morts ne sont pas morts" ["the dead are not dead"]. Martial's spirit thus lives on for his followers. But if for them, the presence of the dead is positive, for the Guide and Chaïdana, it is dreadful. The Guide meets with no tangible punishment for his murder of Martial, but in the fabulous tradition of oral and Gothic tales, *Hamlet* and *Macbeth*, he is tormented in his sleep. In Chaïdana's case, her father's dreadful, incestuous visits symbolize the burden of her history and explain the intensity of her anger and struggle. Given the limits of characterization that *La Vie et demie* accepts, the novel embeds motivation through this narrative mechanism and suggests the ineffectiveness, ultimately, of the regime's brutal tactics. The narrative license of fable allows the novel to refuse death as the final opposition to life and to insist on the continuity between them.

Dwelling in Possibility, or *"le corps farouche"* [*"the untamed body"*]

So far we have been considering the ways in which *La Vie et demie*'s caricature, excess, and fantasy evoke aspects of totalitarian government and
how laughter destroys the credibility of such government. Let us now consider the possibilities for agency that a fable such as this affords, particularly in the case of Chaïdana.

Chaïdana acts out of madness, a madness which Katamalanasia has
induced and the fruits of which it thus deserves. Having witnessed the
murder of her father, mother, sisters, and brothers, having been forced
to eat them in *pâté* and *daube*, forced then into marriage with the Guide
who has performed the murders, Chaïdana complains to Doctor Tchi: "Ils
m'ont mis là-dedans un corps et demi. . . . Vous ne pouvez pas deviner,
docteur, vous ne pouvez pas savoir comme ça vibre une chair et demie"
(22) ["Inside me they put a body and a half. You can't imagine, Doctor,
you can't know how a body and a half vibrates"]. She elaborates on her
difference and alienation, the space which brings with it knowledge that
cannot be suppressed, when she adds, "Comment vous dire, docteur? On
n'est pas du même monde. On n'a pas le même coefficient charnel. Moi,
là-dedans, c'est une fois et demie" (27) ["How can I explain it to you,
Doctor? We are not of the same world. We don't have the same bodily
coefficient. Inside me, it's a time and a half"]. She is, of course, as destructive of herself as she is of others. Haunted by dreams and visions, she
attempts suicide and pays a heavy price for the murders she will inflict—
the rape by her father and what we may presume to be a distasteful intimacy with her "ugly" sexual partners.

Chaïdana begins her attack on Katamalanasia with a writing campaign:

> Elle acheta de la peinture noire pour trois millions. . . . Elle recruta
> trois mille garçons chargés d'écrire pour la nuit de Noël à toutes les portes
> de Yourma la célèbre phrase de son père: "Je ne veux pas mourir cette
> mort." Le beau bataillon de pistolétographes avait fonctionné à merveille:
> ils avaient pu écrire la phrase jusqu'au troisième portail des murs du
> palais excellentiel. Certains d'entre eux, les plus audacieux sans doute,
> avaient réussi à écrire la phrase sur le corps de quelques responsables
> militaires tels que le général Yang, le colonel Obaltana, le lieutenant-
> colonel Fursia et bien d'autres. Amedandio disait avoir écrit la phrase
> sur mille quatre-vingt-dix uniformes.
>
> Pendant ce Noël où la ville buvait et dansait, les pistolétographes
> se battaient pour mettre la phrase de Martial partout. Et Amedandio
> proclamait une obscure "prochaine fois le feu" en déclarant qu'il écrirait
> la phrase sur le cul du Guide Providentiel. (44–45)

> [She bought black paint for three million francs. . . . She recruited three
> thousand boys who, on Christmas night, were to write on all the doors
> in Yourma her father's famous saying: "I don't want to die this death."
> The handsome battalion of pistolwriters worked marvelously: they'd

managed to write the saying even on the third set of gates in the wall of the excellential palace. A few of them, the boldest undoubtedly, had succeeded in writing the sentence on the body of several military officers such as General Yang, Colonel Obaltana, Lieutenant-Colonel Fursia, and quite a few others. Amedandio said he'd written the saying on one thousand and ninety uniforms.

On Christmas, while the city drank and danced, the pistolwriters did their all to put Martial's saying everywhere. And Amedandio vaguely proclaimed "there'd be fire the next time," promising he'd write the saying on the Providential Guide's ass.]

Once again, we are in the realm of hyperbole, random elements and laughter: three million francs (CFA), three thousand boys, one thousand and ninety uniforms, all the doors, and quite a few military bodies. The novel adapts a familiar motif, the writing on doors on a special night. Martial's phrase thus will have still greater authority because, in the morning, it will appear to have been written supernaturally. It is significant that young boys, armed with spray guns, replace the heroine. The novel fuses writing and combat and portrays them as masculine activities. Chaïdana enters these two domains "in disguise," through her surrogates.

Her second offensive, however, exploits her femininity in a hilarious parody of the myth of irresistible female sexuality (and male weakness). The text is explicit regarding this dynamic, because Chaïdana exploits all her "feminine wiles" to lure the innumerable government ministers, one by one, time after time, into her hotel room. In a reworking of the myth in which the male prey dies after lovemaking, "Ils firent l'amour au champagne. Mais c'était du champagne Chaïdana car, quelques semaines plus tard, monsieur le ministre . . . était frappé de paralysie générale et devait mourir trois ans après" (49) ["They made champagne love. But it was Chaïdana champagne because, a few weeks later, the minister was struck with general paralysis and was to die three years later"]. So effective is her campaign against the government ministers—one-dimensional buffoons, like the Guide, whose absurdity implies the illegitimacy and excesses of authority—that "Il fut établi dans toutes les presses du monde et dans l'opinion que le Guide Providentiel avait une satanique façon de remanier ses gouvernements" (65) ["The consensus in the world press and in public opinion was that the Providential Guide had a devilish way of reshuffling his government"].

Chaïdana turns her sexuality, a tool by which she is abused, into the tool by which she avenges herself, and it leads her to discover the untenability of the very notion of power:

Chaïdana demanda au Guide Providentiel l'autorisation d'aller visiter ses parents en Katamalanasie maritime.

—Ton odeur! Je n'arrive plus à me passer de ton odeur amère. Mes narines y sont accoutumées.

—Rien que trois jours.

—Que veux-tu que je fasse? Tu es devenue l'autre moi-même.

Il enfonça la tête dans ses cuisses comme pour prendre une bonne dose de cette odeur vitale.

—C'est un miracle: moi qui n'ai jamais aimé une femme! Un vrai miracle.

Elle souriait aimablement au Guide Providentiel. "Un souverain nu, pensait Chaïdana, c'est le sommet de la laideur." Elle pensait aussi à ce qu'un homme peut devenir moche sous le poids, la secousse et l'odeur d'une femme. (57)

[Chaïdana requested permission from the Providential Guide to go visit her parents in maritime Katamalanasia.

—Your smell! I can't do without your bitter smell. My nostrils are used to it.

—Just for three days.

—What do you want me to do? You have become my other self.

He buried his head between her thighs as if to take in a good dose of this vital smell.

—It's a miracle: I who never loved a woman! A real miracle.

She smiled agreeably to the Providential Guide. "A naked ruler," thought Chaïdana, "is the height of ugliness." She was also thinking of how ugly a man could become under the weight, tremor, and odor of a woman.]

This is a critical moment in Chaïdana's consciousness. With the eyes of the child in "The Emperor's New Clothes," she comes to a liberating recognition. Power, stripped of its accoutrements, is not only unconvincing but pathetic. Conversely, mere flesh—with its physical needs, functions, and dependency—that nonetheless passes itself off as independent and omnipotent is revolting. Given his piteous corporeality, the Guide's power has no justification and is therefore counterfeit. It is only to the extent that power dazzles and blinds that it may go unchallenged.[9]

Bakhtin sums up the sense of Chaïdana's thought when he writes that

(in the plane of laughter) one can disrespectfully walk around whole objects; therefore, the back and rear portion of an object (and also its innards, not normally accessible for viewing) assume a special importance. The object is broken apart, laid bare (its hierarchical ornamentation is removed); the naked object is ridiculous; its "empty" clothing, stripped and separated from its person, is also ridiculous. What takes place is a comical operation of dismemberment. (23–24)

It is precisely during the physical act of sex that Chaïdana kills off the ministers and military men, for in that act they are "emptied" of their clothing and ornamentation and reduced to the frail human parts that they are. The vantage point of this marginalized and abused female allows a unique vision of the nakedness of power.

Chaïdana's acts, like those of Scheub's "culture hero," are bold and personally costly, but they suggest the daring and determination necessary in violent times. Chaïdana's vengeance, violent and "lacking in virtue" (Dabla 135) though it may be, also can be read in light of Bakhtin's analysis of the grotesque images of death and the body in popular culture and their regenerative nature. The text typically refers to Chaïdana or the female body in ambiguous terms, as in the following passage:

> Le docteur savait seulement qu'elle avait un corps farouche, avec des formes affolantes, un corps d'une envergure écrasante, électrique, et qui mettait tous les sens en branle, et il lui disait toujours, à ce corps plus qu'à celle à qui il appartenait: "Ecrasante beauté! . . . Impérative beauté!" (22)

> [The doctor knew only that she had an untamed body, a spellbinding shape, a body with crushing and electric dimensions, that made all one's senses swim, and he would always say to her, to this body more than to the one to whom it belonged: "Crushing beauty! . . . Imperative beauty!"]

The vocabulary of beauty and seduction (fierce, crushing, imperative) intersects with that of war and military might. The body is at once voluptuous and fierce. Doctor Tchi also expresses that equivalence between passion and violence when he says to Chaïdana: "Vous avez des dents à mordre aux endroits les mieux charnus de l'existence" (27) ["You have teeth to bite the most fleshy corners of existence"]. Chaïdana's body is thus destructive of the Katamalanasian hierarchy, and it is that destruction which makes way for a different future. Sony Labou Tansi situates her creativity both in her poetic impulses and, predictably, in the engendering of children (and future grandchildren) who will take up her struggle.

Chaïdana smiles at the Guide as she thinks her treasonous and liberating thought, "A naked ruler is the height of ugliness." In that ambiguous gesture we find a metaphor for *La Vie et demie* itself. Beneath the novel's playful exterior lies a subversive reflex, both in theme and form. Labou Tansi's fable is the anti-epic or anti-chronicle befitting the clown show of the powerful in Katamalanasia.

La Vie et demie's fabled construction allows us to see the "real" world from outside its parameters; it allows us thus to challenge that world in a way we cannot from within the perspective of realism which inscribes that world to begin with. It is thus the density of form, its atypicality, that, *because it alienates* the real world it evokes, makes that world all the more visible. Fable removes us from the space in which we are accustomed to exist and through whose atmosphere we are accustomed to look around ourselves. Placing us on a distant shore, it forces us to look at that world from afar. It makes us aware of that real world, not as the world within which we do and must operate, but as one that can be interrogated, held accountable, and ultimately one that can be changed.

Many African novels typically have one main resource: in order to erase the system they write, they are heavily ironic. They stay within the laws of the system and thus mock from within; there are thus always two levels of meaning, the stated and the unstated, which erodes the former. Irony remains in *La Vie et demie*, but it is "marvelously" buttressed by narrative form, which proclaims from the beginning the nonnecessity of the world it portrays, its man-made-ness and thus arbitrariness.

9

"The Mouth That Did Not Eat Itself": From Object of Representation to Medium in *Devil on the Cross*

Je serai la bouche des malheurs qui n'ont
point de bouche.
Aimé Césaire, *Cahier d'un retour au pays natal*

[I will be the mouth of misfortunes that have
no mouth.]

In *Decolonising the Mind* (1986), Ngũgĩ wa Thiong'o takes what I believe to be a useful and liberating view of the novel in Africa. He explains in the same vein as Paulin Hountondji, with whose position in other regards Ngũgĩ would seem to be at odds, that the "social or even national basis of origins of an important discovery or invention is not necessarily determinant of the use to which it can be put by its inheritors" (68). He gives technological examples, as does Hountondji, of Arab math, Chinese gunpowder, and inventions and sports originated among the peasantry. He concludes that the crucial question regarding the novel "is not that of the racial, national, and class origins of the novel but that of its development and the uses to which it is continually being put" (69).[1]

The argument that Ngũgĩ expounds in the series of essays in *Decolonising the Mind* reflects in part his experience of writing *Devil on the Cross*, published by Heinemann in Gĩkũyũ in 1980 and then in English in 1982. In *Decolonising*, Ngũgĩ describes his journey as an author from *Weep Not, Child* and *The River Between* to *Devil on the Cross*; he indicates different mentors and models at various stages of his novel writing, including Joseph Conrad and George Lamming. Having tired of the omniscient narrator and "linear" biographical or chronological progression in narrative, Ngũgĩ moved toward multiple perspectives, shifts in time and space in his later *A Grain of Wheat* and *Petals of Blood*. As he began *Devil* from his prison cell—he was detained without trial during 1978—he thought consciously about his audience and the possibilities of dissemination and reception of his work. With these issues in mind, he tells us, he decided to turn toward oral traditions, to use biblical elements, the parable, the familiar motif of the journey, and to choose a content related to people's everyday struggles. Structured by this combination of elements, his novel, he tells us, was read aloud in bars, shops, and homes; it was passed from hand to hand; episodes were retold and so reentered the oral tradition.

If we examine his novels to corroborate Ngũgĩ's account of his progression as a writer, it becomes clear that his first works are not derived instinctively from an oral tradition but that his reference to that tradition is more recent and quite conscious. Aspects of the oral tradition, as of the prose tradition, are not simply given, they are chosen. They are present in Ngũgĩ's work not because they are essentially African but because they offer possibilities to achieve specific ends—in this instance, to appeal to a specific audience.

Devil on the Cross is a novel, then, whose "development and uses"—to paraphrase Ngũgĩ—are consciously inscribed into the text. Such comments by authors on the nature of the creative process are sometimes taken lightly, since they may be a better guide to authors' intentions than to their effects, and since it is the public who ultimately judge the writer's success or failure. Yet Ngũgĩ's remarks, regardless of our judgment of *Devil*, remind us of the presence of certain factors, the context, in the text. For Ngũgĩ, texts bear signs—indeed they are signs—of the context that produces them. From his materialist perspective, the audience and conditions of publication and reception—or, as Ngũgĩ himself writes, the mode of consumption—are not external aspects of literary production.

Because such conditions make themselves felt in the text, they should not be relegated to postliterary discussions. They are responsible for the very fabric of texts which idealist criticism has heretofore considered to be "purely" literary and aesthetic (theme, genre, style, etc.). Accordingly, these conditions themselves should constitute the object of *literary* analysis. Ngũgĩ's description of the creation of *Devil* highlights this relationship between context and text.

Oral Genres and Language Revised

Together, *Decolonising the Mind* and *Devil on the Cross* propose different approaches to the novel. First of all, Ngũgĩ insists that a literary invention like "the novel" can be used, regardless of its origins, either to promote and reinforce repressive ideologies or to undo them. Second, he insists that novels can be produced and consumed in elitist or populist ways. Furthermore, Ngũgĩ's essay and narrative suggest that orality can be an idiom out of which writers write and through which they target a specific audience rather than a set of traits or an atmosphere represented by writers to suggest an African identity. These two texts thus challenge the notion of the novel and of orality as essences.

Let me elaborate on certain of these points. *Devil* highlights, first of all, the issue of class both in oral genres and in the uses of oral language.

Differential uses of forms and language are obscured both by universal models of "oral narrative structure" (as opposed to models of generic patterns) and by uniformly flattering generalizations on oral language and cultures. *Devil* thus helps us reread older texts, like Laye's *Le Regard du roi* and Achebe's *Things Fall Apart*, in a new light. Whereas Laye uses the structure of initiation narratives to assert a certain authority and status quo, and Bâ relies for that reason on epic structures in *Wangrin*, Ngũgĩ's parable and those parables situated in the oral stories of his characters parody, ridicule, and challenge authority. This multiplicity of voices and languages thus is illuminated by Bakhtin's discussions of both dialogism and low genres. Such different uses of narrative forms found in the oral tradition suggest that the lessons of narrative have less to do with the mode of language—oral or written—than with genre, than with who speaks and to whom a narrative is spoken. Thus, the griot serves the noble class by reasserting its authority (and, consequently, his own). Significantly, in both *Le Regard* and *Wangrin* there is a highly visible, external target, the colonial situation. Casting a white man in the role of initiate, Laye relocates authority from a colonial to an indigenous order and validates it. *Wangrin* makes a similar bid to steal back power.

In reading Achebe's *Things Fall Apart* and *Arrow of God* alongside *Devil on the Cross*, we become aware of the different ways in which oral language can be conceived and contrived in works of literature. Ngũgĩ surely subscribes to Achebe's well-known remark that the work of the writer in postcolonial or neo-colonial societies is to teach.[2] All three novels are mimetic, consciously documenting the life of Nigerian and Kenyan societies in their many facets, including language. Yet these narratives, as I read them, are profoundly different, although as English-language texts, they are superficially similar in their use of proverbs and their interweaving of the rhythms and turns of phrase of two languages (English and Igbo, English and Gĩkũyũ). Ngũgĩ gives a clue to the difference when he writes— his predatory metaphor notwithstanding—that African writers have concerned themselves until now with "how best to make the borrowed tongues carry the weight of our African experience by, for instance, making them 'prey' on African proverbs and other peculiarities of African speech and folklore . . . enriching foreign languages by injecting Senghorian 'black blood' into their rusty joints" (*Decolonising* 7).[3]

In his combat with colonialist stereotypes, Achebe eloquently represents the speech and oral arts of Umuofia. Given the context in which *Things Fall Apart* and *Arrow of God* appeared, their "oral" language tends to be identified as a fundamental, undifferentiated facet of Igbo culture, before colonialism. Thus readers may interpret orality as a quintessential sign, as does Aguessy, of authentic African cultures.

With *Devil on the Cross*, on the other hand, oral language is a quality of Kenyan culture *now*. The temporal and spatial setting of each story means that with regard to Achebe's first novels, orality becomes identified with what Achebe shows to be a complex time before colonialism (read often as the millennium "before the fall"), while Ngũgĩ's situation of orality in the present challenges such interpretations. The contemporaneity of *Devil* seems to me singularly important, for it demonstrates that orality is neither of the past nor the elementary stage of an evolutionary process.

In addition, Ngũgĩ depicts language, not surprisingly, as dynamic, differentiated, determined by one's class and one's gender; it is one of several registers of wealth and class. Levels of power in current society can be surmised by the foreign languages one knows and particularly by one's attitude toward them. Thus Wangarĩ, the least powerful of the travelers in *Devil*, speaks only Gĩkũyũ during the story—we guess that she does not speak English or speaks little of it. On the other hand, Mwĩreri wa Mũkiraaĩ knows English quite well; he has studied at foreign universities and is schooled in money-making schemes. Gatuĩria, the young composer and student intellectual, also mixes English and Gĩkũyũ but wishes, the narrator tells us, that his speech were rid of the foreign tongue: "Gatuĩria spoke Gĩkũyũ like many educated people in Kenya—people who stutter like babies when speaking their national languages but conduct fluent conversations in foreign languages. The only difference was that Gatuĩria was at least aware that the slavery of language is the slavery of the mind and nothing to be proud of" (56). The so-called modern thieves in the forum of the competition—attended by foreigners and for the benefit of these international visitors—speak English, of course. Language, like the number of women, cars, and guns a man owns, is a sign of status.[4] Thus while choice of language and mode of language do not necessarily measure honesty, they are predictors of the dimensions of crime (when crime exists), since they correlate to one's class and access to international institutions: the names of buildings, banks, money-making enterprises are all in English.

Differences between Ngũgĩ and Achebe with regard to the representation of orality may be due not only to the respective cultural and narrative codes within which they live and write but also to the writers' respective social and historical vantage points and the fact that each was dealt a particular "set of cards," certain elements dictated by the circumstances under which he was writing. Indeed the representation of oral arts, like the representation of women in any number of male writers, may assume a certain character determined by context—in the case of Achebe, by the colonialist views which he struggled to correct. Thus *Things Fall Apart*, for example, is riveted on the past, in which oral language becomes a sign. Later Achebe novels do, of course, portray language acts as determined in part by age, by class, by city or village life, by wealth or poverty.

Thus orality in *Things Fall Apart* is a cultural symbol, represented, encased within the novel, under glass as it were. Such framing, in fact, characterizes the culture as a whole, as it is represented in *Things Fall Apart*. In Ngũgĩ, where orality is similarly a manifestation of a particular cultural matrix, it cannot be read as a curio, prepared for the eye of the outside viewer, for it participates in determining the actual shape of the narrative. In the first instance Igbo culture is replicated by the narrative; in the second, the narrative is elaborated in the idiom of those who are meant to be its primary listeners, in their common codes. Achebe represents a tradition of speech, Ngũgĩ tries to conceive (write) within it.

Now, "oral" language in any written text is obviously neither oral nor—were such a thing possible—a transcript of standard speech, characterized by rhythms, pauses, tones, and unconventional sounds.[5] What is usually meant by the "orality" of Achebe or Ngũgĩ are the proverbs, analogies, and the cadences of phrasing, which literary convention holds to be oral.[6] In the case of *Devil on the Cross*, as Ngũgĩ describes it, the intended audience and the probable means of distribution and consumption of the novel in Kenya seemed to require "oral" language. Just as *Kaïdara*, according to Bâ, is written to be performed, so, too, *Devil* was written to be read aloud for people schooled in oral stories. Here, orality is not "preyed upon," a resource *for* the narrative, inside its frame, "possessed" by it. Oral language is thus not the object of representation that can be read as quaint and *passéiste* [of the past]. Orality here means the language and tradition in which this narrative is articulated, the medium in which Ngũgĩ's audience will hear this story. Intended for telling or reading aloud, *Devil* does not showcase a neat orality. Proverbs, repetitions, riddles, "songs," and so on reveal the addressee and are not uniquely referential.

It is also the very act of telling and listening that Ngũgĩ evokes— the exchange of voices, stories, the interaction of many personalities, the dynamic of presence and voice. The story intimates a *telling* between the speaker-writer and the listener-reader, and inside that telling-listening there are, as Bakhtin would have it, other tellers and listeners.[7] Oral language and African languages are obviously the media of those classes of people disenfranchised by the African bourgeoisie and elites. Gatuĩria, the student composer in the novel, seems to speak for Ngũgĩ when he says,

> "I myself ask a question that I have posed many times: what can I do to compose truly national music for our Kenya, music played by an orchestra made up of the instruments of all the nationalities that make up the Kenyan nation, music that we, the children of Kenya, can sing in one voice rooted in many voices—*harmony in polyphony*?" (60, emphasis added)

Ngũgĩ's preceding two novels, *A Grain of Wheat* and *Petals of Blood*, have been exactly this effort toward harmony in polyphony: the chorus of voices during a collective—if not always unifying—enterprise, the different roles, personalities that come together to create change and independence, to shape history. *Devil* extends an idea that has been present for a long time in Ngũgĩ's work.

As we have seen, then, Ngũgĩ's novel for oral consumption aspires not to incorporate speech so much as to belong to a tradition of speech, the tradition of people who have had no pen, Césaire's *mouth of misfortunes that have no mouth*. For this reason also, Ngũgĩ writes, the novel's first language was Gĩkũyũ. Through its allegiance to a tradition of speech, *Devil* identifies itself with a class of people who, heretofore, have been literarily disenfranchised (in written literature, that is). The use of Gĩkũyũ would make it available to those people, first and foremost. Finally, *Devil* adapts and redirects a narrative form that has its material origins in the rise of the European bourgeoisie and that has been until now the preserve of Western-educated classes in Africa. It exploits this literary technology, the novel, regardless of its origins and standard usage, as Ngũgĩ says, to new ends. In short, it seeks to extend voice to those who, in this forum, have had little.

Decolonising the Mind and *Devil on the Cross* suggest, then, that "oral tradition" is not the sign of a coveted set of values; it is rather a set of aesthetic conventions with which Ngũgĩ's audience is conversant and from which he chooses several elements. Just as he chose multivoiced narration in preceding novels, here he chooses proverbs, parables, and the motif of the journey. *Devil* thus gains a particular currency and comprehensibility by associating itself with traditional storytelling, but it does not muster authority from traditional high genres. It cannot in any case rely on the epic and the initiation story, which posit an immutable hierarchy and unquestionable authority outside the protagonist (and, we infer, outside the narratives themselves), for Ngũgĩ's novel proposes a caricature of power. As I read it, *Devil* does not conceive of orality as a source either of authority or of precious authenticity to be held and treasured.[8] It does not use the "oral tradition" as a bulwark to inspire confidence or action by association with a people's past grandeur or wisdom and virtue. It is neither the "source of truth" nor an exemplary quality of African culture to be retreated into or represented textually; rather, it offers verbal means and procedures for constructing and analyzing an issue. *Devil* treats the same issues that are at the heart of other Ngũgĩ texts, but it does so in parables. In so doing, it demonstrates that oral traditions are not synonymous with static codes and principles.

Devil is deconstructive and reconstructive in other ways as well. Not only does it take orality out of the past, but, like Sembène's *Les Bouts de bois*, it focuses on the constructedness of the order of things, their inner workings and tensions. Ngũgĩ's exposition of the relationship between the Kenyan thieves and international capital is masterful, as is the revelation of their vulnerability in the jealous dispute about belly size and in the thieves' anger at being duped by one of their own who has stolen their unsatisfied wives and offered them counterfeit English schooling for their children. These cleavages in their ranks are analogous to the "appeals to tribe and religion," which the thieves themselves use to divide peasants and workers.

The Uses of Fable, the Fantastic, and Suspense

Ngũgĩ, it will be recalled, finds that the outrageousness of neo-colonialist repression may "beat all fictional exaggerations" (*Decolonising* 80) and that it therefore sorely tests the writer's imagination. Not surprisingly, *Devil* draws on a number of narrative traditions. Ngũgĩ refers to his novel as a parable because he intends it as a simple story to illustrate a lesson. More precisely, *Devil* is a fable of economic and political greed. Its thieves are not the animal characters that readers usually associate with the tradition of fable but are one-dimensional beings, like the dictators of *La Vie et demie*. In addition, *Devil* is a fantastic narrative that continually blurs the line between real and surreal. Finally, like *A Grain of Wheat* and *Petals of Blood*, *Devil* is a teleogenic mystery story, that is, its biggest riddle is solved at the end and forces a rereading of certain events. These elements— suspense and the fantastic—contribute to the novel's effectiveness as fable. We shall consider them more closely.

As the narrative begins, the Gĩcaandĩ Player—Ngũgĩ chooses a "people's" musician-singer for this crucial role—has been reluctant to accede to the request of Warĩĩnga's mother to narrate this story. Like biblical and mythical heroes, he then is visited by visions and voices:

> for seven days I fasted, neither eating nor drinking, for my heart was sorely troubled by those pleading voices. Still I asked myself this: Could it be that I am seeing phantoms without substance, or that I am hearing the echoes of silence? Who am I—the mouth that ate itself? Is it not said that the antelope conceives more hatred for him who betrays its presence with a shout?
>
> And after seven days had passed, the Earth trembled, and lightning scored the sky with its brightness, and I was lifted up, and I was borne up to the rooftop of the house, and I was shown many things, and I heard a voice, like a great clap of thunder, admonishing me: Who has told you that prophecy is yours alone, to keep to yourself? (8)

The Gĩcaandĩ Player is then cast down into the ashes of the fireplace and agrees to tell his community what he has been shown. In this extraordinary portrait of the birth of the narrative to follow, the narrator's voice is mobilized both in response to the call of other human voices and in response to a deeper spiritual impulse, suggested in the fasting and purification, the communion with nature and with the admonishing voice, in the visionary character of the narrative act. This scene of revelation signals both the symbolic nature of the ensuing story, its kinship to allegory and fable, and its moral authority.

Devil is strewn with such dreams and visions. Warĩĩnga, for example, is forewarned of Kĩmeendeeri wa Kanyuanjii's speech in the cave. She foresees Mwĩreri wa Mũkiraaĩ's murder. She sees the devil's death and resurrection. These visions are, of course, confusing and troubling to the characters, but the fulfillment of such prophecy is at once amazing and satisfying to the listener and reader of Ngũgĩ's story.[9] Its presence here seems to have a dual function. Once again, such visions may be elements of the tradition in which Ngũgĩ targets a specific audience. Second, they serve to reinforce the special significance of the Gĩcaandĩ Player's tale.

The preponderance of visions and dreams contributes likewise to the continual, sustained confusion about the frontiers of the real and the imagined.[10] In the following passage we read of Gatuĩria's reactions inside the cave:

> Gatuĩria thought he saw Mwaũra look at him with eyes full of ravenous greed. Then he saw that it was not Mwaũra alone who looked at him in that manner. All the people around him wore the same expression. Whenever one of the thieves yawned, Gatuĩria thought he saw his teeth transformed into blood-soaked fangs that were turned toward where he and Warĩĩnga sat. He heard a voice whisper to him: These are the eaters of human flesh; these are the drinkers of human blood; these are the modern Nding'ũri's; take this girl and flee this place. (175)

In the foregoing passage, the narrator does not, of course, declare what is true; on the contrary, he promotes the uncertainty through indirect discourse. First, he plainly situates the origin of an idea in a specific character (who well may be imagining things): "Gatuĩria thought he saw. . . ." Then he allows for the possibility that those things might be true by abandoning the filter ("Gatuĩria thought") and describing them firsthand in his own voice: "Then he saw. . . . All the people . . . wore. . . ." Uncertainty looms everywhere for the characters and for listener and reader: how did Mũturi come to save Warĩĩnga, and how does he now find himself in the same *matatũ* with her and all these other unrelated and yet related people? Why are they all heading for the same destination? Were the creatures of the old man's stories men or beasts? This final instance of fusion between real and surreal is especially significant.

The characters of the stories that Gatuĩria has heard and retells in the *matatũ* are, for the most part, devils and ogres, who represent—metaphorically it would seem—human beings deformed by monstrous greed, wealth, and power. The point is made explicitly, however, through synecdoche, a more compelling figure, for the "human" competitors in the cave are, above all, corporeal protuberances symbolizing appetite, desire, and thievery:

> The following are things that were revealed by Gĩtutu wa Gataangũrũ concerning modern theft and robbery. Gĩtutu had a belly that protruded so far that it would have touched the ground had it not been supported by the braces that held up his trousers. It seemed as if his belly had absorbed all his limbs and all the other organs of his body. Gĩtutu had no neck—at least, his neck was not visible. His arms and legs were short stumps. His head had shrunk to the size of a fist.
>
> That day Gĩtutu wa Gataangũrũ was sporting a dark suit and a white shirt with frills. A black bow tie, which looked as if it had been stuck

to his chin, stood where his neck should have been. His walking stick was decorated with pure gold. While he talked, Gĩtutu stroked the side of his belly with his left hand and swung his walking stick with his right hand. He panted as he talked, like a person carrying a heavy load. (99)

Gĩtutu wa Gataangũrũ may have a familiar air to those acquainted with oral stories, but such characterization here is not simply a necessary vestige of an imposing oral tradition. Here in *Devil on the Cross*, as in *The Beautyful Ones Are Not Yet Born* and in *La Vie et demie*, humans who prey on their less fortunate fellow citizens are dehumanized by their immoral activities. Relatives, both in nature and in fictional treatment, of the teeth that confront Armah's man and the bruised "queue" of the Providential Guide, Ngũgĩ's thieves are, for the most part, all belly. This deformation is still a meager and inadequate sign of their greed, however, for the thieves seek true monstrosity, as is obvious when Nditika wa Ngũũnji argues for additional human parts:

I have enough money and property to supply food for a thousand people, but I am satisfied with one plateful, just like other people. I have enough money to wear a hundred suits at a time, but I can only put on one pair of trousers, one shirt, one jacket, just like other people. I have enough money to buy fifty lives if lives were sold in the market, but I have only one heart and one life, just like other people. I have enough property and money to enable me to make love to ten girls every night, but one girl exhausts me after only one go, and I end up falling asleep without being completely satisfied.

So, seeing that I have only one mouth, one belly, one heart, one life and one cock, what's the difference between the rich and the poor? What's the point of robbing others?

It was revealed to me that . . . we should have a factory for manufacturing human parts. . . . This would mean that a rich man who could afford them could have two or three mouths, two bellies, two cocks and two hearts. If the first mouth became tired of chewing, and his belly could hold no more, then the spare mouth and belly could take over. . . . We could coin some new sayings: a rich man's youth never ends. (180)

It is once again through the grotesqueness of the body that authority—in this instance, the authority bought by wealth—is undermined. Nditika's spare parts proposition also exposes the fears and strategies of masculine authority, for Nditika's wife becomes enthusiastic about the prospect of having two "female organs." Nditika expresses horror at the idea of such equality between the sexes—it is never clear, of course, that *any* equalities are acceptable to him—and he urges his wife to espouse instead "true" African culture, to heed tradition, which Nditika would like to interpret as meaning an inferior status for women. Nditika would seem to need women as witnesses of his masculine prowess, yet he fears them and their sexual demands. It is to serve his own masculine quest for privilege and power that he—like Mabigué in his exchange with Ramatoulaye—invokes the authority of "tradition."

I have said that the grotesqueness of the body serves here, as it does in *La Vie et demie*, to challenge the authority of privilege. The thieves are pathetic and despicable in both appearance and speech. We should note, however, a distinction with regard to the strategies of these two narratives. In *La Vie et demie*, fancifulness, playfulness, and laughter force us to step outside the sphere of authority and enable us to see its vacuity. *Devil on the Cross*, on the other hand, is hyperrealistic: especially inside the cave, we see in microscopic, unmitigated detail the most profound and ferocious yearnings of the authority of wealth. Ngũgĩ's narrative does not defuse authority (for the reader) but rather displays a certain authority in its full-ness. Greed and power are magnified, taken to their full and logical ex-tremes or, it might also be said, reduced to their essences. There is comedy in Ngũgĩ's portrayal, to be sure, but it is hideous and hallucinatory, akin to madness.[11] The thieves in their greed are therefore more frightening than the tyrants of *La Vie et demie*. *Devil* is a scandalous distillation of a certain reality. This difference in approach to what is fundamentally a similar problem is expressed, of course, in the titles of the novels. *La Vie et demie* announces in its third and fourth words its intention "to play" with what is given. *Devil*, on the other hand, immediately signals its moral impera-tive, and it is emphatically didactic. I see in those two impulses—the first carnivalistic in its treatment, the other reminiscent of fire and brimstone—Catholic and Protestant paradigms.

Let us turn now to the matter of suspense in *Devil on the Cross*, which begins at the moment Warĩĩnga's mother pleads with the Gĩcaandĩ Player to tell the story of her daughter so that people will understand and judge her for themselves. Suspense is heightened when the Gĩcaandĩ Player is told in his vision to reveal what he has seen and then when he begins his tale at its end, the fatal Sunday on which Warĩĩnga . . . (Of course, realizing he has begun at the end, he thinks better of it and starts again with the chronological sequence of events.) The Gĩcaandĩ Player's tale itself contains its share of suspense, as we have begun to see—the mystery of fate and of identity. Six Kenyans find themselves traveling together by *matatũ* from Nairobi to Ilmorog. The circumstances that throw them to-gether are ostensibly random, but the collective journey becomes the occa-sion for conversation and storytelling, and little by little, relationships are hinted at, identities are discovered. There are a great many (too many) coincidences—the common destination of the travelers as well as their ex-periences of the past which intersect in unsuspected ways. The mystery of identity is important in Ngũgĩ's preceding novels as well. Individuals are thrown together at decisive moments, and they bring with them the baggage and burden of their past lives. That history affects their choices and ultimately affects the new history being forged in that moment.

After the lessons of the collective journey and of the cave, then, both

Gatuĩria and Warĩĩnga find a sense of purpose and direction. Yet one bit of information has never been disclosed—the identity of the Rich Old Man who abused and betrayed Warĩĩnga. It is clear that a second set of events will take place, that they will bring about the audacious act which Warĩĩnga's mother wanted the community to understand. Thus in the final moments of the story as Warĩĩnga—Mũturi's gun in hand—goes to meet her fiancé Gatuĩria's father, the identity of the Rich Old Man, hinted at all along, is made known. Bits and pieces of the story then fall into place: this is surely why Gatuĩria's voice sounds familiar to Warĩĩnga (58, 60), why her child resembles him, and so on.

Ngũgĩ has a predilection for the teleogenic ending, as is evident in both *A Grain of Wheat* and *Petals of Blood*. It will be recalled that this type of structure in the context of the early modern European novel is read by many as the sign of the ability to rewrite history, to change the course of events. It has precisely that effect here. The revelation of the Rich Old Man's identity radically reorganizes relationships and power because in this least fantastic sequence of the novel Warĩĩnga assassinates the man who previously had poisoned her life. Indeed the Gĩcaandĩ Player narrator of *Devil* is moved to tell this story precisely in order to reveal the facts, encourage judgment, and enlarge the possibilities for agency and change. The emphasis is thus on the ability to weigh, reconsider, avoid past errors, decide on future direction. If for some, such endings hold out a dubious promise that we may rewrite history, for Ngũgĩ, undoubtedly, to label this promise a false hope is to give up writing, communicating, urging.

The journey to Ilmorog and the experiences of the cave are an initiation of sorts for Warĩĩnga: she grows at last into a lucid, decisive woman. Warĩĩnga's initiation is not, of course, the traditional initiation to which we have referred in preceding chapters. Warĩĩnga does not learn *thanks to a higher authority*, in place all along, though she could not see it. She is not stripped of her propensity to reason and decide, as is Clarence. In fact, quite the opposite is true. Ngũgĩ is above all a partisan of weighing and thinking, of democratic, individual, and collective decision making. This is the thrust of the book as a whole. Thus the initiation that Warĩĩnga undergoes is not the apprenticeship of a Clarence, an entry into a secret but pervasive order. It is, on the contrary, the growth of the heroine, who learns to act on her own.

It is perhaps no coincidence that Ngũgĩ, Labou Tansi, and even Sembène to a certain extent revise narrative structures and that their heroes are heroines. Both Warĩĩnga and Chaïdana have been abused by masculine power, directly and indirectly through the actions and, indeed, the very existence of repressive authority. For both Labou Tansi and Ngũgĩ, these female figures suffer more and, as a result, are more lucid and visionary human beings.[12] Both heroines strike back in similar ways. Yet this act of revolt at the end of a novel such as *Devil*, which—though not strictly realist—seems overall to present itself as such, is ineffective because it seems contrived. In the fantasy of *La Vie et demie*, on the other hand, all subversions of government are credible and admissible. Moreover, such subversion is more empowering because it is abetted by the corrosive effects of laughter.

Whose Authority?

Thus the first passages of the novel raise fundamental questions about language and literature: to whom and why does one narrate? What are the costs of narration? The Gīcaandī Player begins the story by repeating this proverb: "Who am I—the mouth that ate itself?" (8). This is the narrator's and, we presume, Ngũgĩ's reference to himself. Silence is betrayal. As the voice of his community, the narrator can be silent only by denying the function for which he exists. Even though some listeners may prefer silence because his story will be a source of shame or pain, he is duty-bound. The narrator of *Devil on the Cross* shares the view set forth by Sony Labou Tansi in his *avertissement*; even if the portrait is unflattering, it must be shown:

> How can we cover up pits in our courtyard with leaves or grass, saying to ourselves that because our eyes cannot now see the holes, our children can prance about the yard as they like?
>
> Happy is the man who is able to discern the pitfalls in his path, for he can avoid them.
>
> Happy is the traveller who is able to see the tree stumps in his way, for he can pull them up or walk around them so that they do not make him stumble. (7)

It is a bard who speaks, but it is not the voice of the griot who serves noble patrons, who affirms authority based on origins. There is a profound mistrust of authority outside oneself and apart from one's own instincts, as revealed in the narrator's comment: "The Devil, who would *lead us into the blindness of the heart* and into the *deafness of the mind,* should be crucified" (7, emphasis added). The allegiance here is to people, to individual intelligence, to knowledge that can be acquired, to self-reliance.

The remarks of Warīīnga's mother, to which we have referred, go even further in articulating this point of view. She beseeches the Gīcaandī Player to "tell the story of the child I loved so dearly. Cast light upon all that happened, so that *each may pass judgment* only when he knows the whole truth. Gīcaandī Player, reveal all that is hidden" (7, emphasis added). It is a democratic vision which complements Ngũgĩ's sense of agency and the possibilities for historical choice and decision making.

The authority of tradition is invoked, however, by individuals in the story—Nditika's discussion with his wife is one such example. Also, the speech of bandits and heroes alike—and this is once again the fictional equivalent of Ngũgĩ's argument that any technology can be used to progressive or regressive ends—is studded with references to Gīkũyũ: "Gīkũyũ once said: 'The leopard did not know how to scratch; it was taught'" (54), "Gĩkũyũ said that he who has put something aside never goes hungry" (62), and so on. "Nothing good is ever born of perfect conditions" (64) is the motto of both sides. As with all allusions to proverbs and ancestral wisdom, one's speech becomes more persuasive and powerful when it draws on the collective treasury of incontrovertible truths. *Devil on the Cross* recognizes that oral speech, stories, and lore contain the wealth of acquired, collective wisdom, but it also shows that words and narrative are not innocent. They cannot be trusted, regardless of their "origins in ancestral wisdom," unless the vantage point from which they are spoken is taken into account. The merits of speech and the speaker depend on the interests they represent.

Just as proverbs are appropriated by repressive segments of society, so, too, are social institutions. Mũturi, unlike Wangarĩ, turns to peasants and workers to challenge the thieves, for the police, the people's official "delegates," serve moneyed interests and cannot bite the hands that feed them. The text is suspicious of "representatives," even when they are not bought by the other side, and argues that people themselves must act to change conditions.

Devil, unlike *Wangrin* or *Regard*, is thus a highly "democratic" narrative that focuses on individual and collective processes of weighing, sifting, and deciding. Characters arrive at knowledge through oral language and stories that articulate debatable points of view. Ngũgĩ does not evoke oral language as object, but makes a radical reassessment of history and social relations through the telling of stories.

The centrality of "orality" in *Devil on the Cross* does not signal a retreat into a lost, precious past. The novel is well anchored in the present and represents the dynamic of life *lived now*. It is a fable that looks, with faith in process and in people, toward the future.

10

Toward New Readings of the Novel

We need only turn our eyes, and familiar paradigms, taboos, and conventions come rushing in like the tide to reimpose themselves. I have written this book against one such liberal paradigm or critical category which superficially allowed for "difference" but seemed to me to deny a good deal of freedom. Against the familiarity and appeal of the traditional reading of "orality in the novel," then, I have argued that it is no longer viable and certainly not instructive to read "traces" (the forms) of oral traditions in the novel as the sign of African authenticity. What is problematic in that equation is both the reading of *form* as authenticity and the very practice (exclusionary and impossible) of defining the criteria for "authenticity."

Let me elaborate briefly. With regard to the latter—regardless of the criterion established, be it orality or writing in an African language, for example—the uses of a concept such as "authenticity" seem to me far too dangerous, for it divides the world into self and other, good and bad, on the basis of an arbitrary value, practice, or heritage deemed essential by some institution or person who claims authority. Demands for authenticity are a prescription for mystification. I think that if we are attentive to the operations of narrative, its clarity and contradictions, and its resonance with social reality, authenticity will take care of itself. This is as true of Naipaul as it is of Bâ or Ngũgĩ. Clearly, books written in Yoruba or Gĩkũyũ for a Nigerian or Kenyan readership are more likely to be accountable to a specific audience, and that accountability will make itself felt. I would argue, moreover, that authenticity—even racists can be authentic—is less important than accountability.

What distinction can we draw, then, between these two terms? Both, it seems to me, are related to the concept of truth, but with some important differences. Authenticity suggests some quality from the world outside the text, incorporable and incorporated into the text and conferring upon it Truth and Validity. Accountability, on the other hand, stresses dynamic exchange between artist and audience: literary works are viewed more properly as statements to which we may and must reply. If we are guided in our readings by the principle of accountability, misrepresentations or poor representations—which have something to teach us, in fact—are more likely to be explored than simply to be labeled "inauthentic" and dismissed. The preoccupation with authenticity has moral overtones and tends to elevate attributes and writers to the status of fetish and idol, respectively, whereas the less divisive principle of accountability seems to me to encourage our focusing not only on the writer's honesty but also on the spirit of dialogue and open-mindedness, on the necessity of readers' probing their own experience and raising their own voices. We move toward a healthier textual practice, in which we cease to privilege Literature, in which the act of reading is primary, as is the act of writing.

As for the other problem to which I refer above, to read form as authenticity is to misread form, for epic, initiation story, and fable are not narrative equivalents of ethnicity but are more nearly representations of social vision. We likewise must refuse the simple reflex that consists of seeing oral traditions as necessary and sufficient explanations—good or bad—of novels. I would be most pleased if those who read this book should never again say casually of an African novel, "Well, of course it's like that. That's the oral tradition for you."

To argue as I have that "form as authenticity" is a false reading is not, however, to deny the prominence of oral traditions in Africa, their relationship to written verbal arts, or the usefulness of comparing the two. On the contrary, my argument requires that we read the presence or modification of an element or form not as a reassuring proof of enduring and untransformed essence but as cause for *questioning*. It is imperative to study oral texts and written texts side by side to discern how their use of elements is similar and dissimilar, how those elements take on different shapes in different social contexts (small agrarian communities and larger, more heterogeneous and urban ones, for example). And we must do this without yielding to the temptation of seeing one term of the comparison as the positive norm, implicit or explicit, against which the other is read.

Thus my objective with regard to generic tendencies in the novel has been to read them anew, regardless of mode of language and yet sensitive to the social ecology of which it is a part. It becomes clear, then, that form is not the concrete literary simulacrum of African essence but is, rather, a manifestation of social consciousness, vision, and possibility allowed by particular moments and niches in African sociocultural life. The variety of ostensibly similar forms demonstrates particularity rather than a deterministic heritage.

The analysis of these novels has proved instructive in several ways and leads me to concur with Jameson's view of the "reappropriation of [form] in discontinuous historical situations":

genre is essentially a socio-symbolic message, . . . immanently and in-
trinsically an ideology in its own right. When such forms are reappropriated and refashioned in quite different social and cultural contexts, this message persists and must be functionally reckoned into the
new form. . . . The ideology of the form itself, thus sedimented, persists
into the later, more complex structure as a generic message which coex-
ists—either as a contradiction or, on the other hand, as a mediatory or
harmonizing mechanism—with elements from later stages. (141)

Thus we may ask, What is the relationship of sociocultural reality
to literature as we have seen it in this study through the reappropriation
of three genres? With regard to the novels of epic tendency, *L'Etrange Destin
de Wangrin* (1974) and *Les Bouts de bois de Dieu* (1960), both set in the colonial
period, the categories of hero and object of the quest show, in the first
instance, degradation and, in the second, revision. Bâ, in a nostalgic gesture, dresses a contemporary, of dubious repute by some measures, in
the vestments of an emperor. Or, more precisely, he mythifies him in an
emperor's tale. The narrative thereby reveals a decline in possibilities for
heroism under colonialism.

Sembène, on the other hand, does not align himself with—and does
not regret in the least—an old order that also could be charged with abuses
of power. Technology, which colonialism in its quest for profit has put
at the workers' disposal, is neutral in this view and can therefore create
the possibility of greater freedom, the opportunity to reinvent an order.
Thus Sembène reworks categories of hero and heroic action, thereby challenging the hierarchical norms implicit in the epic.

As with the foregoing novels, *Le Regard du roi* (1954) and *La Carte
d'identité* (1980) are revealing in their reuse of and deviation from the traditional form. The initiation story is reappropriated whole in *Le Regard*—
we sense its presence and force in the metamorphoses, both verbal and
physical, in the allegory itself. A significant element, then, is that the subject
of initiation is a wayward outsider. The traditional ideology works thus
in inexorable counterpoint to the "novelistic" ideology (cultural baggage)
that is Clarence's inheritance. Despite—or, perhaps, *because of*—new and
profoundly different historical circumstances, the narrative seeks to recon-
struct the old order, in which it would seem community and nature are
one and supreme and in which Africa may yet redeem Europe.

Marked by atemporality and stasis and projecting social consensus,
the initiation story works for Laye precisely because the initiate is a white
man, that is to say, Europe. Adiaffi, on the other hand, modifies the form,
and his variations on the initiation story model signal important changes
in contemporary society: its heterogeneity and new forces and issues for
which this metaphysical form seems inappropriate. The narrative's inclusion of comic scenes of popular life and "lower-class" violence would
contextualize the initiate's quest, but these modifications serve, in fact,
to challenge the relevance of the object of the quest: African *identity*. Thus

the initiation story, in its pure form, seems obsolete, and in its modified form, expanded by the "popular" dimension, there are contradictions and incongruencies that strain the fiction.

Both *La Vie et demie* (1979) and *Devil on the Cross* (1980) represent a trend in contemporary fiction toward "magical realism" as a response to contemporary political and economic realities. These novels participate in a tradition of fable that in this instance is characterized by both metaphor and metamorphosis. In each novel, the representatives of power are portrayed through a deprecating, minimalizing caricature, through grotesque physical appetites and bodily deformations that serve to expose their puniness and puerility, to mock the authority, political or economic, that they represent. In addition, the principled, knowable worlds that characterize fable and other forms of romance have become in these novels worlds of discontinuity, arbitrariness and excess. Authority is subverted, then, through laughter and references to "lower bodily strata." The impulse to fable in these novels works thus, as Bakhtin has argued with regard to popular forms in early modern European culture, to parody official order. The antagonism between popular views and official doctrine is reinforced in *La Vie et demie* by the text's representation of official and popular practices of language.

To read each of these novels, not as a natural derivation of an oral tradition but as a meaningful reappropriation of an oral narrative genre, is to grapple with one of the most haunting and important issues that continually begs for an answer in African literary criticism, the parameters and values of the novel. It is clear, first of all, that there is not *one* novel of fixed form and values. Ngũgĩ's view of the novel as an "invention" that can be used in various places and times to various ends is valid, in my view. Writers are prisoners neither of oral traditions nor of the so-called European novel. To write a novel is not necessarily to imitate Europe, to foist corrupt values on an ill-prepared audience, to stimulate inappropriate desire. Nor can the rejection of the individual-centered novel and a nostalgic retreat to "pure" traditional forms ensure the transformation of contemporary sociopolitical realities.

But there is unquestionably a web of factors affecting the production and reception of novels—language choice and literacy, education and wealth—which make the novel the most problematic literary form on the continent today, the one in whose very fabric the formidable problems and social inequities that Africa now faces become quite visible. As we know, the novel cannot in its typical practice escape a certain elitism to which poetry and tales, theatrical representations, and cinema are less likely to be heir, since these acts generally come to fulfillment in local performance of one sort or another. Sembène's and Ngũgĩ's turning toward cinema and drama, respectively, remind us of this. To the extent that the novel more easily resists (through European languages, foreign publication, and a hegemonic readership) those "forces of gravity" that are operative on other genres and that would bind it to its place of origin, it will remain a controversial and contested art. For this reason, the interest in "orality in the novel" may be symptomatic not only of the search for authenticity but also of a desire to bridge a gap in society. Perhaps we interpret a fictive orality as whisking away (in literature) the distance in reality between two populaces, one rich, the other poor, one literate, the other oral.

Whatever our final judgment regarding novels, their context and values, this particular intellectual effort to devise more liberating ways of reading and thinking about the interplay of oral and written forms will have been successful if it serves to remind us that form is complex, supple, and meaningful and that literature is a dynamic and always unfinished process that comes to fruition, not in mystification, but in interrogation.

Notes

1. The Search for Continuity and Authenticity

1. Except where indicated by an English language title, all English translations of French text are mine.

2. Cheikh Anta Diop's *Nations nègres et culture* is a major document in the current reassessment of Africa's intellectual and aesthetic life prior to colonization. One of the most important and ancient scripts is, of course, Egyptian hieroglyphics, and Diop demonstrates that Egyptian civilization was both product of and contributor to African culture.

Albert Gérard's *African Language Literatures* popularizes the little-known history of writing in Africa. He describes, for example, the fourth-century development of Sabean script in the region that corresponds to present-day Ethiopia and the later flowering of Ge'ez literature in the thirteenth and fourteenth centuries (7–12). He also cites the fact that after the European contact Fulani, Hausa, and Wolof continued to be written with the use of Arabic script. Similarly, David Dalby documents the development of scripts for "restricted" use in nineteenth- and twentieth-century West Africa. As Harold Scheub indicates, oral and written forms have coexisted and enriched each other.

There is, of course, a more general philosophical debate concerning the role or consequences of orality, writing, and literacy with regard to intellectual traditions. Walter Ong argues, for example, that "writing has to be personally interiorized to affect thinking processes. Persons who have interiorized writing not only write but also speak literately" (56; see also 172). For Paulin Hountondji, writing and literacy are crucial to philosophy and science—not, as Ong claims, because they change thought processes, but because they allow for the development of a tradition of textual commentary and criticism (128–32).

3. There are, however, valid questions which may be asked with regard to the reciprocity between social context and literary forms and the relationship of language choice and literacy to the creation and reception of novels. Mudimbe states, for example, with regard to the epistemological categories that African children encounter in schools:

> L'école . . . introduit graduellement le jeune enfant à des catégories, à des concepts, à des schèmes de pensée, à une manière de vivre et de comprendre le monde et l'univers, qui proviennent en droite ligne d'un champ et d'un ordre épistémologique qui sont, au moins, géographiquement, étrangers à l'Afrique. Le jeune Africain va apprendre une langue étrangère qui lui permettra, selon les normes intellectuelles consacrées, de communier aux valeurs d'une tradition et d'une culture insignes, certes, mais étrangères. Et lorsqu'un jour, au sortir du lycée,

il s'interroge sur sa propre histoire et le passé de son milieu, c'est avec un regard fortement marqué qu'il lira, le plus souvent en langue étrangère, le destin passé des siens, sa propre condition dans le présent et les perspectives futures de sa terre et de sa culture (110–11).

[School . . . gradually introduces the young child to categories, to concepts, to ways of thinking, to a way of living and understanding the world and the universe, that proceed directly from an epistemological field and order that are, geographically at least, foreign to Africa. The young African learns a foreign language that will permit him, according to hallowed intellectual norms, to share in the values of a tradition and culture that are certainly eminent but nonetheless foreign. And when one day, after leaving high school, he asks himself about his own past and the history of his surroundings, it is with a deeply biased gaze that he will read, more often than not in a foreign language, the past lives of his own people, his own condition in the present, and the future prospects of his country and his culture].

Mudimbe's and Roscoe's statements, despite superficial similarity, reveal different concerns. Roscoe's argument is, in the final analysis, patronizing, for he argues that the child's origins, his past, have not prepared him to feel at ease with new forms and information. Basing his argument on history and ontology, Roscoe "sympathetically" wants to spare the child a confrontation with ideas and situations "beyond" his grasp or of dubious value for the presumably more innocent lifestyle of his society.

Mudimbe warns, to be sure, of the dangers in Eurocentric epistemological categories—presumably literary, philosophical, and so on—through which African children come to regard themselves as objects rather than apprehending subjects of history in Eurocentric schools in Africa and abroad. But this is not to say that there are dangerous disciplines from which the young must be sheltered. Nor is it a justification for the *exclusion* of certain data, experiences, epistemological forms (or European novels). It is rather a compelling argument for contextualization and historicizing, because most canonical works, if we take the case of literature, do not come to honor the culture that has produced them; rather, they are canonized *because* they honor that culture. Thus the child who reads Tolstoy, Toni Morrison, or V. S. Naipaul must learn to see their novels as well as the literary categories by which they are judged in their cultural and historical contexts, in their relationships to social practices, inclusion and exclusion, definitions of good and bad. If, as some have argued, nineteenth-century and twentieth-century European novels correspond to and justify certain social and political practices, there is no reason why every novel must do so, as we shall see in the chapter on Ngũgĩ.

4. For a detailed account of anthropological theories as they related to African oral literature, see Finnegan, 35–47.

5. Note, for example, this definition of folklore provided by the London *Daily News* on September 29, 1891: "The peculiarity of Folk Lore is to approach the whole subject from the side of ancient practices, beliefs, and rites, surviving either among the least educated and most stationary classes; or among the educated who retain or have borrowed their superstitions" (cited in Dorson 299).

6. For a discussion of two anthropologists, Paul Radin and Marcel Griaule, whose works were at odds with these prevailing views, see Paulin J. Hountondji, *African Philosophy* 88–101.

7. See Miller, "Orality" 98–100.

8. This is an issue which Derrida does not take up, to my knowledge. Despite the privileging of voice in Western discourse, writing is viewed as essential to learning and technological advances, and illiteracy is viewed with contempt. It

would seem that factors such as class and race are operative in these seemingly contradictory attitudes.

9. Even Ong, who has made the most vociferous arguments with regard to orality/writing and sensorium-thought ("writing makes possible increasingly articulate introspectivity, opening the psyche as never before . . . to the interior self against whom the objective world is set" [105]), comes close to deconstructing his claims:

> To say that a great many changes in the psyche and in culture connect with the passage from orality to writing is not to make writing (and/or its sequel, print) the sole cause of all the changes. The connection is not a matter of reductionism but of relationism. The shift from orality to writing intimately interrelates with more psychic and social developments than we have yet noted. Developments in food production, in trade, in political organization, in religious institutions, in technological skills, in educational practices, in means of transportation, in family organization, and in other areas of human life all play their own distinctive roles. But most of these developments, and indeed very likely every one of them, have themselves been affected, often at great depth, by the shift from orality to literacy and beyond, as many of them have in turn affected this shift. (175)

10. This common and nebulous assertion seems close to Ong's proposition that writing "restructure[s] thought processes." By contrast, Hountondji's view that a true African philosophy requires ongoing critical assessment, made possible by the accumulation of written texts, suggests that writing is technically necessary to provide the means to store and retrieve intricate arguments.

2. An Impoverished Paradigm

1. Jameson's comments on the narratives that form the basis of Lévi-Strauss's research in *Mythologiques* may be of some relevance here. Jameson notes, for example, that they are "preindividualistic" and "emerge from a social world in which the psychological subject has not yet been constituted as such, and therefore in which later categories of the subject, such as the 'character,' are not relevant" (124). These observations are not conclusive, but the principle can be retained, it seems to me. Narratives generated in specific historical conditions could not have been created under entirely different circumstances in another time and space. Moreover, researchers may misperceive because of the narrative categories that we take for granted, given recent literary experience—an issue to which we shall return. Thus while a knowledge (however uncodified) of human behavior and its motives surely has existed in all human communities, what the West has come to call psychology and the manifestation of it, known as "psychological realism," are particular to specific historical circumstances.

To subscribe to this view is not to argue—as is sometimes claimed on the basis of traditional tales—that interest in the individual is absent from discourse in Africa. See Honorat Aguessy's discussion of the *moi* (158–61).

2. Havelock, for example, observes that the prealphabetic scripts of the ancient Near East were incapable of rendering the "basic complexity of human experience" expressed in oral stories and myths (72), and Ong argues that the principle of "unity of action" in Greek art and Aristotelian aesthetics develops with the advent of drama, which is based on written composition. The selectivity involved in streamlining a story and creating a climactic plot is related to the new technology of print because lengthy oral narrative tends toward the episodic (153).

3. For Bakhtin also, (Western) epic and novel are indeed mutually exclusive,

not necessarily because of the novel's supposed complexity but because there is something "open-ended" about the novel and, conversely, formulaic and conclusive about traditional genres. Thus we never achieve a novel simply by expanding episodes of the tale. Bakhtin, of course, privileges what is for him the "more modern" novel and views the epic in hindsight.

4. Karin Barber, who has published extensively on Yoruba oral traditions and culture, notes that "the freedom to allude across modes [of language] is not necessarily one-sided (writers alluding to oral tradition): oral artists also allude to writing and use the idea of it, sometimes, to claim authority. . . . Yoruba *oriki* chanters may say, 'This is what I have given you, write it down and take it away,' after uttering a particularly significant or striking passage. 'Writing' to them as to Derrida is a metaphor for the 'inscription of a durable sign,' but also a mark of value. A slightly different example is the Yoruba popular theatre, where many of the practitioners have some degree of literacy, and some of them are quite highly educated. They talk of 'writing' their plays before putting them on stage. But what they actually do is write a synopsis of the story. All the dialogue and the details of plotting are developed entirely through oral improvisation, and change over time in a characteristically 'oral' manner. However, the orientation toward writing is visible in the form of the plays, which are modelled on the 'well-made play' of European literature; and in a sense they are regarded as *if* they had a script, even though this script is always a mental and not a physical one. . . . [T]here are processes of *mutual* appropriation, allusion and commentary between oral and written modes: not . . . a 'pure' innocent oral state which is then simultaneously absorbed and superseded by the larger domain of written literature."

3. The Importance of Genre

1. See Tine. Although he falls into rather traditional thinking on the necessity of orality in African novels, his analysis of such oral speech in the novel is valuable.

2. I am referring to the textual effects of oral composition or performance, such as rhyme, mnemonic devices, parallelisms, and so on.

3. John Johnson notes, for example, that women bards in the Mande traditions do not narrate epics as do men, although a woman may accompany her husband by reciting the epic as he plays a musical instrument (25). Obviously, the absence of a political focus or of the epic form in women's writing is no indication, as is sometimes suggested, that women are unconcerned for the "great" problems that are the focus of "great" art. A judgment such as this makes clear that aesthetic categories and "taste" are devised within relationships of power.

4. Bugul's *Le Baobab fou*, for example, begins like the hierarchical stories with the *pre-story*, which emphasizes Ken's implacable origins (the amber pearl that symbolizes the child's terrible difference from others—abandonment by the mother, academic achievement, loneliness, lack of family ties). Yet the book is written against "la soumission à un esclavage conditionné appelé destin" (64) ["submission to a routine slavery called destiny"]. Ken's story is clearly an initiation—but not into an established order of grace and goodness. There is no good authority that is always trustworthy and in control.

5. See note 5 of Chapter 8.

6. I am reminded of the situation of women writers in England and Europe in the eighteenth and nineteenth centuries. According to Gilbert and Gubar, not only was novel writing a lucrative occupation—this contributed, of course, to its lowly reputation—but it also did not presuppose, as did verse writing, an aristocratic (male) education. Novel writing was therefore deemed suitable for women and was, in fact, an easier point of entry into literary life than was verse writing (110).

4. A Dubious Heroism

1. Tidjani-Serpos offers an incisive (and complementary) interpretation of the opening sequences of the novel.

2. Todorov notes, for example, in *La Conquête de l'Amérique* that la Malinche, the Aztec woman who translates for Cortez, becomes for Mexicans after independence "une incarnation de la trahison des valeurs autochtones, de la soumission servile à la culture et au pouvoir européens" (107) ["an incarnation of the betrayal of indigenous values, of servile submission to European culture and power"].

5. The Democratization of Epic

1. See Roger Chemain's chapter on Sembène in *L'Imaginaire dans le roman africain*, 165–202.

6. Authority Reconstructed

Elements of this argument appeared in my article "A Narrative Model for Camara Laye's *Le Regard du roi*," *The French Review* 55 (1982): 798–803.

1. Christopher Mfizi, in a *mémoir* at the Catholic University of Louvain in 1970, insists on a Christian message, while J. A. Ramsaran describes the novel as a quasi-religious, universal allegory that ends in the "mystic union after the long struggle between the sensual and the spiritual. . . . The fertility dances, the drumming, insistent as the pounding of the sea waves, the all-pervasive odour of the forest of primitive urges, the ecstasy of the priestess Diolu [sic]—all these, partly or wholly inexplicable aspects of Africa, become the symbol of the inscrutable forces in man, regardless of colour or creed" (208–9). Gerald Moore argues that "quite as much as a search for God, Clarence's pilgrimage seems to be a search for *identification*" (96). In a perceptive reading that stresses indigenous African traditions at work in the novel, Jahnheinz Jahn states nonetheless, "Like everything in this novel this king is a symbol too. He is fortune, merit, favour, mercy, he is king and redeemer. Camara Laye gives the sum of all religion, of all humanity, in this novel. And he shows that here, finally, all religion is one. Various symbols of different religions are used to fuse them into a unified concept of religion" (213). Charles Larson, writing in the early seventies, also emphasizes the spiritual salvation embodied in the king: "Laye merges the elements of purification by fire, passion, and love—fusing Clarence into total oneness with Africa, a total unity with the mystical world of his environment. For the white man willing to cleanse himself of his past, Africa may somehow become the final fulfillment in life—grace. And the king, who represents all of Africa, everything that the continent consists of and symbolizes, is the total fulfillment of the African experience, the total embodiment of the dark world négritude" (223). Sonia Lee also stresses the search for God in her 1984 study, *Camara Laye* (52). Kenneth Harrow, commenting on several of these analyses, proposes a Sufi interpretation of the novel "*not* as a key to unlock the mystery of the symbolism or allegory . . . but as an approach to the experience of mysticism as portrayed in the novel" (135).

2. See Arlette and Roger Chemain, Jonathan Ngaté, and Simon Simonse (462–464) for three secular readings.

3. *Kaïdara* is a Pular initiation narrative from the Senegalese Ferlo. It belongs to a specific narrative genre, the *jantol*, "un récit très long dont les personnages sont humains ou divins; son sujet peut-être une aventure mythique, une histoire exemplaire didactique ou édifiante, une allégorie initiatique" (7–8) ["a very long tale whose characters may be human or divine; its subject can be a mythical adventure, an edifying or didactic story, or an initiation allegory"]. Amadou Hampâté Bâ indicates that this form of narrative is practiced by Pular scholars who write

...hen recite their texts. The story itself is precise and must be respected, al-
...gh the writer/performer is at liberty to sing or recite, in verse or prose, to
...mment on the action, or to digress from it. The *jantol* may be told all at once,
...lthough it is performed more often in fragments.

4. Mamadou Kouyaté's stance with regard to oral and written language (Chapter 2) confirms this view.

5. Birago Diop expresses it well in the tale "Vérités inutiles." Bouki-Hyena,
of legendary hunger, comes across a stray goat who pleads for her life. At the
suggestion of letting the goat go, Bouki remarks that "la chose est tellement
ahurissante que si je la racontais un jour au pays, l'on ne me croirait pas, parce
que la vérité dépend de qui la dit aussi bien que de qui l'écoute" (*Contes et lavanes*
15) ["The idea is so bewildering that if one day I told the tale at home, no one
would believe me, because truth depends on the teller as well as on the listener"].

6. For Simonse, the novel constructs a preindustrial, precommercial world
in which human life has inherent value apart from what it produces.

7. "On mesure . . . la différence fondamentale qui sépare les contes africains
des contes européens dont le thème est apparemment analogue. Les contes
européens traduisent le rêve d'une société où les séparations qui opposent les
classes s'évanouissent devant l'audace, le courage, la patience; en un mot, devant
les vertus morales d'un personnage dont l'ascension inespérée traduit la
valorisation de l'individu propre à la mentalité européenne, et l'accent est ainsi
mis sur la virtualité d'une promotion sociale due au seul mérite personnel. Les
contes africains, quant à eux, indiquent des normes de comportement qui doivent
s'inscrire dans le cadre même d'une société communautaire au sein de laquelle
chacun doit tenir sa juste place et dont les structures, loin d'être remises en question, se trouvent au contraire confirmées, restaurées et réajustées à leur vocation
idéale" (Paulme and Seydou 105) ["One can gauge . . . the fundamental difference
between African and European stories, whose themes are superficially analogous.
European stories convey the longing for a society where class distinctions disappear in the face of boldness, courage, patience; in a word, in the face of the moral
virtues of a character whose unexpected ascension expresses the value of the individual, characteristic to European thought. In this way, emphasis is placed on
the virtue of social promotion due only to personal merit. African stories, on
the other hand, point to norms of behavior that are observed in a communitarian
society within which each person must hold to a given position and within which
societal structures, far from being put into question, find themselves reconfirmed,
restored, and reoriented to their ideal purpose/calling"].

7. An Ambiguous Quest

1. The parallels between Mélédouman's status and that of Caliban in Césaire's
Une tempête are striking: both are dispossessed in their own land and nameless.
Caliban says to Prospero, "Appelle-moi X. Ça vaudra mieux. Comme qui dirait
l'homme sans nom. Plus exactement, l'homme dont on a *volé* le nom" (28) ["Call
me X. That would be better. As if to say, the man with no name. Or to be precise,
the man whose name was *stolen*"].

2. From the outset, given his responses to Kakatika, it is clear that Mélédouman is neither a typical farmer nor city dweller. He argues not only as an exceptionally intelligent man but as one who has been educated in schools. The text
does not inform the reader of Mélédouman's studies in France until Mélédouman
informs the commandant of it at the end of the story. We will refer again to the
teleogenic nature of the narrative.

3. See Bernard Dadié's tale "La Légende baoulé" and Nokan's play *Abraha
Pokou* for references to this legend.

4. Notice that Kakatika's insistence on penetration and ejaculation reveals a

male-centered definition of rape. Moreover, even if there were female "enjoyment" in forced sexual relations, that would be beside the point. The issue remains female consent.

5. There are other occasions in which the narrative defeats its own purposes, as when Adiaffi allows the colonial officer to parody himself: "Comment, on veut les civiliser, on veut leur apporter la culture, la *merveilleuse* culture française, la science, le *beau* travail de l'intelligence française . . . on leur fait *même l'honneur* de les faire descendre des Gaulois . . . et au lieu de *l'adoration*, de la *vénération* qu'on devrait lire dans les regards, c'est de l'odieuse ingratitude" (31, emphasis added) ["Look at that! We want to civilize them, bring them culture, glorious French culture, science, the splendid fruits of the French mind . . . we even honor them as descendants of the Gauls . . . and instead of adoration or veneration, it's an ugly ingratitude we read in their eyes"].

6. See Adiaffi's article "Maîtres de la parole," in which he elaborates on his intention to adapt traditional forms so as to affirm the durability of cultural practices in contemporary society.

7. The narrator says, tongue-in-cheek, that the news of Father Joseph's trance arrived in the African section of town "en un clin d'oeil . . . mais hélas largement déformée, comme toutes les sources orales" (87) ["in a flash . . . but, naturally, distorted as with all oral communication"]. In a more serious vein, Mélédouman thinks toward the end of his journey of his grandfather and says, "Pouvait-il deviner que la croix qu'il fit de sa main royale analphabète . . . était la croix du calvaire de son royaume, le viol de son peuple?" (136) ["Could he, a king, guess that the X he made with his illiterate hand . . . would be the cross his kingdom would bear, the rape of his people?"] The commandant says in his initial interrogation of Mélédouman, "Vous n'avez même pas pu inventer un langage, un signe pour écrire votre nom, conserver votre mémoire. Vous êtes un peuple analphabète, un peuple sans écriture, donc sans mémoire et par conséquent sans histoire. . . . Vos conneries de tradition orale, mon cul! . . . Vous n'avez pas d'écriture, donc vous n'avez pas, bien sûr, de littérature. Pas de pensée" (34). ["You couldn't even invent a language, signs for writing your name or preserving memory. You are an illiterate people, a people without writing. No memory, no history. . . . Your stupid oral traditions, my ass! . . . You do not know how to write, so, of course, you have no literature. No thought"].

8. I am referring to Ngũgĩ's *Decolonising the Mind*, Mudimbe's *L'Odeur du père*, and Hountondji's *Sur la philosophie africaine*.

8. "The Emperor's New Clothes"

1. In describing the tales of certain ethnic groups, especially those in southern Africa, the ethnologist Paul Radin uses the term *humanization*, thereby implying not that animals symbolize a specific human trait but that they are, for all intents and purposes, human beings in "animal face." "Simple" animal stories were transformed, humanized, Radin hypothesizes, when southern African people experienced conflict and disorganization as a result of enslavement and forced acculturation: "Human heroes with plots taken from purely human situations forged to the front. . . . [W]ith uncompromising realism, man was pitted against man, as is inevitably the case when individuals are living in an economically and politically disturbed and insecure world. . . . This emphasis upon man and the mundane contemporary scene did much more . . . than assure to the tales dealing with them a major place. It brought about a humanization of the animal stories" (8–10).

Radin's hypothesis might be an important element in a discussion of Jameson's claim that "preindividualistic narratives . . . emerge from a social world in which the psychological subject has not yet been constituted as such, and therefore in which later categories of the subject, such as the 'character,' are not relevant. Hence the bewildering fluidity of these narrative strings, in which human characters are ceaselessly transformed into animals or objects and back again" (124).

2. See, for example, "How an Unborn Child Avenged Its Mother's Death" (Radin 186–189) or "Let the Big Drum Roll" (Torrend 24–26). Note also that Aminata Sow Fall published *Le Revenant* in 1976.

3. In this regard, see Tidjani-Serpos (120).

4. This problem is highlighted by Sembène's final sequence in the prose narrative *Le Mandat* (1966) and film *Mandabi* (1968) [*The Money Order*]. After Ibrahima Dieng's demoralizing experience, another character, the postman, steps in to say, "We can change this country." The force with which Ibrahima's experience is portrayed tends to inscribe it and to create a sense of impasse.

5. We have the right to ask to what extent this characterization is true of African, as well as European, tales and folk traditions. Bakhtin's thesis refers, of course, to a highly stratified society in which official, elite culture serves to maintain authority and hierarchy.

But the tendency to parody and subvert has been neglected in studies of African tales. In his study of Birago Diop's *Contes d'Amadou Koumba*, Mohamadou Kane makes an argument, widespread in African literary circles (Paulme, Koné): "Le conte est, avant tout, au service de la société, dont . . . il doit contribuer à assurer la survie. . . . Ces thèmes issus de la tradition ont ceci de commun qu'ils concourent à l'exaltation de comportements ou d'idées propres à convaincre ces hommes que leur vie ne peut avoir de sens que conduite dans la perspective du renforcement de leur groupe social" (31–32) ["The tale is, above all, at the service of society and contributes to ensuring its survival. . . . Traditional themes all participate in exalting behaviors or ideas capable of convincing men that their lives are meaningless except when guided by the principle of affirming their social group"].

Michael Jackson's *Allegories of Wilderness* challenges the determinism implicit in this truism. Jackson demonstrates that Kuranko (Sierra Leone) narratives ultimately reaffirm accepted customs and values but that they are more importantly an interplay between "givenness and possibility" (2). Thus they tend to subvert and experiment with normal social rules. They allow the audience to "entertain new possibilities of thought and action" at least temporarily and to see that accepted patterns are not therefore necessary ones (50–54).

6. For a discussion of sexual violence in *La Vie et demie*, see Julien, "Rape, Repression, and Narrative Form."

7. For further discussion of how hyperbole fits into the warring and, not incidentally, comic discourses in *La Vie et demie*, that of the political regime and that of its opponents (the citizens of Katamalanasia and the narrator), see Julien, "Dominance and Discourse."

8. A parallel can be drawn with Borges's "Chinese encyclopedia," discussed by Foucault in the preface to *Les Mots et les choses*.

9. This moment has interesting parallels in two French texts, Jean-Paul Sartre's *Les Mouches* and Albert Camus's *L'Etranger*. In the former, Orestes avenges his father, Agamemnon, once he no longer believes in the authority of the gods. In the latter, Meursault comments that "il y avait une disproportion ridicule entre le jugement qui l'avait fondée [his death sentence] et son déroulement imperturbable à partir du moment où ce jugement avait été prononcé. Le fait que la sentence avait été lue à vingt heures plutôt qu'à dix-sept, le fait qu'elle aurait pu être tout autre, qu'elle avait été prise par des hommes *qui changent de linge*, qu'elle avait été portée au crédit d'une notion aussi imprécise que le peuple français (ou allemand ou chinois), il me semblait bien que tout cela enlevait beaucoup de sérieux à une telle décision" (119, emphasis added) ["there was an absurd disproportion between the verdict of a death sentence and its inevitable occurrence once the verdict had been pronounced. The fact that the sentence was read at 8 p.m. rather than at

5 p.m., that it could have been completely different, that it had been taken by men who *change their underwear*, that it had been made in the name of a concept as vague as the French (German or Chinese) people. It seemed to me that all that greatly discredited such a decision"]. Meursault is shocked both by the variability of so final a decision and by the fact that it is made by nonessential beings, subject to circumstances and accidentals.

9. "The Mouth That Did Not Eat Itself"

1. Sembène's *Les Bouts de bois de Dieu* is precisely such an adaptation, the "democratization" of a literary form that, in its original usage, buttresses the authority of a ruling class.

2. His treatment of the Gĩcaandĩ Player, for example, makes clear that for Ngũgĩ, the writer or artist is not a self-contained visionary and guide; rather he or she is one of a community of people, a funnel of their experience.

3. I take a less dismal view of this aspect of artistic process which is surely ubiquitous and immemorial. Ngũgĩ's attitude is, above all, a response to the imbalance of power between Africa and the West. The appropriation and adaptation by Western art and languages of non-Western elements is often an ambiguous process that does little to transcend the taste for exoticism.

4. All of these symbols of power are brought low and ridiculed, however, by the intense dispute that breaks out among the thieves over the correlation between belly size, another such index, and competence at theft. The thieves' corporeality, a sign of their appetites, and their quarrelsomeness, a sign of egocentrism, function exactly as they do with respect to the Guides in *La Vie et demie*: these attributes serve—à la Bakhtin-Rabelais—to demystify power and the powerful.

5. Dennis Tedlock has devised a system of notation to attempt to convey such traits of speech (20–21). Derrida has argued, of course, that written language is not a representation of oral language.

6. Davis argues that the novel, as a genre, subverts true speech *with a purpose*: textual dialogue is pristine, plainly non-oral language that is meant to reaffirm the reader's sense of superior education and position (162–90). Yet oral performances or retellings also may fail to give the full complement of modulations found in plain speech; they, too, are frequently "cleaned up." This characteristic is perhaps not a matter of the novel's role in a class society.

7. There is a similar dynamic in *A Grain of Wheat*: shared speech is the path to self-knowledge, truth, and direction. The "we saw on that day . . ." of the narrator of *A Grain of Wheat* suggests collective presence and communal participation in what is being recounted (Julien, "Heroism" 139).

8. *Decolonising the Mind* is different in this respect because, its compelling arguments notwithstanding, it prescribes African languages as the source of authenticity.

9. See the discussion of Havelock's "echo principle" in Chapter 4.

10. Interesting comparisons might be made between the uses of such confusion in texts such as this one and in the European genre of the *fantastic* as Todorov describes it in *Introduction à la littérature fantastique.*

11. See Roger Berger, "Ngũgĩ's Comic Vision," for a detailed analysis of comic and grotesque elements in *Petals of Blood* and *Devil on the Cross.*

12. Mouralis argues that Ouologuem's *Le Devoir de violence* presents precisely the opposite view, that suffering does not transfigure, that there can be no *"peuple élu"* (88) ["chosen people"].

Works Cited

Achebe, Chinua. *Arrow of God*. 1967. Garden City, NY: Anchor Books, 1969.
———. *Things Fall Apart*. 1959. New York: Fawcett, n.d.
Adiaffi, Jean-Marie. *La Carte d'identité*. Abidjan: CEDA, 1980.
———. "Les Maîtres de la parole." *Magazine Littéraire* 195 (1983): 19–22.
Aesop's Fables. New York: Avenel Books, n.d.
Aguessy, Honorat. "Visions et perceptions traditionnelles." *Introduction à la culture africaine*. By Alpha I. Sow, Ola Balogun, Honorat Aguessy, and Pathé Diagne. Paris: 10/18, 1977. 141–212.
Armah, Ayi Kwei. *The Beautyful Ones Are Not Yet Born*. Toronto: Collier-Macmillan, 1969.
Bâ, Amadou Hampâté. *L'Etrange Destin de Wangrin*. Paris: 10/18, 1973.
———. *The Fortunes of Wangrin*. Trans. Aina Pavollini Taylor. Ibadan: New Horn, 1987.
———. *Kaïdara*. Ed. Amadou Hampâté Bâ and Lilyan Kesteloot. Paris: Julliard, 1969.
Bâ, Mariama. *Une si longue lettre*. Dakar: Nouvelles Editions Africaines, 1979.
Bakhtin, Mikhail. *The Dialogic Imagination*. Trans. Caryl Emerson and Michael Holquist. Ed. Michael Holquist. Austin: U of Texas P, 1981.
———. *Rabelais and His World*. Trans. Helene Iswolsky. Bloomington: Indiana UP, 1984.
Barber, Karin. Letter to the author. 15 August 1990.
Baudelaire, Charles. *Les Fleurs du mal*. 1855. Paris: Garnier-Flammarion, 1967.
———. "Exotic Perfume." Trans. Alan Conder. *The Flowers of Evil*. Ed. Marthiel and Jackson Matthews. New York: New Directions, 1963.
———. "The Fleece." *Flowers of Evil*. Trans. George Dillon and Edna St. Vincent Millay. New York: Washington Square Press, 1962.
Beckett, Samuel. *En attendant Godot*. 1952. Toronto: Macmillan, 1963.
———. *Molloy*. Paris: Minuit, 1951.
Beckson, Karl, and Arthur Ganz. *Literary Terms: A Dictionary*. 1960. New York: Farrar, Straus and Giroux, 1975.
Berger, Harry, Jr. "Bodies and Texts." *Representations* 17 (1987): 144–66.
Berger, Roger. "Ngũgĩ's Comic Vision." *Research in African Literatures* 20 (1989): 1–25.
Blachère, Jean-Claude. *Le Modèle nègre*. Dakar: Nouvelles Editions Africaines, 1981.
Bugul, Ken. *Le Baobab fou*. Dakar: Nouvelles Editions Africaines, 1984.
Calame-Griaule, Geneviève. *Langage et cultures africaines*. Paris: F. Maspero, 1977.
Calame-Griaule, Geneviève, and Veronika Görög-Karady. "La calebasse et le fouet: le thème des 'Objets magiques' en Afrique occidentale." *Cahiers d'études africaines* 45 (1972): 12–75.
Camus, Albert. *L'Etranger*. 1942. Paris: Bordas, 1980.
Céline, Louis-Ferdinand. *Voyage au bout de la nuit*. 1932. Paris: Gallimard, 1952.

Cendrars, Blaise. *La Vie dangereuse.* 1938. Vol. 8 of *Oeuvres complètes.* 15 vols. Paris: Club français du livre, 1970.

Césaire, Aimé. *Cahier d'un retour au pays natal.* 1947. Paris: Présence Africaine, 1956.

———. *Une Tempête.* Paris: Seuil, 1969.

Charbonnier, Georges. *Entretiens avec Lévi-Strauss.* Paris: 10/18, 1961.

Chemain, Arlette and Roger. "Pour une lecture politique de *Le Regard du roi.*" *Présence Africaine* 131 (1984): 155–68.

Chemain, Roger. *L'Imaginaire dans le roman africain.* Paris: Harmattan, 1986.

Chevrier, Jacques. *Littérature nègre.* Paris: A. Colin, 1974.

Cole, Michael, and Sylvia Scribner. *The Psychology of Literacy.* Cambridge: Harvard UP, 1981.

Conrad, Joseph. *Heart of Darkness.* 1902. Harmondsworth, Eng.: Penguin, 1973.

Copans, Jean, and Hilippe Couty. *Contes wolof du Baol.* Paris: 10/18, 1976.

Dabla, Séwanou. *Nouvelles Ecritures africaines.* Paris: Harmattan, 1986.

Dadié, Bernard. *Légendes africaines.* Paris: Seghers, 1966.

Dalby, David. "Survey of Indigenous Scripts of Liberia and Sierra Leone: Vai, Mende, Loma, Kpelle, Bassa." *African Language Studies* 8 (1967): 3–51.

———. "Indigenous Scripts of West Africa and Surinam." *African Language Studies* 9 (1968): 156–97.

Davis, Lennard. *Resisting Novels.* New York: Methuen, 1987.

Dehon, Claire. "Les Influences du conte traditionnel sur le roman camerounais d'expression française." Unpublished essay, 1986.

Derrida, Jacques. *De la grammatologie.* Paris: Minuit, 1967.

———. *Of Grammatology.* Trans. Gayatri Spivak. Baltimore: Johns Hopkins UP, 1976.

Diop, Birago. *Les Contes d'Amadou Koumba.* 3rd ed. Paris: Présence Africaine, 1961.

———. *Contes et lavanes.* Paris: Présence Africaine, 1963.

Diop, Cheikh Anta. *Nations nègres et culture.* 3rd ed. 2 vols. Paris: Présence Africaine, 1979.

Dorson, Richard. *The British Folklorists: A History.* Chicago: U of Chicago P, 1968.

Ducrot, Oswald, and Tzvetan Todorov. *Dictionnaire encyclopédique des sciences du langage.* Paris: Seuil, 1972.

Eagleton, Terry. *Literary Theory: An Introduction.* Minneapolis: U of Minnesota P, 1983.

———. *Marxism and Literary Criticism.* Berkeley: U of California P, 1976.

Emecheta, Buchi. *Joys of Motherhood.* New York: Braziller, 1979.

———. *The Rape of Shavi.* New York: Braziller, 1985.

Fagunwa, D. O. *Forest of a Thousand Daemons.* Trans. Wole Soyinka. New York: Random House, 1982.

Finnegan, Ruth. *Oral Literature in Africa.* Oxford: Oxford UP, 1970.

Foucault, Michel. *Les Mots et les choses.* Paris: Gallimard, 1966.

Frye, Northrop. *An Anatomy of Criticism.* 1957. Princeton: Princeton UP, 1971.

Gates, Henry Louis, Jr. "The Collective and Functional Fallacies in African Literary Criticism." Div. on African Literatures, MLA Convention. Chicago, 28 Dec. 1985.

Gérard, Albert. *African Language Literatures.* Washington, DC: Three Continents Press, 1981.

Gide, André. *L'Immoraliste.* 1902. Toronto: Macmillan, 1963.

Gilbert, Sandra, and Susan Gubar. Introduction. *Shakespeare's Sisters: Feminist Essays on Women Poets.* Bloomington: Indiana UP, 1979.

Gobineau, Comte Arthur de. *Essai sur l'inégalité des races humaines.* 1851. Paris: Gallimard, 1983.

Harrow, Kenneth. "A Sufi Interpretation of *Le Regard du roi.*" *Research in African Literatures* 14 (1983): 135–64.

Havelock, Eric. *The Literate Revolution in Greece and Its Cultural Consequences*. Princeton: Princeton UP, 1982.

Hazoumé, Paul. *Doguicimi*. Paris: Larose, 1938.

Hegel, Georg Wilhelm Friedrich. *The Philosophy of History*. 1902. Trans. J. Sibree. New York: Dover, 1956.

Hountondji, Paulin J. *African Philosophy: Myth and Reality*. Trans. Henri Evans with Jonathan Rée. Bloomington: Indiana UP, 1983.

———. *Sur la "philosophie africaine": critique de l'ethnophilosophie*. Yaoundé: Clé, 1980.

———. "Table ronde." *Recherche, pédagogie et culture* 56 (1982): 3–14.

Irele, Abiola. Introduction. *African Philosophy: Myth and Reality*. By Paulin Hountondji. Bloomington: Indiana UP, 1983.

Jackson, Michael. *Allegories of Wilderness: Ethics and Ambiguity in Kuranko Narratives*. Bloomington: Indiana UP, 1982.

Jahn, Janheinz. "Camara Laye: Another Interpretation." *Introduction to African Literature*. Ed. Ulli Beier. 2nd ed. London: Longman, 1967. 210–13.

———. *Manuel de littérature néo-africaine*. Paris: Resma, 1969.

Jameson, Fredric. *The Political Unconscious*. Ithaca: Cornell UP, 1981.

JanMohamed, Abdul. *Manichean Aesthetics*. Amherst: U of Massachusetts P, 1983.

Johnson, John, trans. *The Epic of Son-jara*. Bloomington: Indiana UP, 1986.

Julien, Eileen. "Dominance and Discourse in *La Vie et demie* or How to Do Things with Words." *Research in African Literatures* 20 (1989): 371–84.

———. "Heroism in *A Grain of Wheat*." *African Literature Today* 13 (1983): 136–45.

———. "A Narrative Model for Camara Laye's *Le Regard du roi*." *French Review* 55 (1982): 798–803.

———. "Rape, Repression, and Narrative Form in *Le Devoir de violence* and *La Vie et demie*." *Rape and Representation*. Ed. Lynn Higgins and Brenda Silver. New York: Columbia UP, 1990. 160–81.

Kane, Mohamadou. *Les Contes d'Amadou Coumba*. Dakar: L'Université de Dakar, 1968.

———. *Roman africain et tradition*. Dakar: Nouvelles Editions Africaines, 1982.

———. "Sur les formes traditionnelles du roman africain." *Revue de littérature comparée* 48 (1974): 536–68.

Koné, Amadou. *Du récit oral au roman écrit moderne*. Abidjan: CEDA, 1985.

Kourouma, Ahmadou. *Les Soleils des indépendances*. Paris: Seuil, 1968.

Labou Tansi, Sony. *La Vie et demie*. Paris: Seuil, 1979.

———. *L'Etat honteux*. Paris: Seuil, 1981.

La Fontaine. *Fables choisies*. 2 vols. Paris: Nouveaux Classiques Larousse, 1971.

Larson, Charles. *The Emergence of African Fiction*. 1971. Bloomington: Indiana UP, 1972.

Laude, Jean. *Les Arts de l'Afrique noire*. Paris: Librairie Générale Française, 1966.

Laye, Camara. *The Dark Child*. Trans. James Kirkup and Ernest Jones. New York: Noonday Press, 1969.

———. *L'Enfant noir*. Paris: Plon, 1953.

———. *Le Maître de la parole*. Paris: Plon, 1978.

———. *Radiance of the King*. Trans. James Kirkup. New York: Collier Books, 1971.

———. *Le Regard du roi*. 1954. Paris: Presses Pocket, n.d.

Lebel, Roland. *L'Afrique occidentale dans la littérature française*. Paris: Larose, 1925.

Lee, Sonia. *Camara Laye*. Boston: Twayne Publishers, 1984.

Lévi-Strauss, Claude. *Anthropologie structurale*. Paris: Plon, 1958.

———. *Race and History*. Paris: UNESCO, 1952.

———. *Race et histoire*. 1952. Paris: Gonthier, 1961.

———. *Structural Anthropology*. Trans. Claire Jacobson and Brooke Schoepf. New York: Anchor Books, 1967.

———. *Tristes Tropiques*. Paris: Plon, 1955.

————. *Tristes Tropiques.* Trans. John and Doreen Weightman. New York: Atheneum, 1974.

Lévy-Bruhl, Lucien. *La Mentalité primitive.* Paris: F. Alcan, 1922.

Lichtheim, Miriam. *Ancient Egyptian Literature: A Book of Readings.* 2 vols. Berkeley: U of California P, 1976.

Liking, Werewere. *Une vision de Kaydara d'Hamadou-Hampâté-Bâ.* Abidjan: Nouvelles Editions Africaines, 1984.

Lord, Albert. *The Singer of Tales.* New York: Atheneum, 1965.

Loti, Pierre. *Le Roman d'un spahi.* 18th ed. Paris: Calmann Lévy, 1888.

Lukacs, Georg. *The Theory of the Novel.* 1920. Trans. Anna Bostock. Cambridge: MIT Press, 1971.

Madubuike, Ihechukwu. *The Senegalese Novel.* Washington, DC: Three Continents Press, 1983.

Malraux, André. *La Condition humaine.* Paris: Gallimard, 1946.

Mazrui, Ali. "The Novelist as a Mediator between Art and Social Philosophy." *Artist and Audience: African Literature as a Shared Experience.* Ed. Richard O. Priebe and Thomas A. Hale. Washington, DC: Three Continents Press, 1979.

Mbele, Joseph L. "The Hero in the African Epic." African Studies Association meeting. Boston, Dec. 1983.

McKeon, Michael. "Generic Transformation and Social Change: Rethinking the Rise of the Novel." *Cultural Critique* 1 (1985): 159–81.

Ménil, Alain. "*Rue Cases-Nègres* ou les Antilles de l'Intérieur." *Présence Africaine* 129 (1984): 96–110.

Mfizi, Christopher. *L'Oeuvre romanesque de Camara Laye.* Louvain: Université Catholique de Louvain, 1970.

Midiohouan, Guy Ossito. *L'Idéologie dans la littérature négro-africaine d'expression française.* Paris: Harmattan, 1986.

Miller, Christopher. *Blank Darkness.* Chicago: U of Chicago P, 1985.

————. "Orality Through Literacy: Mande Verbal Art After the Letter." *Southern Review* 23 (1987): 84–105.

Montesquieu, Charles Louis de. *Lettres persanes.* 1721. Paris: Garnier-Flammarion, 1964.

Moore, Gerald. "Camara Laye: The Aesthetic Vision." *Twelve African Writers.* Bloomington: Indiana UP, 1980. 85–103.

Mouralis, Bernard. "Un Carrefour d'écritures: *Le Devoir de violence* de Yambo Ouologuem." *Recherches et Travaux* 27 (1984): 75–92.

Mudimbe, Valentin Y. *L'Odeur du père.* Paris: Présence Africaine, 1982.

Neal, Larry. Personal interview. October 1976.

Ngal, M. a M. *Giambatista Viko ou le viol du discours africain.* Paris: Hatier, 1984.

————. "Les Tropicalités de Sony Labou Tansi." *Silex* 23 (1982): 134–43.

Ngaté, Jonathan. *Francophone African Fiction: Reading a Literary Tradition.* Trenton: Africa World Press, 1988.

Ngũgĩ wa Thiong'o. *Decolonising the Mind.* London: Currey/Heinemann, 1986.

————. *Devil on the Cross.* Trans. Ngũgĩ wa Thiong'o. 1980. London: Heinemann, 1982.

————. *A Grain of Wheat.* London: Heinemann Educational Books, 1967.

————. *Petals of Blood.* New York: Dutton, 1978.

————. *The River Between.* London: Heinemann Educational Books, 1965.

————. *Weep Not, Child.* London: Heinemann Educational Books, 1964.

Niane, Djibril Tamsir. *Soundjata ou l'épopée mandingue.* Paris: Présence Africaine, 1960.

————. *Sundiata: An Epic of Old Mali.* Trans. G. D. Pickett. London: Longman, 1965.

Nixon, Cornelia. "The Cult of Virility in Modernist Literature." Bunting Institute Colloquium. Cambridge, MA, 5 Nov. 1986.

Nokan, Charles. *Abraha Pokou*. Honfleur: Oswald, 1970.

Obiechina, Emmanuel. *Culture, Tradition and Society in the West African Novel*. Cambridge: Cambridge UP, 1975.

Okeh, Peter I. "Les origines et le développement de la littérature négro-africaine: un regard critique." *Revue canadienne des études africaines* 9 (1975): 409–20.

Ong, Walter. *Orality and Literacy*. London: Methuen, 1982.

Ouologuem, Yambo. *Le Devoir de violence*. Paris: Seuil, 1968.

Owomoyela, Oyekan. *African Literatures: An Introduction*. Waltham, MA: Crossroads Press, 1979.

Oyono, Ferdinand. *Une Vie de boy*. Paris: Julliard, 1956.

———. *Le Vieux Nègre et la médaille*. Paris: Julliard, 1956.

Palmer, Eustace. *The Growth of the African Novel*. London: Heinemann, 1979.

Paulme, Denise. "Morphologie du conte africain." *Cahiers d'études africaines* 12 (1972): 131–63.

Paulme, Denise, and Christiane Seydou. "Le conte des 'Alliés animaux' dans l'Ouest africain." *Cahiers d'études africaines* 12 (1972): 76–108.

Rabelais, François. *Gargantua*. 1534. *Oeuvres complètes*. Paris: Seuil, 1973. 32–208.

Radin, Paul. *African Folktales*. 1952. Princeton: Princeton-Bollingen, 1970.

Ramsaran, J. A. "Camara Laye's Symbolism: An Interpretation of: 'The Radiance of the King.'" *Introduction to African Literature*. Ed. Ulli Beier. 2nd ed. London: Longman, 1967. 206–9.

Roger, Le Baron J. F. *Fables sénégalaises recueillies de l'ouolof*. Paris: Dundey-Dupré, 1828.

Rosaldo, M. Z. "The Use and Abuse of Anthropology: Reflections on Feminism and Cross-cultural Understanding." *Signs: Journal of Women in Culture and Society* 5 (1980): 389–417.

Roscoe, Adrian. *Mother Is Gold*. Cambridge: Cambridge UP, 1971.

Salih, Tayeb. *Season of Migration to the North*. Trans. Denys Johnson-Davies. London: Heinemann, 1976.

Sartre, Jean-Paul. *Les Mouches*. 1947. *Twentieth Century French Drama*. Ed. Germaine Brée and Alexander Y. Kroff. Toronto: Macmillan, 1969. 227–81.

———. *La Nausée*. Paris: Gallimard, 1938.

Scheub, Harold. "A Review of African Oral Traditions and Literature." *African Studies Review* 28.2–3 (1985): 1–72.

Schipper, Mineke. "Toward a Definition of Realism in the African Context." *New Literary History* 16 (1984–1985): 559–75.

Scholes, Robert, and Robert Kellogg. *The Nature of Narrative*. London: Oxford UP, 1966.

Sembène, Ousmane. *Les Bouts de bois de Dieu*. 1960. Paris: Presses Pocket, n.d.

———. *God's Bits of Wood*. Trans. A. Adu Boahen. Garden City, NY: Anchor Books, 1970.

———. *Mandabi*. New Yorker Films, 1968.

———. *Le Mandat*. Paris: Présence Africaine, 1966.

Senghor, Léopold Sédar. *Anthologie de la nouvelle poésie nègre et malgache*. 1948. 2nd ed. Paris: Presses Universitaires de France, 1969.

———. *Chants d'ombre*. 1945. Rpt. in *Poèmes*. 1963. Paris: Seuil, 1974.

———. "Comme les lamantins vont boire à la source." *Ethiopiques*. 1956. Rpt. in *Poèmes*. 1963. Paris: Seuil, 1974.

———. *Poems*. Trans. Melvin Dixon. Charlottesville: U of Virginia P, 1991.

Seydou, Christiane, ed. *Silâmaka et Poullôri: récit épique peul raconté par Tinguidji*. Paris: A. Colin, 1972.

Simonse, Simon. "African Literature between Nostalgia and Utopia: African Novels since 1953 in the Light of the Modes-of-Production Approach." *Research in African Literatures* 13 (1982): 451–87.

Sow, Alpha I. "Prolégomènes." *Introduction à la culture africaine*. By Alpha I. Sow, Ola Balogun, Honorat Aguessy, and Pathé Diagne. Paris: 10/18, 1977. 9–46.

Sow Fall, Aminata. *Le Revenant*. Dakar: Nouvelles Editions Africaines, 1976.

Soyinka, Wole. *Myth, Literature and the African World*. Cambridge: Cambridge UP, 1976.

Tedlock, Dennis. *The Spoken Word and the Work of Interpretation*. Philadelphia: U of Pennsylvania P, 1983.

Thompson, Robert Farris. "An Aesthetic of the Cool." *African Arts* 7 (1973): 41–43, 64–67, 89–91.

Tidjani-Serpos, Noureini. "Evolution de la narration romanesque africaine: l'exemple de *L'étrange destin de Wangrin* d'Amadou Hampâté Bâ." *Présence Francophone* 24 (1982): 107–21.

Tine, Alioune. "Pour une théorie de la littérature africaine écrite." *Présence Africaine* 133–34 (1985): 99–121.

Todorov, Tzvetan. *La Conquête de l'Amérique: la question de l'autre*. Paris: Seuil, 1982.

———. *Introduction à la littérature fantastique*. Paris: Seuil, 1973.

Torrend, J. *Specimens of Bantu Folk-lore from Northern Rhodesia*. 1921. New York: Negro U P, 1969.

Tutuola, Amos. *The Palm-Wine Drinkard and his dead Palm-Wine Tapster in the Dead's Town*. New York: Grove, 1953.

Tylor, Sir Edward Burnett. *Primitive Culture*. 1871. 2 vols. New York: Putnam's Sons, 1920.

Voltaire. *Candide*. 1759. London: U of London P, 1958.

Watt, Ian. *The Rise of the Novel*. Berkeley: U of California P, 1957.

Zola, Emile. *Germinal*. 1884. Paris: Garnier-Flammarion, 1968.

Zumthor, Paul. *Introduction à la poésie orale*. Paris: Seuil, 1983.

Index

Accountability: concept compared to authenticity, 154–55

Achebe, Chinua: European literary tradition, 3; Ngũgĩ and representation of orality, 143, 144–45

Adiaffi, Jean-Marie: initiation story and *La Carte d'identité*, 107–22; sociocultural reality and reappropriation of genres, 156–57. See also *La Carte d'identité*

Affinity: African and European texts, 4

"African": early definition of as Europe's opposite, 22–23

L'Afrique occidentale dans la littérature française (Lebel): European views of Africa, 91

Agency: narrative structure of *Wangrin*, 63–67; helpers and epic tradition in *Les Bouts de bois*, 76–78; *Le Regard* and initiation story, 103–106; *La Vie et demie* and fable, 136–40

Aguessy, Honorat: novel and assumption of African orality, 10; European awareness of African oral literature, 11; orality and authentic African cultures, 143

Anthropology: domination of study of African cultures, 11; cultural relativity, 16; Third World nationalists and "progressive" Western, 20. See also Lévi-Strauss

Arbitrary: use of term, 41

Armah, Ayi Kwei: approach to neo-colonialism compared to Tansi's, 127–28. See also *The Beautyful Ones*

Arrow of God (Achebe): *Devil on the Cross* and representation of orality, 143

Art: principles of traditional and *La Carte d'identité*, 118. See also Sculpture

Assimilation: Wangrin's wealth and status as *assimilé*, 58

Authenticity: Lévi-Strauss's assessment of orality and writing, 15–18; searches for origins, 24–25; Igbo culture and orality in *Things Fall Apart* and *Arrow of God*, 143; oral tradition and new reading of African novel, 154–55

Authority: initiation story and *La Carte d'identité*, 108–11; fears and strategies of

masculine in *Devil on the Cross*, 149–50; *La Vie et demie* and *Devil on the Cross* compared, 150; narrative structure of *Devil on the Cross*, 152–53. See also Power

Autobiography: Kane's discussion of early African novel, 34

Bâ, Amadou Hampâté: epic tradition and the novel in *L'Etrange Destin de Wangrin*, 51–67; West African initiation story and *Le Regard*, 95–97; class and narrative structure, 143; relationship of sociocultural reality to literature, 156. See also *L'Etrange Destin de Wangrin*

Bakhtin, Mikhail: as important theoretician, 46–47; time and epic, 52–53, 78; narrative structure of novel, 63–64; novel and other genres, 69; initiation story and the novel, 94; laughter as liberating strategy, 128, 129, 138; analysis of grotesque images of death and the body in popular culture, 139; discussions of dialogism and low genres, 143; popular forms and parodies of official order, 157

Baudelaire, Charles: European images of Africa and *Le Regard*, 88–89

The Beautyful Ones Are Not Yet Born (Armah): approach to neo-colonialism compared to *La Vie et demie*, 127–28; immoral activities as dehumanizing, 149

Beginnings: transformation and narrative structure of European novel, 64

Beowulf: narrative prototypes and historical events, 69–70

Berger, Harry: language and knowledge, 99

Béti, Mongo: satire in realist novel, 84

Bildungsroman: oral tradition and initiation story, 95

Birth: hero and epic tradition, 53–55

Blachère, Jean-Claude: European views of oral literature, 13

Blindness: initiation story and *La Carte d'identité*, 111–12

Bol, Victor: psychological development of characters in African novel, 37–38

EILEEN JULIEN, Associate Professor of Modern
Foreign Languages and Literatures at Boston
University, is a past president of the African
Literature Association (1990-91). She writes
primarily on sub-Saharan literature of French
expression.